KENYA TODAY

Breaking the Yoke
of
Colonialism in Africa

KENYA TODAY

Breaking the Yoke
of
Colonialism in Africa

Ndirangu Mwaura

Algora Publishing
New York

ISBN: 0-87586-319-1 (softcover)
ISBN: 0-87586-320-5 (hardcover)
ISBN: 0-87586-321-3 (ebook)

Library of Congress Cataloging-in-Publication Data —

Mwaura, Ndirangu.

Kenya today-breaking the yoke of colonialism in Africa / by Ndirangu
Mwaura.

p. cm.

Summary: "Examining the impact of foreign aid, trade policies, study-abroad
programs, religion, entertainment, the media and other forms of foreign
influence on Kenya and other under-developed African nations, the author
finds that initiatives billed as "assistance" in many cases serve instead to keep
in place the colonial status of dependency"

Includes index.

ISBN 0-87586-320-5 (hard cover: alk. paper) — ISBN 0-87586-319-1 (soft
cover : alk. paper) — ISBN 0-87586-321-3 (ebook)

1. Kenya—Colonial influence. 2. Economic assistance—Kenya. 3. Technical
assistance—Kenya. 4. Kenya—Relations—Foreign countries. I. Title.

DT433.586.M87 2005

967.6204'3—dc22

2005004134

Front Cover: Kenyan Protesters Run Away From Police During A Demonstration In Nairobi

Kenyan protesters run away from police during a demonstration in Nairobi July 3, 2004.
Kenyan riot police armed with teargas, batons and a water cannon vehicle fought running
battles on Saturday with hundreds of people defying a ban on a rally called to press for
constitutional reform.

© ANTONY NJUGUNA/Reuters/Corbis Date Photographed: July 3, 2004

ACKNOWLEDGMENTS

I thank God for opening doors. I am grateful to Wambui Mwaura for crucial practical help throughout this project. Thanks also to Papa for all the research assistance.

TABLE OF CONTENTS

INTRODUCTION

Development and underdevelopment are two terms that have found common usage in Africa. In Kenya, nearly all politicians plead their cases by promising to bring "development" to the people. Although there is no fixed meaning of the term, development can be described as the capacity to deal with the environment. The ability to fully comprehend science and apply this knowledge in the production of tools, which are then used to deal with the environment, is economic development[1]. An underdeveloped country is one which has an untapped potential for using more capital or more labor or more available natural resources to support its present population on a higher level of living[2].

Western propaganda uses the term "developing" instead of "underdeveloped" to describe Africa, in order to give the false impression that African countries are making progress, moving away from a state of economic backwardness, and that they are freeing themselves from the relationship of being exploited by the countries of Europe, North America and Japan — which is simply not true. In fact, exploitation of African countries increased in the last decades of the 20th century and first part of the 21st century, both in scope and degree.

---

1. Walter Rodney, *How Europe Underdeveloped Africa*, Heinemann Kenya Limited, Nairobi, 1992.
2. A. N. Agarwala and S. P. Singh (eds), *The Economics of Underdevelopment*, Oxford University Press, New York, 1963.

1

The present underdeveloped state of Africa is a result of slavery, colonialism and neocolonialism. There are several factors that hinder development and these include:

- neocolonialism
- foreign investment
- liberalization
- lack of leadership
- lack of capital
- under population

African poverty stems from the time when Africans first came into more than sporadic contact with Europeans — who proceeded to capture and enslave them. African labor was utilized in the Americas for the benefit of Europeans. Africa lost its most productive people on a large scale and over several centuries, and as a result suffered social disruptions and wars, all of which combined to cause massive economic retardation.

During the colonial era the Europeans made profits from selling enslaved Africans; they invested some of those profits in Africa, but the profits made from those investments were quickly taken back to Europe, thus further draining off African wealth. Similarly, in today's era of neocolonialism, Europeans and Euro-Americans are using the money taken from Africa during colonialism to invest in Africa, only to take away the profits again, leaving African nations further impoverished.

The results of this exploitation have been severe. They include:

- political and military weakness
- economic weakness
- mass poverty

The causes and effects of underdevelopment are inextricably linked, and sometimes reinforce each other. Lack of capital and technology hinder development while at the same time they are consequences of underdevelopment.

Because the principle cause for economic stagnation is the lack of capital for productive investment, the first part of this book focuses on where the money has gone.

PART ONE: FACTORS HINDERING DEVELOPMENT

Chapter 1. Neocolonialism

Europe's former colonies may have formally reclaimed political independence decades ago, but in many ways the colonial system still survives. After African countries nominally acquired independence, the former colonial powers continued to exploit them at will, politically, culturally and economically. The African countries remain dependent on the imperialist powers in every sector. Financially, the dependence is seen in the form of loans and "aid" tied to the donor; culturally, in the practice and spread of European culture; militarily, through the permanent occupation of Africa by foreign armies.

African economies are dysfunctional because of certain flaws within their structures. Economic activity in any country is influenced by the political and social structure in the country. As is sometimes maintained, a country is economically backward because it is politically, socially and physically backward. If a country is under the domination of foreign powers, then its economy will also be geared to serve those foreign interests that have established the political and or cultural hegemony over the said country. This is the reality of Africa today. Africa remains under the political, cultural and economic domination of the states of Europe and North America. It follows that African economies have been distorted to serve these states. This distortion is the main flaw in African economies.

The current economic structure was established during the era of colonialism for the purpose of transferring wealth from Africa to Europe. Colonialism itself was a system of organized exploitation through foreign investments backed by military force. All the wealth created in the colonies was

5

expatriated to the metropoles. When the colonies acquired flag independence, nothing significant changed except for the fact that colonial Governor was replaced by a neocolonial ambassador. The colonial economy remained intact.

Independence was not granted to colonial territories out of a romantic vision of the equality of peoples. It was simply the realization that capitalism in the 20th century no longer required colonialism to serve its purposes and that the political and military costs of maintaining colonialism were both high and unnecessary; there are other, cheaper methods of maintaining economic domi-nance[3]. The formal political domination of African countries was transferred from European governments to foreign businesses in whose interests European governments determine their relationships with African nations. What is com-monly called "aid" functions as an instrument of coercion and domination. Direct investment takes back more from African countries than it gives, producing a reverse transfer of resources, counterbalancing the transfer of technical and managerial skills.

Europe's colonialism in Africa lasted a mere seventy years. This is remarkable when one considers Europe's overwhelming military advantage over Africa. The geographical size of Western Europe is miniscule vis-à-vis Africa, but Europe's population in the 19th century was much larger than Africa's. Hence, the invading colonial armies were larger than local ones. Colonialism would have gone on much longer had Europe not destroyed itself in the 1939-45 war. Within Africa, the collapse of European rule meant that "reliable" Africans were selected to take over the artificial states that were carved out. Those who were chosen could be trusted to subvert their own people's interests in favor of the old colonial power. Therefore, at independence, a majority of Africa's new rulers were, in a sense traitors, pretending to a false patriotism — one that never promoted domestic interests over foreign ones. The few rulers who were genuine nationalists were soon eliminated by coups and assassinations with the result that the political, cultural and academic elite, throughout the continent, with few exceptions, became dominated by reactionary, mentally-colonized elements who did everything to undermine Africa's success. This remains the situation today.

This work therefore is a comprehensive study of the survival of the colonial order under African management, otherwise known as neocolonialism. This system operates with the willing participation of Africans, without which it

---

3. Rodney, *How Europe Underdeveloped Africa.*

cannot survive. Its consequences can be seen in the deplorable state that Africa is in. This paradoxical situation, in which Africans promote that which is killing them, has been created through sustained and systematic brainwashing, resulting in mental colonization which manifests itself in the hero worship with which most Africans regard foreigners. Education, mass media and religion form the foundation for this brainwashing. One cannot fully understand the quandary in Africa without comprehending the role mentally-colonized Africans play in sustaining this system. Since religion is important in Africa, it creates the most mentally-colonized Africans who, after a steady diet of images of Jesus as a blond European with blue eyes, and the mandatory requirement to be baptized using only a European name (African names are not accepted), end up manifesting the most bizarre forms of self rejection and mutilation.

The mass brainwashing and mental colonization of Africans is the main reason why Africans support neocolonialism. The ironical twist is that, in the final analysis, Africa's current deplorable state is to be blamed on Africans and not the West. Admittedly, exploitation does exist, but it does so because Africans are at all times happy to hand over vital economic resources such as mineral wealth to foreigners.

The current economic structure is geared to produce and serve external interests. All African countries have invested heavily in the export sectors. This type of investment does not add to the internal development of a material and technical base (which is a prerequisite to self-sustaining economic growth). For any development to occur, the economy must be internally responsive. Home demand to stimulate economic growth cannot be induced merely by creating supply without introducing far-reaching changes into the economic structure.

The whole approach must be changed in several fundamental ways.

• There must be enlarged effective demand for the products of sectors which yield a foundation for a rapid rate of growth in output. This would mean the imposition of high tariffs to stop the inflow of cheap imports that deny market for local products.

• There must be an introduction into these sectors of new production functions as well as an expansion of capacity. This can only happen by the massive infusion of new capital. Money for such a venture can only be acquired by the diversion of money meant for unnecessary imports to more productive purposes within the country.

• The society must be capable of generating the capital initially required to jump start a weak economy. Then there must be a high rate of plough back by the state or private entrepreneurs; in Africa, foreign investors control all big business and they disappear with all the profits. The policy of allowing foreigners to own the means of production must be re-examined.

- The conviction that Africa has more to gain by small- and medium-sized activities than giant ventures must be abandoned. Emphasis on *Jua kali* — although well intentioned — is no basis for industrialization. (*Jua kali* is Swahili for "hot sun". It refers to an informal system of business production, organization and set up. It is low tech and undercapitalized.)

- Finally, the leading sectors must be such that their expansion and technical transformation induce a chain of input-output needs for increased capacity and the potential for new production functions in other sectors to which the society progressively responds.

Ever since African countries acquired flag independence, most of their economies have experienced retarded and low levels of growth and many times negative growth. The ruling elites in most of these countries have been similar in their incompetence, short-sightedness, and continued failure to recognize the factors that hinder growth.

Economic take-off is defined as the interval during which the rate of investment increases such that real output per capita rises, and this initial increase carries with it radical changes in production techniques and the disposition of income flows, which in turn perpetuate the new scale of investment and thereby perpetuate the rising trend in per capita output. Initial changes in method require far-reaching changes in the structure of society and the economy. In most cases countries which have managed to achieve take-off and free themselves of the grip of exploitation by foreigners have changed their political structure. This requires that a group of progressive people in the exploited country have the will and the authority to install and diffuse new production techniques that offer a path to development different from the one championed by the International Monetary Fund (IMF) and World Bank (WB), that is, international capitalism with no capital in the hands of Africans.

A perpetuation of the growth process requires that such a leading group expand in authority and that the society as a whole respond to the impulse set up by the initial changes. These changes in the scale and direction of finance flows are likely to imply a command over income flows by new groups of institutions; and sustained growth requires that a high proportion of the increment to real income during the take-off period be returned to productive investment. In Africa, this is not possible because of the extraction of massive profits by foreign companies and the dissipation of gains made in the export sector through the increased propensity to import (a propensity that is encouraged by the policy of trade liberalization). The take-off needs, therefore, a society prepared to respond actively to new possibilities for productive enterprise; and it is likely to require radical political, social and institutional changes, which will both sustain an initial increase in the scale of investment and result in the regular acceptance and absorption of innovations[4].

The beginning of take-off is usually a sharp stimulus. The stimulus may take the form of a political revolution in which an old ideology would be substituted for a newer one, and which will affect the balance of social power and effective values, the character of economic institutions, the distribution of income, the pattern of investment outlays and the proportion of potential innovation actually applied.

As a precondition to take-off, a country's surplus should not flow into the pockets of those who will take it out of circulation by hoarding, luxury consumption, low productivity outlays or expatriation to foreign countries. Institutions which are unavailable under the colonial economic structure must be developed to provide cheap and adequate working capital.

Lastly, one or more sectors of the economy must grow rapidly and local investors in such sectors must plough back a substantial proportion of their profit in further productive investment.

Agriculture is the backbone of most African economies. Cash crop growing is geared to serve foreigners and fluctuates or responds to the pattern of production and consumption in Europe and North America. It is the Europeans who set the buying price of these crops and constantly subject them to massive cuts. The terms of trade between Africa and the wealthy states have been specifically designed to cause Africa's export to lose in value while imports increase in value. For example, when African countries began to win independence, their exports started to lose value and by 1970 they were down by 11%. This is a very direct form of exploitation. Sustained absolute demand for primary products by Europe, Japan and North America is the main reason why exports in these products have grown. Productivity has increased more rapidly in the export sector than in the rest of the economy. The increased supply of exports has never translated into an increased capital supply to the rest of the economy, because of the dissipation of gains made in the export sector on increased propensity to import and also because of several factors that drive down the prices. Too many

---

4. A. N. Agarwala and S. P. Singh (eds) *The Economics of Underdevelopment.*

countries produce the same crops for export, meaning that supply has grown faster than demand. Cash crop producers are poorly organized and divided, hence they cannot effectively raise prices. Their only strategy is to hope for misfortune to other poor countries; coffee prices in Kenya rose only after frost destroyed the Brazilian crop.

Agriculture in Africa is characterized by the ownership of small-holdings that are shared between cash crops and food crops. Hence a significant proportion of the national crop out put is not produced for the market but for self-consumption. In these circumstances, the multiplier principle does not work and poverty among peasants is sustained. This type of agriculture, (subsistence) is practiced because of the low prices offered for agricultural produce and the inability of local industries to increase production. This is caused by the lack of sufficient internal demand due to high poverty levels, small population and the restrictions imposed by wealthy states on processed African produce. The capacity to buy depends on the capacity to produce and the division of labor depends on the extent of the market, which depends on the division of labor. Because of the inability of local industries to increase production and therefore use more farm produce, the capacity to buy is reduced, accentuating the negative effects of the already tiny market. Peasants have to limit the crops they grow to a level of subsistence and self-consumption.

The standard of living in rural areas has always been extremely low, despite the fact that almost every peasant holding grows some type of cash crop. These crops are the cause of misery to many Africans. In order to obtain foreign exchange, which is quickly wasted on unnecessary imports, many African countries have brought more acreage under crops meant for export and which are largely inedible. "Cash" crops are only profitable when farmed on large scale, and only politicians, European settlers and foreign-owned companies control large landholdings. Most of the rural population owns tiny holdings. Peasant poverty has intensified since they were misled into growing these crops.

The rural people have to contend with three forms of exploitation; in their role as unskilled labor they encounter the big foreign-owned farms which are exploiters of their labor; in their role as peasant producers they face small groups of exporters and processors who are the monopolistic buyers of their produce and who take advantage of their position by paying as little as possible; and in their role as consumers of imported manufactured products they are exploited by those who sell over-priced low-quality goods.

Given the low the price paid for cash crops, most small farmers show little interest in them. Opposition to farming these cashless crops became so great in Kenya that the Government found it necessary to enact laws that forbid peasants to uproot, cut or by any way cease the farming of cash crops. Since they are forced to grow these crops, the land is not released to other crops that would increase their income as well as boosting local food production. About a third of the rural poor hold plots of land too small to maintain a family above subsistence level. Some 40% of peasants work for big landowners for very low wages. There is a gross mal-distribution of land and labor. At one end of the spectrum, 30% of the cultivated land is splintered up to be shared by 70% of land-holders, and at the other end 70% of the land is shared among some 30% of landowners that include large local joint land-buying companies, foreign companies, the local rich and European settlers. This combination of over-concentration and over-diffusion of land and ownership and land tenure, has serious effects upon standards of living, employment and food production especially when the main crops grown on large holdings are not fit for human consumption — flowers, for instance.

This present system of land tenure, which reflects the colonial nature of the entire economy, is characterized by poor management, failure to mechanize and failure to undertake capital expenditure on irrigation, and it is also keeps children from being educated by utilizing child labor. This, and not "overpopulation," is the cause of recurrent food shortages and mass starvation in Kenya.

Apart from serving foreigners outside Africa by growing primary products in response to the patterns of consumption in the wealthy states, African economies are also structured to serve foreigners *inside* Africa. African governments work hard to encourage Europeans and North Americans to visit Africa as tourists. In 1994, tourism earned Kshs 25 billion ($417 million). The underlying belief, frequently stated, is that tourism (in the case of Kenya) is the "number one foreign exchange earner". It may be true that tourism is the largest foreign exchange earner; but who is it that earns from this industry? Africans in Kenya get less than 20% of the total profits from tourism. Any gains made by the government are automatically negated.

Foreigners get receive 80% of all profits earned from tourism. Most Africans are mere spectators and are completely marginalized. The few who benefit are the drivers, waiters, housekeepers and hawkers. It is the *mzungus* (Swahili for non-African foreigner) who own the resorts and lodges in the game parks and also the big luxury hotels in Kenya. They also own the tour companies.

Local politicians are also to be considered *wazungus* (plural for *mzungu*). Most visitors come to Kenya on prepaid packages, meaning the people who control the transportation and accommodations are the major beneficiaries. When tourists arrive in Kenya, for example, on Kenya Airways, the Dutch benefit — they have colonized the national carrier through KLM. When tourists stay in the big hotels in any town, ordinary Africans do not benefit since most of these hotels are foreign owned, for example, Intercontinental, Hilton, Norfolk, New Stanley. Africans have been convinced that they will gain from tourism; the reality is that tourism is just a transfer of money from Western tourists to Western businessmen who own and dominate the tourist industry.

In one case, a foreigner leased 800 acres of land and paid the local community Kshs 170,000 ($2,800). The Kenya Wildlife Service, traditionally controlled by foreigners, pays this man an average Kshs 6 million ($100,000) *annually* for this ranch as an incentive for the rancher to keep it under wildlife rather than farming it[5]. The conspiracy of silence here is clear. No one bothered to inform the local community, which lives in extreme poverty, that they stand to benefit more if the foreign parasite is eliminated. The worst scenario is the current re-colonization of the most profitable parks in Kenya.

These Game Parks or National Parks are the exclusive property of certain European governments. This means that all revenue from these parks go directly to the coffers of the imperialist nations. And every year Kenyans ritually and collectively cheat themselves on Madaraka Day by congratulating themselves on being a "free" nation.

The only benefits that tourism has brought Africa are cultural imperialism, degradation of the environment and the spreading of AIDS. In other words, Africa loses from tourism particularly because it allows unrestricted entry of foreigners[6] (while the most difficult barriers are placed in the way of any African curious to see Europe or North America). Take this case: recently (1998) a British criminal was sent on a Kshs 700,000 ($11,667) holiday to Kenya and other African countries to "rehabilitate" him.

Another flaw in African economies is the institutionalization of the international division of labor. People the world over occupy themselves with specific economic activities allotted to them by wealthy states. The role allotted to

---

5. Ken Opala, "Who skims tourism's fat?" *Daily Nation*, May 17 1996 p. 22.
6. Acquired from a letter to the editor, by "Disgusted citizen", "Human rights abused in the UK", *Daily Nation* 1996.

Africans is the one of producing primary produce, which mainly requires physical effort. Africans hack minerals out of the ground, grow cash crops and perform assorted odd jobs. In Kenya, Africans are either peasant farmers or *jua kali* artisans, while the foreigners, be they in Europe, North America, Japan, or elsewhere, process the raw materials and produce finished products. This system exists to ensure that there is maximum increase in the level of skills, employment and wealth in North America, Japan and Europe but not Africa. Foreign companies in Africa leave nothing but gaping holes in the ground and exhausted soils; yet, in the industrial states the resources thus extracted have contributed to the development of a massive industrial complex.

While Japanese children are able to make digital watches, Kenyans busy themselves with the production of pots and pans, repairing shoes, roasting maize and other forms of non-productive work. For their own reasons the IMF and WB have championed the policy promoting small workshops as a precondition for industrialization; it's called *Jua kali*. *Jua kali* is the equivalent of the cottage industries that existed in feudal Europe. In effect, Kenya has been persuaded to regress by at least 300 years, all the while congratulating itself on finally finding a path to development. Foreigners manufacture bicycles in large air-conditioned factories while the African in Kenya repairs the same bicycle at the side of the road, choking with dust in the hot sun; that's *Jua kali*.

Colonial economic systems use a minimum number of natives in the upper echelons and rely mostly on big companies from the "Mother" country. Up to 90% of the permanently employed in Kenya are in non-productive functions, mostly in the bloated bureaucracies of government departments; their services do not add to the productive capacity of the economy.

In Kenya, secondary schools absorb only 20% of the primary school leavers. Universities and other tertiary education institutions take in only 5% of the secondary school leavers[7]. And 99% of the tertiary education institution graduates fail to find employment in their field of study before two years after graduating.

This means that the colonial economy of Kenya absorbs less than 2% of all school graduates in any meaningful capacity. The high level of unemployment induces governments to expand their departments with unnecessary staff. Administration is commonly recognized as the principle "industry" that Africans

---

7. Mutuma Mathiu, "Salary crisis: Is money the solution?" *Sunday Nation* July 26, 1998, p.12.

engage themselves in; public servants constitute the largest portion of employed persons in Africa. Rather than encourage growth, high inefficiency and corruption in government act as brakes on development. A large part of the national income that is retained within African countries goes into the hands of government employees. Most of the wealth left over falls into the hands of non-Africans, the foreigners who have settled in South Africa, Asians in East Africa and the Lebanese in West Africa. Africans scramble for what little is left, and most of them survive in slums and shanties in urban areas. The peasants in the rural areas get next to nothing.

Most of the town dwellers actually provide auxiliary services and are not involved in the direct production of wealth. Peasants produce wealth through farming. What little come their way always finds its way back to the towns and the foreign companies. Yet, town dwellers who live off the sweat of rural people despise them because for their poverty. Urbanites claim they run the country by paying taxes, but without the sale of agricultural commodities produced by peasants, the town dwellers would have no income to be taxed. The government in Kenya is aggravating the disparity between rural and urban areas by going through spates of expansion in the hiring of public employees.

Like any other non-developing country, Kenya concentrates on consumption rather than production. This means that the little wealth created by peasants and workers that is retained within the country is squandered on imported luxuries rather than being directed towards productive purposes. This is because most of the people who acquire wealth are not directly involved in its production. Defects in the economic system have ensured that the principal producers of wealth acquire the very least but those who provide auxiliary services get the most. An industrial laborer is paid less than a divorce lawyer. It has been calculated that Kenya loses up to 320 million shillings ($5.33 million) annually just through cinemas showing imported movies[8]. Foreign musicians, too, make easy money in Kenya.

When the North American Barry White was in Kenya, he had special diet of non-African food and was accommodated in a foreign-owned hotel. To see him perform, Africans were asked to cough up Kshs 2,500, ($42) or the equivalent of two weeks wages of an ordinary worker[9], and the hall was filled. Senegal

---

8. The figure 320 million shillings was arrived at by multiplying known attendance numbers by the average cost of tickets at the main accredited cinema halls. Consider John Kariuki, "Field day for blockbuster films", *Sunday Nation*, February 1, 1998.

and Uganda have also been targeted. Performers, non-Africans mostly, have demanded up to Kshs 7 million ($116,667) *per concert*. Among them were Maxi Priest, Buju Banton, Chaka Demus and Pliers[10]. These foreigners also doubled as cultural imperialists; yet, Ugandan newspapers proclaimed that Uganda had finally entered the "world music map."

Foreign musicians promote the vulgar culture of Europe and America. One Shabba Ranks simply brought pornography on stage at a show described in newspaper advertisements as a "family show."[11] Singers like Coolio show their "coolness" through the profuse use of foul language. Many parents were misled into taking their children to his concert;[12] it turned out to be a heavy-handed promotion of much that American parents also deplore, characterized by the sustained use of degrading language. Since American singers are role models for many African youth, the younger generation will follow in their style, use their language, and take pride in doing so. Coolio left Kenya several million dollars richer, and the sales of cassettes and CDs goes on.

Colonialism and neocolonialism are both systems of foreign investment. Direct foreign investment and portfolio investment is not a charitable exercise. It is all about getting and disappearing with African money. Foreign capital becomes concentrated in plantations and mines producing for export, and in transport infrastructure connecting export-producing areas with seaports and airports. The nations of Europe, North America and Japan are quick to finance transport infrastructure that draws more and more areas into the colonial economic structure, particularly when one of their own companies stands to benefit. For example, the British may offer to finance a hospital in Kenya, with the aim of providing an outlet for drugs and medicines produced by British companies. That the hospital will provide healthcare facilities to African people is purely incidental but it gives the government-corporate partnership a handy propaganda cover, allowing them to claim they are expanding access to healthcare.

---

9. John Kariuki, "Why is Kenya such a poor destination for international stars?", *Sunday Nation*, April 12, 1998. p. 11.

10. *Ibid.*

11. John Kariuki, "It's nothing but gender bias, say local stars", *Daily Nation*, May 31, 1996, p. 2.

12. Njoki Karuoya, "Coolio show delights fans," Lifestyle Magazine, *Sunday Nation*, April 12 1998, p. 9.

Rich foreign governments decline to fund projects that could genuinely help develop Africa and change the lives of Africans positively. For instance, the extraction and removal of African copper in Zambia during the colonial era required supplies of coal from South Africa. At the time Zambia was granted flag independence, its only railway system was the one that linked the copper belt and South African coal mines and to the Beira seaport in Mozambique.

There were no other rail routes that could contribute to the development of Zambia. When they were approached to finance a railway linking Zambia with East Africa, all the European countries, the USA, and Japan all refused; the venture would have aided the economies of Zambia and Tanzania, but not their own. It would have enabled Zambian Africans and Tanzanian Africans to trade without the use of foreign intermediaries.

Colonialism and neocolonialism by their very nature obstruct the acquisition of skills by the colonized, and thus curtail development. Africa today is partitioned into several unconnected sectors. Hence, even if the volume of trade in one sector increases, other sectors derive no benefit. Lack of economic integration between African nations and regions is a major element in the neocolonial structure.

Instead, African countries are integrated into the industrialized Northern economies. And the skills acquired in Europe, North America and Japan have not been diffused to their African neocolonies.

In the US, the states are fully integrated economically as well as politically and react beneficially to each other in all spheres of the economy. For example, the discovery of oil deposits in the southwestern state of California spurred the growth of industries in the northeastern states. Yet the oil deposits in west and central Africa have not helped any other African region. Even the oil producing countries have not benefited, because the oil revenues are repatriated by the foreign oil exploitation firms. Nigeria has constant petrol shortages despite being one of the world's biggest oil producers. The presence of large mineral deposits in DR Congo has not stimulated the development of a vast industrial complex there or in the surrounding nations. But it has fueled the vast military-industrial complex of Western Europe and the US because, like all other African countries, DR Congo is fully integrated into the economies of Western Europe and the US.

This integration of Africa's economy into those of the US, the EU and Japan exposes individual African economies to exploitative maneuvers. When the US government devalued the dollar, the gold currency reserves of the underdeveloped economies were reduced by a third, thus reducing their purchasing power by Kshs 34.8 billion ($580 million); their debt automatically increased by Kshs 210 billion ($3.5 billion). When the dollar was revalued, the amounts outstanding on loans and credits were increased.

For a long time the currencies of all the sixteen Francophone countries were tied to the French Franc. This kind of closed currency zone is a facade for increased exploitation. Within this franc zone, the African countries could not use their reserves independently; and French workers in these African countries were allowed to take money out of the country without restriction. This classic example of economic colonialism has been introduced throughout Africa through SAPs and "liberalization".

This is the exploitative neocolonial structure that was threatened when Tanzania and Zambia proposed to construct a railway linking their countries. It was China that ended up constructing the Tazara/Tanzam railway and not the Westerners whom Africans so admire. Tanzania and Zambia have not benefited from the railway as much as expected, in any event. The industrialized states have come up with many means of countering any African initiative. The British government always kept an eye on the East African community which was threatening to end the compartmentalization of Africa into unlinked regions tied to the economies of Europe, the US and Japan. The East African community attempted to integrate the East African region, which would have expanded markets for locally produced commodities.

Of late, the EAC has been revived under the name East African Cooperation. This development did cause considerable consternation among the wealthy states as it threatened yet again the structure of neocolonialism. The wealthy states quickly urged the WB and IMF to press for the implementation of trade liberalization, meaning that the market that had been created and guaranteed by the cooperation between the East African states was lost. Kenyan-made products would have had a ready market in Uganda and Tanzania, and vice versa, but with trade liberalization the East African market is saturated with foreign products and so the main problem plaguing locally produced commodities — lack of guaranteed market — persists, thus nullifying the most important aspect of the EAC.

The "new," much-touted US policy on Africa concerning "development through trade" is not new at all. It is as old as slavery and colonialism. Exploitation through trade occurs when the imperialist nations establish the price of agricultural products and, frequently, cut those prices. Concurrently, they establish the price of manufactured goods and the freight tariffs. Ships of a particular nation, of course, stimulate the commerce of that nation. Most African nations do not own any shipping lines. Lufthansa Cargo, a subsidiary of the German national carrier specializing in cargo transport, takes in Kshs 360 million ($6 million) on average annually by transporting fresh fish from Kenya to Europe[13]. Sometimes foreign companies transport produce from one African country to another and derive enormous profits. This will soon become common, as foreign companies begin re-colonizing parastatals (business organizations formed by the government to provide services in the public interest) such as national railway networks.

When products from Africa reach Europe and North America, they are met with numerous non-tariff barriers to these markets. These include health, safety, packaging, labeling standards, and custom regulations. All these are intended to prevent processed goods from Africa from gaining entry and in effect they raise tariffs to more than 200%, making the products too expensive to sell[14], while trade liberalization in Africa ensures the unhindered entry of goods from Europe and North America without even being taxed.

Neocolonialism would collapse, left to its own devices, due to systemic inefficiencies; this alien system needs to be propped up by various mechanisms. The first prop is "aid", which also functions as an avenue for reverse finance transfer, as explained below. The second mechanism of maintaining neocolonialism both as an economic and political system is through brute force. The industrial states are not shy to kill Africans directly for their opposition to neocolonialism. Other methods of coercion in maintaining neocolonialism are distorted education, cultural imperialism, misinformation, false religion and military threats.

The solution to the current economic stagnation boils down to the destruction of neocolonialism, which can only be achieved through the elimination of cultural imperialism in all its forms.

---

13. Mishael Ondieki, "EU fish ban sparks crisis, *Business Week Magazine, Daily Nation,* January 20, 1998. Also look at Alfred Omondi, "EU fish export ban hurt firms", *Business Week Magazine, Daily Nation,* March 10, 1998, p. 16.
14. Paul Vallely, *Bad Samaritans: First World Ethics and Third World Debt,* 1990.

CHAPTER 2. FOREIGN INVESTMENT

The colonial and neocolonial economy is based on foreign investment. Direct foreign investment is not a charitable exercise; it is all about getting and disappearing with African money. Foreign investment has very negative effects on a weak economy. The economy is distorted to serve foreign interests; growth is retarded; unemployment is increased; it fosters a massive loss of capital and ensures the complete domination of the economy by foreign interests. Foreign capital always concentrates in certain countries and in certain industries — mainly extractive ones. While positively directed foreign investment may be helpful to an ailing economy, foreign investment directed at making profit for the foreigner at the expense of the host often destroys a country's economy.

Whenever the economies of Africa secure an increase in exports, the expatriation of profits by foreign companies dampens the effect of both the multiplier and the accelerator. Although the basic ingredients for a multiplier-accelerator process are present, the income generating forces are retarded, as mentioned above, by the massive loss of capital through the repatriation of profits, interest and dividends as well as the high marginal propensity and high income elasticity of demand for imports. In a sound economy, gains made from exports should be ploughed back into the economy as productive investment.

Thus, investments in an African country generate far less income than equivalent sums invested in developed countries. Underdeveloped African economies have a high marginal propensity to consume what they have not produced; hence, loss of capital which, in turn, renders the multiplier and accelerator effects negligible. The adoption of the policy of trade liberalization only aggravates an already serious capital flight situation. Whatever induced investment is made is geared entirely to changes in the Japanese, European and American demands. Investment should be induced by changes in home demand.

Because the three principle exploiters (Japan, Europe and the US) know the difficulties and disadvantages of foreign investment in Africa, they have come up with a means to ensure that underdevelopment and poverty remain permanent features of Africa. The Trade Related Investment Measures (TRIM) is one such arrangement that is meant to sustain African poverty[15]. TRIM prevents African governments from restricting the operations of foreign investors. For example, an African government cannot establish the African content of raw materials used in manufacturing and also cannot limit imports by the foreign companies according to TRIM. Suppose, for instance, that Kenya and Japan both produce tea. If a Japanese company establishes itself in Kenya to produce processed tea for export to Europe in order to reduce transport costs, the Kenya government shall not have the power to determine the amount of tea this company may import; the Japanese company shall be allowed to import tea from Japan to resell in Europe while ignoring tea grown in Kenya, such that Kenyans shall not benefit from this investment. In another scheme, the Kenya Government according to the Multilateral Agreement on Investment (MAI) shall have to provide this Japanese company with facilities and incentives to ensure that Japan is the beneficiary of this trade[16].

Foreign investment has meant that Africans have to contend with at least three types of exploitative forces. As unskilled labor they have to face the big foreign mining, plantations and business concerns and also individual European settlers; as peasant producers they are vulnerable to a small group of exporters and processors who are the monopolistic buyers of produce; and as consumers of imported commodities, they are exploited by being sold overpriced low quality goods.

In the budget read in the Kenyan parliament in June 1998, the Finance Minister admitted that foreign investors "repatriated about Kshs 15,000,000,000 ($250 million) leading to a 20% depreciation in the shilling". This in turn raised interest rates by a whopping 9%. The minister added that "the overall position in 1997 was weaker than targeted because of *net capital outflows....* and... [the] current account deficit, which increased from Kshs 4.2 billion [$70 million] to Kshs 22.2

---

15. Oduor Ong'wen, "Investment plan will hurt Africa," *Sunday Nation.* April 5, 1998, p. 15.
16. *Ibid.*

billion [\$370 million] in 1997. This deterioration was... due to *strong import growth* while exports stagnated" (emphasis added). The government still pursues such damaging policies, so that in 2004, the overall balance of payments had deteriorated by Kshs 7.4 billion (\$93 million), mainly because of a widening of the current account deficit by Kshs 12.4 billion (\$155 million) as a result of high growth of imports[17]. Ignoring the fact that it was the IMF and WB policies that had forced Kenya to open its markets, the Minister enthusiastically continued: "[As far as] ... the IMF and WB ... we are happy to work with [for?] them.... We should at all times endeavor to ... collaborate with the Bretton Woods institutions... because an agreement with the two institutions opens ... quick ... foreign direct investment". In other words, foreign investors require to know if the country is safe for plundering, and any country controlled and run by the IMF and WB are easy targets

On hearing this budget that guaranteed advantages to foreign investors, the de facto finance minister, the World Bank Country Director, was inspired to say that "the budget is positive." In Kenya as in the rest of Africa, the premise that foreign investment is a positive force has led to the complete re-colonization of African economies. This pattern has continued and in the financial year ending July 2004, the Kenya shilling lost 6% of its value against foreign currencies, which also contributed to the increase of the public debt by Kshs 20.7 billion (\$250 million)[18].

In Kenya, foreign companies have colonized nearly every sector of the economy. In foodstuffs, cooking oils and margarine, there are Coca-Cola, Nestle, Cadbury's, Proctor and Gamble, Unilever. In oil and petroleum, Mobil, Total, Shell, BP, Caltex, Agip. In transport, Stagecoach (before it was bought in late 1998) and Kenya Airways (since it has been colonized by KLM). In medicine and pharmaceuticals products, Smithkline Beecham, Glaxo Wellcom, Sterling Winthrop. In cigarette production, the main manufacturer is British American Tobacco. In advertising, McCann Erickson. Banking is dominated by ABN Amro, Barclays, Standard Chartered, Citibank, First American Bank, Guilders International Bank and, of course, the World Bank. In hotels, Intercontinental, Hilton, New Stanley, and Norfolk dominate Kenya. Price Waterhouse Coopers and Lybrand dominate accounting services. In parcel transport there is United Parcel Service, and Wells Fargo. Other examples include Kenya Television Network,

---

17. Central Bank of Kenya, *Monthly Economic Review*, July 2004, p. 29
18. *Ibid.*, p. 15

Standard Newspapers, Lonrho, Reckit Coleman, Rhone Poulenc, Hoechst, Colgate Palmolive, Bata, Delmonte, and Wrigley's. The IMF and World Bank are pressing for the privatization of all parastatals, which implies making them available for foreign investors to buy, thus completing the re-colonization of Kenya. This has already happened in electricity generation, and also management of the Mombasa container terminal which was taken over by Felixton Ports Authority. In Tanzania, the second largest airport, Kilimanjaro International Airport, has been taken over by Mott MacDonald, a UK Company[19].

Because the Government of Kenya is "happy to work with.... and at all times endeavors to collaborate with the Bretton Woods institutions", commerce and banking have been concentrated on transport, port and other facilities used by foreigners. This pattern of complete foreign ownership of African land, companies and resources is the same in Uganda, Malawi and elsewhere in Africa.

North America and Western Europe jointly consume two-thirds of the world's fossil fuels, three-quarters of the metal ores, iron and steel, and four-fifths of non-ferrous metals and non metals. For Africa this brings about a danger of depletion. The rich nations shall finish off African minerals without any benefit to the source country. The former Zaire is the world's largest supplier of industrial diamonds and cobalt. It has large deposits of gold, zinc, tin, and uranium. All these mines and deposits are owned by foreigners and so, despite their natural wealth, Zairians are extremely poor and their situation will only get worse when the foreign investors exhaust their minerals and leave the country in the dust.

All the oil in Angola, Nigeria, Cameroon, and Congo is not African oil, in reality. None of the owners is African. All the rubber in Liberia belongs to Americans. Apart from owning all the mineral wealth of Africa, foreign companies have concentrated most of the processing facilities in their home countries. Minerals are exported from Africa in raw or nearly raw state: the cheapest state. Hence, the exporting country at the very most gets only 30% of the mineral value; the other 70% is pocketed by the Westerners. Africa is a very rich continent but as long as this goes on, Africans shall continue to be the poorest, most despised people to walk the earth.

In the late 1990s, a sophisticated scheme was unveiled by the developed countries. Africans, who have already been taught the importance of encouraging "investor confidence" and "promoting foreign investment", will most likely

---

19. *Daily Nation*, July 1997

wholeheartedly agree to it, failing to comprehend the long-term implications. This scheme includes the proposed Multilateral Agreement on Investment[20]. The chief proponents are the OECD members (Organization for Economic Cooperation and Development), a group of twenty-nine nations that are heavily involved in Africa.

Colonialism was essentially a system of foreign investment whereby the European parasite state and its citizens would invest in the vassal countries, which would not have the power to oppose the investment nor the right to invest in that European state. It is hard to see where the current scheme differs. This Agreement between OECD members gives foreign companies the right to go into any African country; their operations are not to be limited by the host government. During the colonial era, European countries could move freely into any African country and take what they liked. British companies established themselves in any part of British colonial Africa without restrictions and they would repatriate all profits. The new plan proposes that the same foreign companies would be accepted as local companies in any part of Africa, meaning they would be entitled to reduction in taxation and be allowed to make off with 100% of the profits.

The Multilateral Agreement on Investment (MAI) can be summarized in three main points:

1. Foreign companies would have the undeniable right to begin exploitative operations in any African country and in any sector of that country's economy. This means that African countries shall lose their sovereignty and shall have no control over their borders. It shall be "illegal" for an African country to bar a particular foreign company from entering the country and starting operations, even though that company's operations may go against the national laws. A European company may even go into Kenya and open brothels, or abortion clinics, without the local populace having any say.

2. Once the foreign company has established itself in the country, the respective African government has to provide it with facilities and incentives to encourage its growth. Required incentives may include tax deductions, guaranteeing minimum profit and others. The government shall be required to comply, regardless of the nature and legality of the product or business.

3. Lastly, once the proposed agreement is accepted by African nations, the rights of the foreign investor will be supported and enforced by the *mzungu*-con-

---

20. Ong'wen, "Investment plan will hurt Africa", p. 15.

trolled World Trade Organization (WTO). This means that if any African country was to refuse to comply, they will be reported to the Europeans and Americans who control the UN and WTO. Punitive sanctions shall then be imposed and the chances of that particular African government collapsing are very real. Other African governments are more likely to help enforce sanctions than go against their Western "business partners," as was seen with the long standing sanctions against Libya.

If this MAI is adopted by African countries then real development, that is poverty alleviation, shall be relegated to a permanent mythical status. African-owned companies will be hindered in their efforts to develop their capacity for manufacturing high-tech commodities. Foreign companies will have unlimited access to African resources and markets. Foreign investment can only help an economy if it adds to the enlargement of that economy's domestic productive capacity; but by its very nature foreign investment is not interested in building up Africa's domestic productive capacity. Its main interest is to get the best deal it can for itself, that is, to take advantage the continent, and that is precisely what it is doing.

Many large multinationals have African blood on their hands, either by the direct killing of Africans or by taking away African resources during colonialism. There are several examples. In 1756, David and Alexander Barclay were actively participating in the abduction, sale and enslavement of Africans. This venture provided the capital with which they started Barclays Bank. Similar activities transformed a small London coffeehouse into one of the largest banking houses, Lloyds. Others, like Unilever, were nourished by the colonial plunder of Africa[21]. Companies such as Total, Elf, Shell and BP have financed and backed brutal anti-people regimes in Congo (Brazzaville) and Nigeria.

Foreign companies operating in Africa have long propagated cultural imperialism as a way of increasing profits. Most large multinational companies aim to produce the same lines of products for sale everywhere with only minor variation. This is very difficult because of the cultural and linguistic differences between one region and another. It is in the interest of foreign companies that most Africans become mentally colonized. The social model adopted by any country determines the choice of consumer goods, so if the model is European then European goods and services shall find a ready market. These companies have therefore embarked on cultural imperialism to mould the market to suit

---

21. Rodney, *How Europe Underdeveloped Africa.*

24

their products[22]. In Kenya this policy has produced some curious advertisements.

Kenya Airways goes to great lengths to show the superiority of things European over things African. In one advertisement a European stag is superimposed on an African Zebra; in another, a Scottish piper is placed over a Maasai herdsmen and so on. Credit card advertisements always show Africans on trips to Europe, Australia, North America and Japan. No African destination is glamorized in a similar way.

Airlines frequently hold competitions where the top prize is a trip to a European destination, causing people to feel that their greatest aspiration should be to get out of Africa. It is this wisdom that led British Airways to sponsor a visit for several children affected by the August 7, 1998 bombing in Nairobi to Eurodisney, in Paris. Advertisements from Peugeot and Ford feature scantily clad women[23]. Unilever offers a soap called Geisha, and uses coarse language in its ads for various products[24]. In addition, this company markets a "skin lightening" cream called "fair and lovely" targeted at the youth, who are encouraged to despise their skin color through various adverts which seek to associate African skin color with ugliness. In these ways the companies promote cultural imperialism, and that always takes the form of undermining values, not strengthening them.

Foreign companies drive up their profits in a variety of ways, many of them illegal. They may declare substantially lower income than they have achieved, thus evading taxes. Then, there is transfer pricing. Most affiliates of global companies trade imports and exports with other parts or branches of the parent company. The parent company, headquartered abroad, overcharges its subsidiary in Africa for imports supplied to it and also underpays it for exports to the headquarters[25]. In a British multinational involved in mining and machinery in DR Congo, for example, the head office in London may trade with the branch office in Kinshasa, exchanging mining machinery for minerals. The London head office buys the minerals at a price below market and sells machinery to the subsidiary at a price above market. The profit is considerable, and even better: it is tax-free.

---

22. Paul Harrison, Inside *the Third world*, Penguin Books, London, 1993, p. 191.
23. *Daily Nation*, June 10, 1994 p. 15.
24. *Sunday Nation*, March 29, 1998 p.11.
25. Harrison, *Inside the Third World*, p. 345.

Then there is bribery. Multinational companies have found many ways to shower prosperity upon government ministers and officials who allow them to sell overpriced, low quality goods. Bribes are also offered to make government officials overlook irregularities. When the Guinness Company bought 45% of Kenya Breweries Limited, it failed to inform the public[26]. Kenya Breweries was the last major African-owned business in Kenya and the move would have been unpopular in the extreme; the purchase of KBL shares by foreigners would also have led to KBL being withdrawn from the Nairobi Stock Exchange. To avoid the issue, Guinness hosted a "Guinness Sunbeat 1998" concert in which musicians were imported as part of the campaign of moulding the market and gaining favorable press through cultural imperialism. The media took the bait, and the fact that all African companies in Kenya have been re-colonized is no longer considered an issue worth discussing.

Export of raw materials is also part of this picture. Minerals and agricultural produce are exported from Africa in a raw or nearly raw state so that all the income made from processing and selling processed raw materials remain firmly in the hands of non-Africans. For example, several years ago, purchases of tea worldwide were dominated by three multinationals which controlled 60% of the market. These companies shipped the tea to the London auction where prices were much higher than in the producing country[27]. Thus the profits were "earned" outside the tea producing country, therefore evading taxes and maximizing revenue.

Throughout Africa, multinationals declared profits are much higher than in the West. In fact, they are so high that foreign companies working in Africa rarely incur losses[28]. In 1997, many of these companies boasted of making mega-profits. Sony Corporation posted 8.61 billion dollars (Kshs 5,166 million) in net profit[29]. The corporation conceded that sales of its products in Europe and America were stagnant; thus, much of the profit was made in Africa. Coca-Cola Company posted a 7% increase in its earnings. Its Africa department saw double-digit growth in unit case helping it earn Kshs 49,020 million ($817

---

26. Samuel Nduati, "KBL rights issue: Saga a lesson for listed firms", *Business Week Magazine, Daily Nation*, December 23, 1997 p. 2. Also Mutahi Mureithi, "KBL 45 pc equity goes to Guinness", *Business Week Magazine, Daily Nation*, December 16 1997, p. 1.

27. Harrison, *Inside the Third World*.

28. *Ibid.*, p.361

29. Report by correspondent, "Corporation makes 2 billion profit", *Daily Nation*, March 24 1998.

million) by the end of 1997[30]. The Cyanamid Transnational Corporation also did handsomely: the Africa regional president said the profit withdrawn from Africa was 14% of total profits. This company made about Kshs 110 billion ($1.83 billion) and repatriated the money to its US owners.

A survey of all foreign companies in Africa will readily reveal that their profits are extraordinary. And that is the declared profits. Using tactics as described above, the real income is two to three times the declared amount. It would appear that Africans need do very little more to boost investor confidence. Many multinationals get a huge proportion of their income from Africa. They have an enormous stake in preserving this aspect of the business climate.

In Africa, labor is cheap and associated costs are very low, unlike in Europe where trade unions have secured a high level of job security. As part of the Structural Adjustment Programs (SAPs) African governments were ordered to crush the power of trade unions and spare the foreign companies the need to consider the welfare of their workers. This was promptly done and in most of Africa, foreign companies can sack any amount of workers at will, and the foreign companies take full advantage of the opportunity to bring in more machinery and employ fewer workers. They also use unskilled laborers, paying them survival wages, and even where skilled workers are used they are granted minimal salaries and fringe benefits.

Caucasian employees of multinationals operating in Africa are paid more than their African counterparts who perform the same duties. One Euro-American company's figures revealed that workers in the USA were paid three times as much as African workers for doing exactly the same job. Furthermore, workers in Europe and the US work from 9.00 p.m. to 5.00 p.m. while those in Africa, working for the same companies, work from 8.00 p.m. to 5.00 p.m. Many are overworked, without adequate pay or with no overtime compensation at all.

The alien model of the economy in Africa has led to an over-dependence on foreign skilled labor. Foreign companies operating in Africa provide employment for foreigners at the expense of Africans, including more than 7 million expatriates living in African countries, and millions more living abroad.

There are more expatriates living in Africa today than there were during colonial times. They take jobs away from local citizens and are paid up to ten times more than an African would be paid to do the same job. Foreign companies always reserve the top managerial and financial positions for Europeans/Amer-

---

30. Report by AP, "Coca-cola revenue up by 7 pc", *Daily Nation*, January 30, 1998.

icans. The multinationals have finally begun employing Africans in a symbolic number of managerial positions so that they would buffer local hostilities and legitimize the companies' other activities. The African branches of foreign multinationals are also used as pressure valves. Job cuts at headquarters may be transferred to Africa where the subsidiary will have to maintain him — usually by firing several Africans, so that their combined salary will cover his.

The best way to solve the problem of foreigners occupying jobs Africans can perform is to follow in the steps of Zimbabwe. The Zimbabwe Government has announced that, "Once we have a Zimbabwean on our register with a skill that is occupied by an expatriate worker, we will not renew that expatriate's work permit".

Multinational companies operating in Africa use their immense clout in the metropoles where they are headquartered to control African governments in their own interests. Most of the largest companies are deeply involved in the local politics, and the wars, in nearly all African countries. Consider the following examples. Congo (Brazzaville) held its first democratic election in 1997 and General Sassou Nguesso, the French puppet, was replaced by Pascal Lissouba. When Lissouba was elected to the presidency he found the oil industry firmly in the hands of European companies. Congo was receiving only 15% of all revenues from its own oil. Lissouba tried to negotiate the increase of Congo's share to at least 30%. The oil companies refused, and arranged for the murder of Lissouba. With the help of French President Chirac, the oil companies hired mercenaries and started a "civil" war in which thousands of Africans were killed. Eventually, Lissouba was overthrown but he escaped with his life. He was replaced by Nguesso and Congo's share in its own oil went to less than 10%. Lissouba is now a refugee. Shell and BP have colluded with the military governments of Nigeria ever since the murder of President Murtala Mohammed by the CIA. This long-term cooperation proved beneficial to the oil company when members of the Ogoni ethnic group began to protest the wanton destruction of their environment by Shell and BP. The oil companies simply paid the dictator Sani Abacha to have protestors killed. The military then started bombing villages of and burnt down thousands of huts full of people. By the time the campaign ended 1000 people had been killed, of whom the best known was Ken Saro-Wiwa. Four thousand port workers were also fired after they protested against this oil company[31].

In August 1998, it was revealed in Tanzania that foreign companies were taking advantage of tax incentives to import arms in collusion with certain government officials. The European-owned African Fishing Company had acquired 10,000 hectares of land and the community that had traditionally owner the land was evicted. This company then imported Kshs 34.2 million ($570,000) worth of arms and ammunition — apparently to attack the local people should they try to return to the land which they had occupied for centuries.

Many foreign companies take advantage of the fact that different regions of Africa are poorly connected economically. They buy a commodity from one region, take it to Europe for processing, flavoring, and packaging, then resell it to other regions of Africa — or even to the area of its origin. Cocoa originating from West Africa first passes through Europe; the finished cocoa powder or chocolate is then resold in Africa. The East African peasant farmer sells his coffee beans to the European company at an absurdly low price; the beans are processed and the finished product is imported back to East Africa, where is sells for up to 50 times the amount paid to the farmers. Nestlé alone boasted of a 40% increase in profits in the first half of 1997, to Kshs 75.6 billion ($1.26 billion). Firestone and Bridgestone have flourished as intermediaries in the rubber trade. Rubber from West Africa is processed in Europe, then sold throughout Africa. The same holds true for other raw materials derived from Africa.

It is through foreign investment that North America and Western Europe consume two-thirds of world fossil fuels and three-quarters of metals ores; they generally control 75% of the wealth of this planet, much of it taken from Africa[32].

Foreign investment also creates a barrier to the development of exports. A good portion of African manufacturing output is produced by firms which are either subsidiaries of foreign companies or work under license from multinationals. These foreign companies often bar the African companies from competing with them either in the metropoles or in third countries.

In short, foreign investment enables the citizens of Europe, Japan and America to own all these means of production in Africa and this is the most direct way that the wealth of Africa is transferred to Europe, Japan and the US. It is therefore that in the best interest of Africans that foreign investment be banned; and African countries should strive to eliminate foreign middlemen in what should be pure inter-African trade.

---

31. Some figures have been obtained from this article, "British [environmental] group snubs Shell over Nigeria", *Daily Nation*, December 1996.
32. Harrison, *Inside the Third World*, p. 363

Chapter 3. Liberalization

Liberalization is an economic policy that sanctions the free movement of goods to and from any country. Ideally, it is supposed to stimulate growth in exports. In reality, there is a net outflow of raw materials from Africa and an inflow of finished goods from North America, Japan, China and Europe into Africa. Africa produces very little in terms of finished products that could be exported, and what little they produce is subjected to high tariffs by the wealthy states, stifling growth in Africa's exports while guaranteeing markets for Western products.

Historically, the imposition of tariffs has played a major role in economic takeoff. Examples include the American tariffs of 1828, which protected infant industries from competition from the larger, more established industries of Europe[33], and in Japan during the Meiji Restoration, when Japan was first developing its industries. Africa, with its tiny, undeveloped industries, is doomed to failure by opening up its markets to foreign products.

Liberalization acting jointly with cultural imperialism guarantees sales of Western products. Mental colonization ensures that Africans strive to emulate European-type people and anything thought to be associated with them. Africans justify this approach by claiming that foreign products are of higher quality, but this is not entirely true. Nairobi supermarkets stock eggs imported from France; yet, a French egg is of no higher quality than an African egg. Poultry

---

33. Agarwala and Singh (eds), *The Economics of Underdevelopment*.

rearing in Nakuru town has actually dropped ever since importation of eggs and frozen chicken was begun[34].

Liberalization was forced upon Africa because Western markets are saturated. The capacity of individuals to absorb material goods is not infinite. As stagnation threatened to hinder growth in the West, governments began to force Africa to open up so as to provide new markets for their products.

In the 1998 budget, Kenya's Finance Minster admitted that the policy of liberalization was choking Kenya's fledgling industries. Growth in the manufacturing sector fell to 1.9% after a modest growth of 3.7 percent in 1996 (before liberalization took effect).

Import liberalization and declining consumer demand were major factors in this slowdown. Exports in the year ending May 2004 grew by 8.4% while imports swelled by 19%, resulting in a trade deficit of Kshs 109,520,000,000 ($1.369 billion)[35]. Because of this massive importation, local industries have collapsed and factories closed down increasing unemployment, poverty and crime. Of this amount, the major portion goes to the rich North. Kenya also gave these countries Kshs 7.7 billion ($97 million) in debt servicing payments *on the interest*[36], while foreign companies working in Kenya and based in these same wealthy countries make off with several billions from Kenya as repatriated profits. At the same time unemployment rose by about 20%, robbery increased by more than 50% and reported rape cases increased by more than 1000%.

This massive loss of capital is one of the main reasons why the economy of Kenya has collapsed. This deterioration is mainly due to strong import growth while exports have stagnated. When a country consumes imports disproportionately, the government loses tax money since less production is undertaken within that country.

As noted above, the massive loss of capital through importation, repatriation of profits by foreign companies and debt servicing have all reduced the amount of money going to the government. This creates a need to borrow, since revenue performance cannot remain on target due to reduced economic activities. This coupled with declining external receipts make the Government resort increasingly to short term domestic borrowing to finance its expenditure. This borrowed money is rarely used for productive investment; rather, it goes to pay

---

34.Nixon Wainaina, Poultry farming drops in Nakuru", *Business Week Magazine*, p. 5 *Daily Nation*, March 24, 1998.

35. Central Bank of Kenya, *Monthly Economic Review*, July 2004, p. 31.

36. *Ibid.*, p. 33

interest on other loans and to balance the national budget and to cover recurrent expenditure such as salaries for civil servants.

The solution proposed by the Kenya Government to reduce the budget deficit is firmly within the confines of economic colonialism. The real cause of economic stagnation is ignored: the policies of liberalization of imports and foreign investment. The minister claimed that "The slowdown in economic growth which began in 1996 is continuing..... and is likely to persist unless urgent measures are taken to tackle factors constraining growth. The excessively high interest rates, the poor state of our roads, power supply shortages, insecurity and adverse weather conditions have all had their toll on [foreign] investment and economic performance. Furthermore, the suspension by the IMF... loans.... also played a role in adversely affecting [foreign] investors' confidence." Based on this erroneous line of thinking, the proposed solutions included increased borrowing, increased taxation, the freezing of salary increments and the sacking of government workers. Hence the Kenya Government announced its intention of retrenching 125,000 public servants, including 66,000 teachers.

These measures would have the effect of increasing government revenue momentarily. But they would also have the effect of increasing unemployment and poverty; and higher taxes and utility bills reduce the real income of the few employed. This diminishes the Governments revenue base, in the long run, forcing it to borrow more and more. The country is then caught in the aid trap, which leads shortly to the loss of genuine sovereignty.

Massive loss of capital due to the repatriation of foreign firms' huge profits and the unregulated importation allowed by liberalization has also caused a depreciation of the shilling, pushing up interest rates to an average of 21%, which in turn has prevented the newly unemployed from getting modest loans to start or run small businesses[37]. The long-term effects of massive capital flight and the government measures to reduce the budget deficit are higher unemployment, as more factories collapse under the weight of cheap imports; inflation due to high interest rates and depreciation of the shilling, which causes a shift of income and wealth from wage earners, salaried workers, and holders of small pensions and savings accounts to the already wealthy — who are able to exploit the rise in prices; and a drop in the savings rate, as people lose confidence in the currency. When people lack effective protection for their liquid assets, they tend to prefer consumable goods and assets having fixed monetary value. Inflation operates

---

37. Central Bank of Kenya, *Monthly Economic Review*, July 2004, p. 13

arbitrarily to distort the direction of investment and generates economic waste. It brings profit to entrepreneurs even if they are inefficient and so dulls the incentives to efficiency. It diverts talent and personnel from productive endeavors to non-productive speculation.

In most parts of Africa, millionaires are not making their money from legitimate business; rather, they have found ways to exploit the system. In countries which are predominantly agricultural and where land is held in large estates, the rich, who should be saving and investing, commonly are non-savers and spend their income in luxurious living with the result that economic development in these countries is retarded. They are discouraged from productively investing in their own countries by mistrust of industrial ventures and the lack of confidence in the stability of the country. In any case, most of them prefer to bank their money outside their countries. The rich in Kenya are known for their big cars, holidays in Europe, and their complete alienation from the rest of the society.

If the government acquires from its citizens in taxes a part of what they would have wasted on luxurious consumption and uses the proceeds in public works of use, then that government is performing the saving function for the community. But in Africa this never happens, because African governments are the largest wasters of funds through unnecessary purchases of luxurious vehicles, expensive weapons and other items. And where the government hikes taxes for the supposed purpose of performing the saving function, the tax revenue is first absorbed by officials and what little remains goes into useless public-funded projects.

When the products of advanced countries are sold in Africa, they directly drain away capital that could be used for productive investment. When contact is made with foreign consumption patterns, the propensity to import is increased. This contact is promoted vigorously by import liberalization in a process called "want development". Cultural imperialism greatly aids in this want development. A decade ago, most African women were not particularly concerned about their weight but after a strong assault by cultural imperialists, women now buy products intended to reduce their weight. All these manufactures are imported. Other examples are less innocuous.

Massive importation also has the effect of aborting economic take-off, so that the multiplier principle fails to work. In an ideal situation, an increase in investment leads to an increase in income and employment. The next increase ought to come from a secondary increase in income, employment and output in consumption goods industries, to be followed by tertiary increase and so on. But

34

somewhere along the line, this fails to happen. This is because domestic consumption is satisfied through imports instead of locally-produced goods (which would have enabled domestic firms to expand output and increase employment); and the prevailing high poverty levels, small population and restrictions imposed upon African exports through protectionism all conspire to prevent local industries from increasing production.

Although the tertiary increase in money income may occur as a result of increased investment, no noticeable increase in either output or employment occurs. Thus, the primary increase in investment and, therefore, increase in income and employment leads to a secondary and tertiary increase in income but not output or employment, to the extent that the increases in money income are not absorbed by a rise in prices and leave a margin of additional real income. This real income is dissipated either by an increase in food consumption or by an increase in imports; hence no increase occurs in either real income or employment for the society as a whole. Most imports are paid for by the activities of peasants but are enjoyed by town dwellers.

The exploitation of the rural areas by the urban areas has tremendously increased the amount of people living in desperate poverty, both in absolute numbers and in the proportion of the population. One of the effects of mass poverty is the loss of markets, forcing companies to cut their output and lay off workers, adding to the number of the poor and unemployed. The second effect is the diminishing revenue base of the government, which forces it to borrow repeatedly to make up for the loss in tax money. The government is also forced to cut spending on health and education, which increases death from preventable disease, and illiteracy both in absolute numbers and in the proportion of the population. Mass unemployment and underemployment destroy families and drive up alcohol abuse and other social ills.

The Government has raised taxes by instituting the Value Added Tax on all goods, and income taxes, but it has failed to tax foreign imports or profits made by foreign companies. This is because the Government is required to follow the advice of the IMF and World Bank, which happen to be based in and financed by the countries in which those imports to Africa are manufactured. The IMF and WB induce African governments to borrow more, and then they are obliged to cut domestic spending just to repay the interest on these external loans.

In Kenya, as the Government ran out of options for financing its own expansion, it started to borrow more, often at grossly inflated interest rates.

Hence, the local rich have become richer and foreign financiers have flocked to the country. In urban areas the value of real estate has soared, creating a phenomenon of land grabbing; rents have risen and many families have been reduced to destitution — especially when "investors" flatten shanties and slums in order to acquire the land.

Apart from fueling land grabbing, the collapse of local production in favor of imported products causes the distribution of income to shift in favor of rents. As the level of non-productive activity rises, a group of intermediary traders emerge who benefit from inflationary pressures. In Kenya this has seen the rise of many retail outlets that contribute to urban decay. For example, in the housing estate of Komarock in Nairobi, every third house has a shop retailing confectionaries and other goods, while in the housing estate of Umoja, the houses have been demolished and replaced by massive multi-storeyed flimsily-built houses or apartments for rent.

The majority of Kenyans are today desperately poor, hungry, unemployed, without access to healthcare facilities or education. When a country has come this far on the road to national collapse, as directed by the IMF and World Bank, civil upheavals loom large. Sensing this; the political leadership becomes more autocratic, and corrupt, and starts to accumulate wealth outside the country. Arms are bought to bolster the collapsing regime while a disregard and disrespect of law and order becomes common in all classes as the society moves towards collective destruction.

The biggest offender today, the US, has come up with a complex scheme to speed up its harvest of Africa's wealth. It has proposed the Africa Growth and Opportunity Act, which aims at crystallizing the international division of labor. African countries, according to the Act, would be allowed to sell cheap handmade products in the US in unlimited quantities, duty free. In return for Africans being allowed to sell cheap trinkets, US companies would be allowed to invest in Africa and would be accorded the same treatment as domestic companies. Africans would only be allowed to sell in the US products which would not offer any competition to US products while the US would be allowed to sell in Africa products which offer competition to domestic industries, and also would be allowed to invest and would receive various other incentives. According to the Growth and Opportunity Act, US companies would have the right to buy every government parastatal and thus complete the re-colonization of Africa. Meanwhile, the American ambassador to Kenya has generously said that the US stands ready to help the Maasai sell their art work. This proposition is very similar to the Multilateral Agreement on Investment discussed above. If African governments lose the power to set the rules by which their own economies are run, and the authority to supervise those economies, Africa will be irretrievably lost.

A UN chaired economic conference in 1996 held in Addis Ababa revealed that Africa is being exploited to the tune of Kshs 1560 billion ($26 billion) annually through the adoption of the policy of import liberalization[38]. The West has forced Africa to open up its markets to foreign products, but has avoided opening up their markets to African products. They know that import liberalization hurts any economy. In fact, the high degree of self-sufficiency of the US is due in part to a deliberate national policy of high tariff protection. The structure of the global economy ensures that Africa fits into its allotted role in the international division of labor which has determined that Africans shall only export raw materials to feed the industries of the US, EU and Japan.

The EU effectively neutralizes the whole concept of liberalization through protectionist tariffs which ensure that Europeans control the most profitable operations, that is, processing. If an African exports unprocessed fruit to Europe, the tariff charges are 9%; if the fruit is processed and canned, the tariff charges jump to 32%; if the fruit is made into a beverage, the tariff increases to 42%[39]. This means that Africans are forced to sell unprocessed fruit, for the least profit. In contrast, Europeans are allowed to come into Africa, take ownership of farms growing fruit and factories that process the fruit, sell the processed and unprocessed fruit, and disappear with the profits. Such tariffs against African products are common throughout the wealthy world.

In 1997, the United States imposed restrictions on the sale of manufactured textiles from Kenya, while at the same time the importation of textiles into Kenya was intensified, directly causing the collapse of Rivatex, which laid off 1500 workers. In the long run, exports of Kenyan textiles fell from 511,000 pieces to only 68,000 pieces and 10,000 jobs were lost[40]. And even now, America has a very favorable reputation among Africans in Kenya.

Recently, the European Union banned Kenyans from selling fish inside the Union. This caused a fall in the price of fish as the catch intended for export was diverted onto the local market. Shippers, clearing and forwarding companies and

---

38. Report by Reuters, "Africa to lose $ 2.6 billion from trade", *Daily Nation*, 1996.

39. Vallely, *Bad Samaritans: First World Ethics and Third World Debt*.

40. Jacintah Sekoh-Ochieng, "Minister welcomes US textile move", *Daily Nation*, March 14, 1998, p. 12.

others dealing in fish lost income[41]. Samaki Industries, the largest local exporter of fresh fish to Europe, cut its workforce by 25%. Due to the switch to frozen fish, the company laid off 15% more of its worker[42]. The pretext for banning Kenyan fish was that the fish would transmit cholera, although scientists say that is impossible.

Many African countries spend up to 60% of their export earnings on oil imports. Now that second hand vehicles are imported with impunity, this situation has worsened. The influx of used cars is also increasing air pollution and crippling traffic jams on the underdeveloped road network; this further increases fuel consumption and pollution. Most of these vehicles have carburetors designed for use in low attitudes, where air has more oxygen. In a country such as Kenya, most cars are used several thousand meters above sea level. This has the effect of reducing the oxidation of the fuel, increasing the amount of carbon and other gases that cause pollution. Reduced efficiency leads to increased fuel consumption and more pollution.

Before the policy of import liberalization was implemented, Kenya was an exporter of sugar. After its implementation, the unregulated importation of sugar led to the collapse of the sugar industry — driving its estimated 1.5 million dependants into unemployment and poverty. Many sugar factories have gone bankrupt and are unable to pay their farmers; they are producing at less than 30% of their total capacity. Even at this lowered capacity of production, most local sugar is not bought as Kenyans rush to buy imported sugar. When the sugar industry collapsed, the West rushed in and convinced Kenyans that the problem was "lack of finance". This obviously meant that outside sources of money had to be sought. This rationalized the argument for inviting foreign investors. By 1999, the sugar industry in Kenya was re-colonized and its foreign senior staff were being paid Kshs 40 million ($666,667) per annum while the average Kenyans lives on less than Kshs 40 ($0.60) per day.

Considering how the twin policies of foreign investment and import liberalization have destroyed African economies, why do Africans still pursue these policies? The first mistake that governments in Africa made on acquiring independence was the failure to dismantle the then emerging neocolonialism. Most African rulers were products of colonialism themselves, having been hand-

---

41. Ondieki, "EU fish ban sparks crisis", p. 1.
42. Omondi, "EU fish exports ban hurts local firms", p. 16. Also Ondieki, "EU fish import ban sparks crisis", p. 1.

picked by the former colonialists specifically because they could be relied upon to pursue economic policies that would favor them. Thus, the first problem in African is the rulers.

The majority of people in Africa have been subjected to cultural imperialism and intense mental colonization. Africans worship Europeans and respect them far more than they respect themselves. This is the single biggest problem in Africa and all other problems, political, social, and economic, derive from it. It keeps Africans from questioning what the Caucasians tell them; in Kenya, when the "evil twins," the IMF and WB, ordered the adoption of liberalization, no one opposed the proposition.

Now that these policies have destroyed the country, rather than refusing to be governed by the IMF and WB, Kenyans still exhort one another on the importance of "encouraging foreign investor confidence". Africans can scarcely conceive that the foreigner investor is the true cause of their suffering. This denial shows up in how many Africans view the economy. The popular view as to the causes of economic collapse in Kenya is the collapsed infrastructure, poor road network, power shortages and corruption — especially corruption. The truth is that these factors are symptoms of a collapsed economy, rather than the cause. These false readings of the situation are propagated and entrenched by local economists, newspapers, politicians and other apologists of neocolonialism who support, and who sometimes are, the enemy.

Furthermore, African governments are bribed and threatened by the imperialist powers into accepting the destructive policies of the IMF and WB. The US State Department gave Kshs 600 million ($10 million) to officials in DR Congo so that US companies would be granted access to Congo's vast mineral resources. This is the same arrangement that the US had with Mobutu Sese Seko. In the rare case that a particular African leader refuses to allow the West access to his country's assets, the rich countries quickly embark on covert and overt operations aimed at killing or toppling that president. One example is the 1997 bloody overthrow of Congo (Brazzaville)'s president Pascal Lissouba, while the best known example is the attempted murder of Libyan leader Muaml16mar al-Qathafi in 1986 by the combined efforts of the British and Americans.

The solution to the problem of the adoption of wrong economic policies is a golden rule: that all economic policies be aimed at establishing a material and technical base inside Africa for the benefit of Africans without the inclusion of other races currently occupying Africa and siphoning off its wealth.

CHAPTER 4. LACK OF LEADERSHIP

All other economic and social problems in Africa are pegged to political leadership. It is the weak, visionless leadership of Africa that has allowed the sustained plunder of this continent.

African rulers are a product of colonialism; therefore, they can only propagate neocolonialism. The majority of these rulers are Europeanized and are unable to relate culturally with the people they govern. In Kenya, many politicians cannot complete one sentence in Swahili — the common language. Most of them speak to the rural populace in English and are astonished at the lack of response. They are more at ease in Paris, London and New York than in their own capital.

Many rulers in Africa genuinely try to uplift the people's standards of living but, in the long run, they betray them — either willingly or otherwise. In their efforts to help their people, they seek the advice of imperialists and so are unwittingly turned into accomplices of the international capitalist system; their good intentions are misdirected and negated. Repeated failure to solve the problems facing the people causes the ruler to give up and to turn, instead, to the accumulation of personal wealth. Many African rulers use political power to enrich themselves while colluding with the West to exploit and plunder their own country and people. The pattern is widespread, even if it varies in degree. Among the worst were Mobutu of Zaire and Colonel Bokassa of the Central African Republic.

Exactly what turns a committed freedom fighter into a puppet of the West? Many of the people who nominally govern Africa today were educated during the colonial or neocolonial periods; they are unable to offer anything better than that which they know. The other group is the military, where semi-illiterate and illiterate individuals rise through the ranks and, upon seizing power, they are even more easily manipulated than their educated counterparts.

When the colonial empires began to collapse, the metropolitan powers started to systematically eliminate genuine nationalists. They were arrested, exiled or killed. Mentally colonized Africans and others of dubious loyalties were moved into positions of importance in the local administration and armed forces. Then independence was proclaimed and power was handed over to these reactionaries surrounded by European advisors. Of course, not all independence rulers were traitors. Those who firmly opposed neocolonialism were quickly toppled through coups or assassinations or were rendered ineffective by civil wars or economic collapse. There are several examples.

If an African ruler is firmly opposed to neocolonialism and is a progressive, then he is sure to fall from power. Kwame Nkrumah was a pan-Africanist who believed that if Africa were to unite, many common problems could be solved. He actively campaigned for unity and thus brought about his own downfall. He was overthrown in a military coup arranged by the US and UK. It should be kept in mind that the British were always opposed to handing power to him when they were withdrawing their colonial apparatus. Nkrumah had won national elections twice and both times the British colonial government refused to have him named Prime Minister for the simple fact that they could not control him. When he did become leader, he was soon thrown out and exiled.

In Algeria, Ben Bella, the man who led the armed resistance that overthrew the French, was targeted by a French- and US-orchestrated coup soon after independence. Today there is a "civil" war in which freedom fighters under the banner of Islam are fighting the neocolonialists who control the military government. In effect it is a war to end France's neocolonialism of Algeria. In cases where the African ruler enjoys massive support in his country and is opposed to neocolonialism, such that no ethnic/political divisions can be exploited to foment a civil war, then that country is invaded directly. The best example would be the invasion of Egypt by the combined might of Israel, Great Britain and France in 1956 after Nasser abrogated the treaty which had allowed the French and British to own the Suez Canal through the concept of foreign investment. However, the invasion did not manage to overthrow Nasser. Other examples include the aerial invasion of Libya by the US, the invasion of Uganda by Israel, Chad by France, Angola by the US, Zaire by Belgium and the US.

The other case is when an African ruler refuses to bow to the demands of the imperialist nations. If he tries an alternative path to development, disapproved by the West, a civil war is fomented in order to render impossible the move from a colonially-structured economy to a normal, growing economy. The West simply exploits the ethnic and political divisions — and where none exist, they create them. Just before the Biafran War (1967-1970), the British embassy in Lagos concentrated on propaganda that directly increased ethnic tensions that fueled the war. Money, arms and military training are then supplied to fuel and escalate the war. Outstanding examples of externally caused and sustained "civil" wars are Angola and Mozambique, where war has raged for more than 20 years because the government sought to try a non-neocolonial path to development — one that did not include the West. Other examples are the brief but bloody civil war that overthrew President Lissouba of Congo (Brazzaville), the genocides of Rwanda.

It is rare for an African leader to refuse to obey the West and not find the CIA instigating a civil war, a coup or an assassination. In Tanzania's case, an economic blockade was effected. When Tanzania sought help from the West to construct the Tazara/Tanzam railway, that help was denied. Later machinations by the British brought down the East African Community in 1977 and this, among other factors, brought Tanzania to its knees, effectively crippling Mwalimu Nyerere. Tanzania reverted to neocolonialism after a brief spell of freedom. The economic blockade was also recently used against Libya with the aim of bringing down its leader.

In cases whereby a Westward-leaning ruler is installed but with considerable local opposition, the West provides arms, organization, and money to create a war machine to prop him up; and the "leader" then holds down the people so that the multinationals can take away the national wealth. Mobutu's long reign in Zaire is exemplary. Whenever local opposition materialized in the form of an ill-equipped rebel army, the French and Americans quickly moved in and destroyed the freedom fighters.

The betrayal of African people also occurs when the rulers identify with the people's enemies. As a result of cultural imperialism and mental colonization, Africans have come to believe that a person gains value if he is a *mzungu* or if he transforms himself into one. Africans have also come to associate poverty, squalor, disease, ignorance and suffering with anything African; and the "good life" has come to be related with all things European. When an African becomes rich, he immediately changes and becomes a *mzungu*. Many rich Africans have

European wives, eat European food, speak European languages only, and take their children to European schools and later to Europe and America for "further studies" in the European way of life. It is from this rich, mentally-colonized elite that rulers in Africa are drawn. Because this rich clique identifies with the Europeans and Americans, and has been educated according to their notions, it follows the fallacious advice of the IMF and WB and thereby reinforce the economic collapse of Africa. This curious situation of an African country being run by people who would rather be in Europe creates many problems; the wealthy people in government are more interested in shopping in London and Paris than in getting the poor people out of the slums.

The lack of leadership on a continental scale has also aggravated the effects of poor leadership in individual African states. Continental leadership was expected to coordinate joint action between African countries to overthrow neocolonial hegemony, because no single African country can overthrow neocolonialism by its own efforts. Instead, the defunct OAU and the AU became tools used by the neocolonialists. This was proven when in 1997 the Assistant Secretary General of the OAU proclaimed that "Africa is the last great frontier for [foreign] investment", a statement that reveals that continental leadership is compromised and is now a tool for furthering the re-colonization.

In many countries of Africa, the private enterprise has become weak and development has stagnated because such governments remain passive. Derived development needs government intervention. A considerable part of the total investment is the social overhead which only a government can undertake. Weak private enterprise is mostly due to the allocation of large amounts of capital to the consumption of imported goods. Thus a progressive government would use the tax power to increase productive investment. Unfortunately, most African governments use tax money for debt servicing, and the rest either buys vanity items such as limousines or is taken by high officials. Apart from finance, the strength of government is organization. It is also in a good position to orient the development of the economy through the means of direct and indirect economic planning and greater regulation. But this power of the government will be destroyed by the Multilateral Agreement on Investment. The government also has a responsibility of ensuring that income shifts from those who will spend less productively to those will spend more productively. The state should also act to mobilize supplies of finance and undertake major entrepreneurial acts.

With the onset of privatization, most African governments have taken a back seat in matters concerning the steering of development. A weak private enterprise and a passive government leave a vacuum which foreign investors are filling.

Much has been said about corruption, and the blame is usually put on African rulers' excessive powers. In their fierce competition with each other the multinationals offer large bribes to government officials in order to secure contracts. It is the people who bear the cost of the bribe. It has been estimated that as a result of corruption, African rulers have stashed outside the continent more than Kshs 1,200 billion ($20 billion).

In many respects, African rulers are the greatest obstacle to development. We shall look at a few from the four main regions of Africa as well as a few minor ones. From West Africa we shall study "Leopold" Sedar Senghor, Central Africa; Mobutu Sese Seko, East Africa; and Jomo Kenyatta.

SEDAR SENGHOR[43]

Senghor was the first African ruler of Senegal. The French specifically chose him because he was culturally alienated and mentally colonized; he fulfilled his role well as Senegal has never deviated from the neocolonial path and is one of the poorest countries in the world. He received his primary education at the seminary at Nyasobil, where all his teachers were Europeans. He developed a high proficiency in the French language, and was taken to the Liberman College in Dakar and then to Paris; he studied at the Ecole Normale Superieure and finally the Sorbonne University. He later became a professor of French language. When the second world war broke out in 1939, he joined the French army; France later sent him to the French National Assembly. The French acted in the belief that the colonies would never be independent of them; this is what inspired them to institute the policy of assimilation. Senghor was sent to the French Parliament to represent Senegal as though it were a province of France. Afterward, he was appointed Mayor of Thies. The French also used him to infiltrate and subvert the Negritude movement. Naturally, he married a *mzungu*.

---

43. Ciugu Mwagiru, "Sedar Senghor's proud legacy to Africa," Lifestyle Magazine, *Sunday Nation*, January 4 1998, pp. 2-3.

When nominal independence was granted to Senegal, the French gave Sedar Senghor power and in neocolonial fashion he won subsequent elections. As ruler of Senegal, he also served as a minister in the French government and a member of the Council of Europe.

When he quit the Presidency he left power to a trusted heir who has never deviated from the path set out by their foreign friends. In 1983, Senghor became the first "African" to be elected to the Académie Française. As a poet, he never wrote in his native African language but opted for French. Today, he spends his time in Normandy, France because he is more at ease with Europeans than Africans. This man is famous and well liked in Europe. In Africa, he is famous for being famous in Europe. An African's greatness among Caucasians is pegged to the extent to which that African is compromised and to the degree to which he has betrayed his own people. Sedar Senghor, like Mandela, is popular among Westerners because of the level to which they have subverted the freedom and independence of their countries. This explains why patriots and nationalists such as Al-Qathafi are hated by the West.

MOBUTU SESE SEKO

Many people would say Mobutu Sese Seko was born a traitor. By 1959, Mobutu was working secretly for the Belgian police whom he supplied with detailed reports on the activities of fellow Africans. He had been sent to Brussels by the Belgians, and while there he studied journalism and infiltrated Lumumba's political party. He was then recruited as a CIA informant. This relationship bore fruit when the CIA and Mobutu arranged for the murder of Lumumba and the rise of Mobutu to power[44]. This aided the Americans in acquiring control of all the mineral deposits in the former Zaire. The Americans dumped Mobutu when they realized that they did not need him since the policy of foreign investment had taken root. During Mobutu's reign, Zaire was the eighth poorest nation on earth, while it was the richest nation in Africa in terms of mineral deposits and other resources. Mobutu's personal wealth (held in Europe and other places) was estimated to be Kshs 240 billion ($4 billion). Mobutu was the classic example of post-colonial rulers selected and managed by

---

44. Sean Kelly, *America's Tyrant*, American University Press, Washington DC, 1993.

the colonial powers, thus condemning the continent to a future of upheavals, wars and massacres to maintain neocolonialism.

JOMO KENYATTA

Kenyatta was born "Johnstone" Kamau. Through historical accident this man ended up as Kenya's first African ruler. It cannot be denied that he was nationalist but he ended up subverting all the hopes of progressive Africans. He was an accomplice of the international capitalist system that is the principal cause of the current difficulties in Africa. Kenyatta became an agent of neocolonialism when he abandoned his family and went to Britain in 1931; he married a *mzungu* and lived there for fifteen years. When he returned, in 1946, he married a daughter of a colonial chief and became the leader of the British loyalists, the Kikuyu. The increased fervor of nationalistic agitation that occurred immediately after his return occurred in spite of rather than because of him. Kenyatta had that aura of prestige that crowned the colonial government and Europeans in general. The British increased his prestige by jailing him and transforming a loyalist into a gallant nationalist hero overnight. The British had recognized that Kenyatta could be relied upon to ensure that progressive Africans did not come to power and also to keep Kenya firmly in the neocolonial fold. The British knew that if elements of the Kenya Land and Freedom Army (erroneously known as Mau Mau) came to power, they would lose their hold over Kenya. They also knew that Kenyatta was part of the Kikuyu and had even married a British woman. It was with this knowledge that they prolonged his stay in detention as a ploy to cause Africans to demand his release, thus increasing his prestige as a nationally acceptable leader. Upon his release, Kenyatta went about the country pleading with the racist settlers not to leave and assuring them that his government was not their enemy, that it harbored no grudges. The settlers eventually left anyway, rather than being governed by "black monkeys", and Kenyatta forced landless Africans to buy their farms — farms which the British had never paid for when they took the land from the Africans.

The Kikuyu will be the focus of our analysis of the post independence years, because it is they who went on to dominate the government during Kenyatta's presidency. However, it was not the entire Kikuyu community that dominated the government; most Kikuyu are destitute, like other Kenyan Africans. A tiny, wealthy elite controlled the state, and we will trace the roots of this elite which was instrumental in perpetuating and aiding the continued presence of neocolonialism in Kenya.

During the colonial era, there were chiefs, home guards and other British loyalists associated with the colonial churches. These were the people through whom the British ruled after they overran Kenyan communities at the turn of the last century. The British, during their occupation, appointed weak and vulnerable men to rule over the community. For example, the fellow who was declared to be "Senior Chief" Kinyanjui was a poor hunter, and thus had a very poor social standing. Kinyanjui wa Gathirimu started as a porter and was first made headman in Dagoretti, then a chief and finally paramount chief. His rise was due to the fact that he helped the British take Gikuyu land. With British help he also acquired land — and over 100 wives. Other outcasts who were made into chiefs were Karuri wa Gakure and Wang'ombe wa Ihura. They had absolute power in the "native reserves" and formed a privileged group together with the home guards and others whose loyalties had been diverted. Members of this elite sent their children to foreign schools and lived an easy life. When the war for land and freedom broke out, this mentally colonized group firmly opposed it and the Kenya Land and Freedom Army (Mau Mau), and supported the British. History made a mockery of KLFA because, after the end of the war and on attainment of self government it was the traitors to Kenya who came into power. This elite became even more affluent in neocolonial Kenya and it continued to ally and identify with the neocolonialists during this neocolonial era. It was and still is the main beneficiary of both the colonial and neocolonial exploitation of Kenya.

This is also true in other African countries. Today this elite is wholly Europeanized and mentally colonized. It is still in power throughout the continent and is responsible for the collapse and relapse of Africa into re-colonization. In Kenya its most treacherous action (apart from overthrowing the independence of this country) is the continued ignoring of the role played by KLFA in the acquisition of independence as embodied in the burial of Dedan Kimathi in the Kamiti Maximum Prison.

Because the ruling elite in Africa is a product of retrogression, it has led Africa into retrogression. When most African countries attained independence, they attained complete freedom. The first actions of the ruling elite were aimed to defeat this freedom, leading to what is known as mere "flag independence". The next step taken by the new rulers was to entrench neocolonialism, and now the rulers of Africa are in the process of returning Africa into colonialism.

In the early 1990s, a wave of civil upheavals swept all through Africa in which people started demanding "democracy". It should be noted that this "democracy" is a Western value. This imported "democracy", like "human rights", seeks to uphold individual rights over communal rights. It is a product of Western culture and is not democracy in fact. In the West, the family institution has collapsed and the prevalent culture there tries to deny that man is a social being and must live in harmony with the wishes of the society as a whole. The imported concept of "human rights" is part of the plan to cause the disintegration of closely-knit communities (in Africa, as everywhere) by attempting to popularize the idea that the individual is more important than the group. This is why prostitution and pornography are legal in the West.

Western states call for "democracy" in Africa as an avenue for extending their influence. Before their invasion, Africa could be categorized into four stages of socio-political organization.

In the first category I include various the forms of government by the absolute ruler, for example Shaka, or Buganda's Kabaka, or many Western Sudan kingdoms.

In the second category there was an elected ruler or government. In Buganda, for instance, all elements of modern governments were present. There was a cabinet of three ministers — the *Katikiro;* and there was a parliament called the *Lukiko*. The society's rights were more important than individual rights, meaning that an individual had to obey societal norms and standards which had grown out of experience. In this stage or category, power was not concentrated on any one person. In this case a medicine man, prophet or chief was elected and ruled with the help of a council. Another good example is the Nandi, whose *Orkoiyot* (supreme chief) was assisted by a council, the *Maotik*, to govern. Although this was not quite democracy in a Western sense, it was still a democratic form of self-governing.

In the third category I include communities that managed to thrive without being under the control of one person. This is the purest form of democracy, and is absent in the world today. The Kikuyu are a good example. They had no central authority and the tools of coercion and oppression, the police and army, were absent because when morals are respected and upheld, enforcers are unnecessary. In place of a single ruler there was a supreme council of elders, *Kiama*, which guided rather than governed the people. This council did not represent the people, in the sense of working to implement their wishes, but strove for what was in everyone's best interest. Decisions were made after extensive consultation and were obeyed by everyone, without question. This pure form of democracy was common throughout Africa and ensured that no one could exploit another; all men were equal in fact, and no one could die of starvation while others enjoyed a surplus and threw away the excess. This social organization was developed in response to the needs of the people and their environment.

The fourth category comprises those human groups that hunted and gathered and had no form of government. In this case class stratification did not exist and democracy was absolute. The only people accorded superior status were elders, and age, and not wealth or class, determined seniority.

In conclusion, it is correct to say that democracy is not alien to Africa and the brand of Western democracy that seeks to hold an individual's rights to be superior or more important than the societal morals and rules has little place in the traditional Africa.

In Europe, industrialization and capitalism changed social relations. In the past thousand years, most Europeans never knew any form of democracy. At the time of the Roman Empire slavery was widespread and later gave way to serfdom, whereby the freed slaves were tied to the land permanently. Most of the land was owned by the few people who made up the ruling elite. Feudalism gave way to capitalism, under which the principal factor in producing wealth was not the land, but factories, etc. Like feudalism, capitalism is characterized by a few people owning the means of producing wealth. The bulk of the people remain poor and exploited. Under capitalism, the serfs were released from the land by the mechanization of agriculture, and taken to work in the factories where the capitalists exercised total control over their lives. Democracy is not inherent or complete in Western nations.

It was once assumed that capitalism should have given way to communism, where the principle of economic equality would be restored. In Russia, the declaration of the "dictatorship of the workers" was a result of the European urban environment and proves the superiority of the traditional democracies of Africa. Communism aimed at creating new social relations in Europe — relations that were already existent in the old traditional societies from rural Russia to rural Africa. In many African communities, people lived and worked together and shared everything that was produced, each according to his needs. Communism sought to give the Europeans a system equivalent to that communalism under which Africans had lived for a thousand years.

International capitalism has survived simply because it has managed to provide the workers of Europe, Japan and North America a higher standard of living by taking advantage of weaker countries.

The capitalists upheld individual freedom over society's control. Moral standards had to be dismantled and lowered so that decadence could become acceptable. The elites of the world have allowed immorality to take root with official encouragement; broad sections of those who are not among the elite, Africans certainly included, have confused this moral decay with "modernity" and accepted it as a sign of "development". One may still ask, however, whether society as a whole must accept every individual's personal inclinations or whether it is up to individuals to abide by society's rules and standards. Freedom must always come with responsibility.

In Kenya, the politicians who emerged after the legalization of multipartyism are not driven by the dream of serving Kenyans; they are driven by avarice. Opposition politicians did not demand multipartyism out of altruism, but opportunism. The opposition parties had nothing in common except the unbridled desire to gain power. Now that they have come to power, the basic problem in Kenya — the continued strangulating presence of neocolonialism — has not been solved, because the politicians are from the same mentally colonized elite that took over after the attainment of independence. They had personal differences with the Kanu government, not programmatic differences based on political or economic issues. The leadership deficit in Kenya is bound to continue for some time. The government has not spoken against neocolonialism and the ongoing relapse into colonialism. Only a meek attempt has been made by the Economic Independence Party, which has not made the connection between cultural imperialism and economic colonization.

OTHERS

Many Africans who have had the fortune of becoming rulers are drawn from among the mentally colonized. Idi Amin wanted to construct "Africa's Empire State Building", while Ivory Coast's President Houphouet Boigny chose to spend almost half his country's annual earnings to construct the biggest cathedral in the world. In the Central African Republic, the ruler, Bokassa was so mentally colonized that he bought the French President Valery d'Estaing a presidential jet. In 1977 Jean Bedel Bokassa decided to crown himself Emperor; during the coronation ceremony, he wore a Kshs 120 million ($2 million) gold crown topped by a 138 carat diamond; his robe imported from France cost Kshs 8.7 million ($145,000). The total cost of this coronation was Kshs 1.4 billion ($23.3 million). He later held a party that cost the CAR half of its annual budget and bankrupted the country[45].

In this general pattern of betrayal and relentless cupidity, at least one leader has distinguished himself by his loyalty to his people. Since coming to power in 1969, Muammar al-Qathafi has successfully blocked cultural imperialism and other forms of imperialism. Libya enjoys a welfare society and sane economic policies are pursued. Unnecessary importation of luxuries is outlawed and any surplus income is therefore not sent out of the country but is ploughed back in to further productive investment. This has provided a sustained high living standard for ordinary Libyans as well as many migrant workers. Libyans do not suffer from starvation even though the country is a desert; neither do they die of preventable diseases as a result of poor medical services. Because of his success in developing and protecting Libya from foreigners, Al-Qathafi has acquired many enemies. The West showed its teeth in 1986 when the Americans attempted to murder him and when this failed, Western states imposed an economic embargo on Libya and cut diplomatic links in an attempt to bring about economic collapse, which, it was hoped, would bring Al-Qathafi down. It failed.

In sub-Saharan African countries, governments directly work to subvert the independence of Africa. This is exemplified in the use of colonial place names. The three East African countries do their fellow Africans no favor by retaining the colonial name for the second largest fresh water body on earth; it remains "Lake "Victoria". Africans particularly like the name "Victoria": apart from Lake Victoria there is Victoria Falls, and there are many statues of Queen Victoria in South Africa. It is ironic that Africans honor a woman who openly said she thought Africans were a species of baboons or monkeys. In Kenya, you will also find a "Thompson" Falls. In other areas whole cities are named after *wazungus*, such as Brazzaville and Johannesburg. No wonder so many Africans prefer to use European names.

In Kenya, the mental colonization runs deep. Even after forty years of independence, students are still taught which Europeans "discovered" what. Judges

---

45. Graham Hancock, *Lords of Poverty*, Mandarin Paperbacks, London, 1991, p. 177.

wear wigs which look like a white man's hair. It was a tragic, if fitting, symbol of a century of colonization economically, culturally, politically and mentally when the Government of Kenya lowered the flag in honor of Princess Diana, a member of the ruling family that has sent an army to dominate the country for seventy years.

Perhaps the best symbol of the glorification of neocolonialism by the Africans of Kenya is the naming of the second highest peak of Mt. Kenya in honor of *Oloibon* (Supreme Chief) Lenana of the Maasai. He is singularly remembered for betraying his people into the hands of the British, causing the Maasai Nation to lose half its territory. That such a quisling would be idolized raises many questions; for one, in whose name do the "post-colonial" rulers rule? The Mau Mau struggle was instrumental to the achievement of independence. It was peasants who rose up against the brutal British colonial regime and sacrificed their lives in order to set Kenya free, but it was the loyalists and other traitors who were given power when the British withdrew and therefore not even one monument has been constructed in the insurgent peasants' honor. Instead, colonial and neocolonial relics such as Fort Jesus and the Macmillan Library are still standing and are even maintained by the state. The only soldiers honored by the Kenya Army are those misguided individuals who were drafted to fight in the European wars of 1914–1918 and 1939–1945. They are buried in dignified, well-maintained war cemeteries while Mau Mau fighters remain in the mass graves where they were dumped by the British after the massacres which cost 12,000 lives.

Multipartyism was supposed to solve the leadership crisis in Kenya, but has been a failure. It should be abandoned. Human and citizen rights must be upheld, but endless argument and partisan politicking weaken central leadership more often than not; and more important, multipartyism fails to solve grave national problems like the overthrow of neocolonialism.

CHAPTER 5. LACK OF CAPITAL

A major hindrance to economic development is the lack of capital for productive investment. This is a common problem throughout Africa. How is capital drained from Africa?

Money flows out through various paths that include the repatriation of profits by foreign companies working in Africa; economic policies that have allowed these companies to repatriate 100% of their mega profits have only aggravated the situation. It has been estimated that the rich countries of the West derive some Kshs 1,080,000,000,000 annually from African countries. This figure includes profits from the distorted global trade, profits accumulated by foreign multinationals, sales from exports to Africa; it does not even include debt repayments. The battle may not be primarily fought by the military, but the absence of overt war does not mean the nations of the world are at peace.

As for debt servicing payments, in 2004, Africa owed foreign countries and financial institutions Kshs 15,576,000,000,000 ($194.7 billion) with a service ratio of 30% a staggering 58.6% of GDP excluding Nigeria and South Africa[46]. It costs Africa up to three times the amount it receives in "aid" to service this debt. Africa pays the wealthy states annually an average of Kshs 3,120,000,000,000 ($52 billion)[47].

With a domestic debt of Kshs 306 billion ($3.8 billion), Kenya pays Kshs 23 billion ($285 million) as *interest* on this debt, that is, 8.8% of the total annual

---

46. IMF, *Sub-Saharan Africa Regional Economic Outlook*, October 2004.
47. Mutuma Mathiu, "Have Kenyans lost business sense?" *Sunday Nation*, July 1998.

Government revenue[48]. Kenya, as of 2004, also has an external debt of Kshs 456 billion ($5.7 billion), the repayment of which accounts for 5% of the Government's annual expenditure, and some 37.9% of Gross National Product[49]. As well as a trade deficit of Kshs109 billion ($1.4 billion)[50]. This large scale financial hemorrhaging causes death, in a country as it would in a human being.

Another avenue for capital flight is thorough unhindered importation. The policy of trade liberalization has allowed much needed capital to be misspent on unnecessary items and vanity goods, such as luxury vehicles. As 2004 Central Bank of Kenya figures reveal, unrestricted imports had cost Kenya Kshs 310,720,000,000 ($3,844 million) for that period[51]. Such funding, if invested locally, could jump start the domestic economy.

Another route for capital flight is through the exportation of wealth by the rich, most of whom are mentally colonized. In most of Africa, there are very few who gained their riches legitimately. Most of them are politicians and high government officials. They not only take advantage of the weakness of their nations to enrich themselves, they stash their money away in Europe and spend lavishly. It has been calculated that African rulers and other wealthy Africans have hidden over Kshs 1,200,000,000,000 ($20 billion) in foreign bank accounts.

In any discussion of capital flight, the role of the two Bretton Woods institutions, the International Monetary Fund (IMF) and the World Bank (WB), must be a major consideration. The economic theories and policies that they promote only bring further damage wherever they have been adopted. The main functions of the IMF and WB in Africa are to propagate false economic theories, represent the imperialists' interests, and foster the re-colonization of Africa.

FALSE ECONOMIC THEORIES

As a "solution" to African poverty and underdevelopment, the IMF and the WB advised that loans and aid be increased, population growth retarded, exports of primary products increased, and structural adjustment programs be

---

48. Central Bank of Kenya, *Monthly Economic Review*, July 2004, p. 51.

49. IMF, *Sub-Saharan Africa Regional Economic Outlook*, October 2004. These figures are differs with Central Bank of Kenya's figures which puts Kenya's external debt (June 2004) at Kshs 403.4 billion, 34.8% of GDP.

50. Central Bank of Kenya, *Monthly Economic Review*, July 2004, p. 31.

51. *Ibid.*, p. 31.

implemented. This bundle of prescriptions has caused the economic ills from which Africa suffers today. We shall break down this "solution" into its constituent factors and study each one of them in depth.

Loans and Aid

First, loans are given both as a way to bolster the alien neocolonial economic structure and also as a means of making easy money. Colonial powers during the colonial era provided money to facilitate the exploitation of the colonies. For example, the British government financed the Uganda railway that stretched from Mombasa to Kisumu. The objective was to tie the Kenya colony's economy to the British one in a lopsided way, such that Britain was to benefit more than Kenya. The colonial powers were willing to spend money on African colonies to set up the colonial economic structure. Today, African countries have to be given aid and loans to avert collapse. If all the neocolonial economies throughout Africa were to collapse, their "business partners" would lose, and eventually Africans would gain control of what was lost by the non-Africans. Thus, "aid" and loans are not given to Africans to help Africans; they are given to maintain, sustain and prop the colonial economies. "Aid" is like lubricating oil applied to a rusty system to keep it working.

There is also money to be made in maintaining economic colonialism, and so the means of sustaining economic colonialism has become an end in itself. The West began lending primarily to make profit. This is similar to what happened to cultural imperialism; at first, this policy was pursued as a way of mentally colonizing and controlling Africans to facilitate continued neocolonial exploitation. The means became the end when the West found out that they could mentally colonize African and make money while they were at it. TV programs, movies, music, clothes and all the constituents of cultural imperialism were promoted as a way of making profits through sales of the same.

Those countries that have refused or were denied aid and loans have experienced tremendous growth rates. A good example is China, whose main preoccupation over the years is an "overheating" economy, growing at a rate of 9.1% in 2003[52] (while Africa's neocolonial economy "grew" at 0.02% per annum for 1990-02[53]).

---

52. UN Department of Economic and Social Affairs, *Economic Report on Africa; Recent Economic Trends in Africa and Prospects for 2004*, p. 27.

Second, aid and loans are also given in order to help foreign companies entrench themselves. The West assists its giant corporations in exploiting African countries by giving bilateral aid tied to procurement of goods and services from the donor country. In addition, the imperialist country negotiates agreements with African countries whereby the foreign-owned corporations pay little or no tax and are even guaranteed a minimum profit, and the right to repatriate all profits. If the leadership of the exploited country changes and embarks on a program of nationalization of the interests of the foreign companies, then the rich state in which the multinationals are based resorts to covert and overt schemes to overthrow the country's leadership. That happened in Chile in 1973.

"Donor" countries also assist their companies in other, subtle ways. Foreign companies invest primarily to make profit and take it home. Any benefit that the African population may accrue is purely unintended. The example of the hospital is explained above; a donor country may finance the construction of a hospital in Kenya but the main underlying objective would be to provide an outlet for medicine produced by companies based in that donor country and also help that company secure a foothold for future penetration of the Kenyan market. In reality, this is not aid at all.

The IMF, WB, and other donors also coerce African governments to pursue policies that will aid foreign countries to entrench and strengthen their grip on African resources. In 1992, the Government of Kenya was given five months to undertake far-reaching reforms in order to qualify for new aid. What were the conditions? The government was ordered to abolish the provincial administrations within five months. The unstated reason for this was to create a vacuum at the grassroots level so that NGOs (nongovernmental organizations recognized by the UN) would have a freer hand in pursuing their anti-African agendas. Most of the NGOs in Kenya are financed by the West, which also defines and controls their activities. This is important to the donors who are currently working at reducing the number of Africans on the planet. If the provincial administration was dismantled, NGOs directly funded by the donors would be able to pursue "family planning" activities which include the giving of contraceptives to primary and secondary students, with deadly side effects. The second demand was that the Government negotiate and complete the sale of the Nyayo Bus Corporation to the Kenya Bus Service, which at that time was British

---

53. The World Bank, *World Development Indicators Online*, 2004 found at http://devdata.worldbank.org/dataonline/.

owned. The donors' objective, as they claimed, was to "rationalize the rates on which the companies operate, hence reduce the losses of [the British owned company] arising from duplication of their services". It was a very open attempt at transforming the bus company into a monopoly, which would have increased profits, and also the dividends paid out to British shareholders. The donors resisted the suggestion that NBS be sold to Africans through a public issue of shares. They did not want NBS to be commercialized; they preferred it to be privatized, since that would enable the British-owned bus company to strengthen its grip on the transport industry in Kenya. The third demand was that the Government allow exporters to retain 40% of the foreign exchange earned, increasing in the course of a year to a full 100%. It must be noted that many exporters in the industrial sector are not Africans, and in the agricultural sector as well, although some Kenyan politicians have infiltrated that fraternity. This change in policy would mean that if Unilever, which parades itself as East Africa Industries, sells soap outside Kenya, Kenya would earn nothing and all the profit acquired would be repatriated to Unilever's London headquarters without even passing through Kenya. An increase in Kenyan exports would not necessarily bring a commensurate increase in the amount of revenue Kenya earns from the exports; all the profits would directly go into foreign hands that own the factories, industries, land and mines.

Thirdly, aid and loans are provided as a means of securing markets and cheap sources of raw materials. Aid is simply one more weapon in the global struggle by the West to capture more and more markets for their goods and cheap sources of raw materials. Africa is still functioning in its allotted colonial role as a limitless market and bottomless pool of cheap labor and raw materials. "Aid" serves to guarantee that this situation becomes permanent forever. This is how it works.

A donor country, say Germany, donates funds for the construction of a road and several bridges in Kenya. The construction is expected to require several thousand tons of tarmac and cement and employ thousands of workers and one or two hundred highly qualified engineers. Kenya is requesting foreign support is because it lacks the money to construct the road and bridges; the country does not lack skilled personnel, cement and tarmac. Yet the German donors will demand that the Kenyans accept machinery, cement, tarmac and majority of the skilled personnel from Germany although all these are available in Kenya and at far lower cost. This means that Kenyan cement manufacturers shall not benefit by supplying cement for the construction of a Kenyan road in

Kenya, but German cement manufacturers shall benefit from what the Kenyans have lost. In any case, the loss is slight since all the cement-making firms in Kenya are owned by foreigners, anyway! Kenyans accept such conditions either because a high government official has been bribed or because they have no other sources of finance to construct the road themselves. And this loan from Germany will have to be repaid, at a high interest. In effect, the Kenyans shall be paying Germany more money than was lent in the first place and will have provided high-paying jobs to German engineers, and a market for German cement and tar as well as the imported machinery. More than 90% of the initial money provided for the road construction project shall actually remain in Germany and an additional sum shall have to be found somewhere to cover the interest on the loan. In total, Kenyans have actually received only 10% of the money because the machinery, materials and skilled manpower were procured in Germany although they were available cheaply in Kenya. Furthermore, the goods imported from the donor country are normally overpriced by up to 40%, pushing up the costs to Kenya and the profits to the "donor".

The London based Overseas Development Institute (ODI) estimated that over 60% of the European Union aid to Africa is tied, as described in the above example. One French package required 45% of the funds to be spent on contracts with French companies[54]. The Commonwealth Development Corporation is wholly owned by the British Government but operates as an autonomous agency. It is not a supplier of goods but if it is managing a project it will be responsible for the placing of orders. It normally orders only from British-owned companies even if the material required is available more cheaply in the African country. A Japanese contribution to partly cover the costs of one aid project set a percentage on the total cost of the scheme, so the recipients actually returned more than twice the funds Japan gave to Japanese firms[55]. The term "tied aid" means that the recipients of that aid are prevented from acquiring more cost-effective services from countries other than the donors themselves. If the recipients of EU aid (more than 60% of which was tied), had been allowed to spend funds elsewhere, the value of that aid would have increased by at least Kshs. 120 billion ($2 billion)[56]. More than $12 billion of aid to developing countries is tied including most "technical" and "emergency assistance". For example in 2001,

---

54. Julian Samboma, "Economist downplays foreign investment," *Daily Nation*, 1996.
55. *Ibid.*
56. *Ibid.*

only 30% of Canada's ODA was untied. Between 1995 and 1999, the US on average gave less than 25% untied aid annually[57]. Tied aid in effect means that recipient African countries lose more than they gain.

The fourth reason why rich nations are so eager to provide loans and aid to African countries, apart from the profit motive, is to maintain neocolonialism. As asserted before, even after the acquisition of independence the previous colony remains an economic and social appendage of the old colonial power, having a socio-economic structure that is totally dependent on that power. Naturally, a national economy should be able to stand on its own feet, but because African economies are colonial, and therefore abnormal, they have to be propped up. Otherwise, they would collapse under the weight of their contradictions. Neocolonialism is a total system whereby political power is used to facilitate the economic exploitation of a weaker country by a stronger one. "Aid" is also given to poor countries which support the imperialist powers in their oppression and exploitation of other poor nations. For example, all those African countries that supported the USA, Western Europe and Japan in the UN in their bid to overthrow the Libyan government by imposing economic sanctions were assured of future aid packages. Aid also serves to increase the economic and political vulnerability and dependence of recipient countries by keeping them politically weak, by making their economies increasingly reliant upon assistance and the world market in which their individual position as buyers and sellers is weak, and by expanding the importance of private exploitative foreign investment. Increased dependency creates more room for further dependency, until a country gets caught in the aid trap. This is soon followed by the sovereign status of that country becoming a myth. This aid trap has caught nearly all African countries, including Kenya. Development is severely retarded even though the GDP may rise.

African governments have become so weak that some of their ministries (such as defense, finance and foreign affairs) are run by the donors. It is the IMF and WB that authorize the disbursement of loans and also determine to what use the money will be put, completely second guessing the Government. In effect, it is foreigners who run Africa and it is under their control that Africa has followed its current path.

---

57. UN Department of Economic and Social Affairs, *World Economic and Social Survey 2004*, New York, 2004.

If it is foreigners who run the financial, foreign affairs and defense matters of each African country, what does this mean? A return to colonialism. In countries of vital importance to Western interests, they ensure peace — because a war renders the raw materials inaccessible. Sometimes war is deliberately as a way of boosting the sales of Western military equipment, and also because once the war is over the West still benefits by supplying aid and loans as well as sales of machinery, factories, industries and other commodities such as medicinal drugs and skilled personnel [expatriates] to replace what was destroyed in the "civil" war. That Africans will die in that war is hardly a problem; see the section on underpopulation.

Aid is also given to governments that ensure their countries remain firmly in the neocolonial fold. The major recipients of American aid were and are those whose loyalty in the cold war and the "anti-terrorism" campaign have been most reliable. Urgency of need is not a criterion in determining the size and allocation of aid; rather, decisions are based on the American imperialist strategy and are strongly influenced by an economic relationship which has grown out of the new military imperialism. For example, "South" Vietnam was allocated about Kshs 24 billion ($400 million) annually between 1965 and 1975, most of which was used to fuel the "civil" war in Vietnam[58].

"Aid" functions and exists to serve the donor and not the recipient. The American "Economic Policy Initiative" shows Africans how to pay off their debts. A country only qualifies for loans on satisfying the conditions that (1) its government reduces spending by cutting down the civil service, and (2) that food farming be replaced with cash crops so that foreign exchange may be obtained to pay off the interest on the debts. The Kenya Government has been pursuing this policy, and with disastrous results. It has embarked on reducing the civil service and more than 100,000 workers are faced with unemployment. It has also raised taxes and cut spending on healthcare. The effects are obvious; Kenyans are dying of easily prevented diseases and illiteracy has increased. Wages in the public sector have also been held down and the massive loss of capital due to import liberalization and repatriation of all profits by foreign companies has caused the shilling to be devalued and has increased inflation, thus reducing the real income of wage earners. In the agricultural sector the Government is trying to increase the amount of land under cash crops rather than food crops. To encourage farmers to switch over, taxes were reduced on agricul-

---

58. John Pilger, *Heroes*, Pan Books Limited, 1987.

tural implements and inputs used in cash crop farming. This has been the policy pursued since the early 1990s and has resulted in widespread hunger and star-vation, a well known case being a hungry boy who ate a dead dog and died immediately afterwards[59]. Hundreds of villagers have also died as a result of con-suming spoiled food rather than throw it away. Another effect was to drive up food prices, thus creating a ready market for European and American surpluses.

It is our intention to show how donors in collusion with African govern-ments are the cause of much misery to most Africans. The cooperation between donor countries and international institutions is aimed at preserving the colonial economies of Africa. The function of these organizations is to force the recipient country to obey the instructions of the donor countries. The imposition of the will of the wealthy states does not appear ominous when it comes under the aus-pices of international organizations such as the IMF and WB. Thus, it is usually easier to bring about changes through their mediation. These two institutions also exercise direct control over the African continent in their own right. This is achieved by placing rigid requirements on African countries as conditions for loans and other services.

The IMF and WB also exist to provide business opportunities for Western investors. In the face of demand by African countries for a maximum amount of capital on the easiest possible terms, in the shortest period of time, these institu-tions tell them that they do not need as much capital as they imagine and that the capital they need is private [foreign investment] and not public. To force a change in policy, loans are withheld until the recipient government gives in. The country that applies to the IMF for a short-term loan, for example to stabilize its currency, is usually desperate. This country may try various emergency measures such as controls over imports, and increased exports; but when these fail, the country turns to the IMF. The IMF may lend a country up to 25% of its quota in the fund (which is backed up by that country's gold subscription or deposit to the Fund).

The monetary and fiscal policies demanded by the IMF are familiar:

1. The elimination of controls over imports, free exchange rates and currency devaluation. The result of these policies is to reinforce the existing price

---

59. Joe Ombuor, "Starving boy died after dog meat meal," *Sunday Nation*, February 23 1997, p. 1.

and trade relationships that exploit Africa and also strengthen economic and financial dependency.

2. The strengthening of monetary and fiscal controls within the country, wage and price controls and balancing of the budget. Balanced budgets are usually achieved by increasing taxes, and cutting expenditure in healthcare, education and other welfare bills.

Both the IMF and WB have their headquarters in Washington. The US provides the largest share of funds for both; therefore it has dominant voting rights. The IMF and US Treasury staff are interchanged and non-US staff are only employed if they are sympathetic to US interests. So, in effect, Africa is run by the US government through the IMF and WB.

The donors have proposed several "solutions" to Africa's poverty that strain credulity but have nevertheless gained wide acceptance among African governments. The goals are:

1) That population growth should be retarded and the population reduced.

The West is particularly hostile to the growth of African population. Aid always has a fixed percentage that goes into population control services. This aid is not provided in monetary form but is contraceptives and propaganda pamphlets. There are several reasons why the West is trying to reduce the number of Africans. First of all is the profit motive. Western contraceptive manufacturing companies wish to open new markets in Africa. For this end, cultural imperialism is used. In the Western-dominated media in Africa, wrong values are deliberately promoted with the approval and encouragement of African governments. The youth are encouraged to be promiscuous. Music, movies, books, magazines imported from the West all encourage illicit sexual activity as part of the campaign to foster new wants. The development of want requires that foreign companies and governments create an artificial need for devices and drugs which enable a society to accept promiscuity; and that opens up a market for contraceptives and abortion services. In this case, cultural imperialism serves to mould society's attitudes such that acts that had been considered outrageous will be tolerated and even encouraged by social pressures. As part of this campaign to mould African attitudes, Western states are pressuring African governments to adopt "Family Life Education" and to legalize abortion and homosexuality.

The second reason why the West wants to reduce the number of Africans is tied up with their own internal problems. While African countries except Nigeria are underpopulated, Europe, North America, Japan and China are heavily populated. They can dump their excess population or take resources for them only if Africans are substantially reduced. In 1986, all these countries met secretly to discuss on the best and fastest way to reduce the population of Africa. After lengthy deliberations, they estimated that by the years 2005-10, over 70% of Africans shall have been wiped out by several factors such as AIDS, deaths from easily preventable diseases, mass starvation and genocidal wars. The population of Africa seems to be surviving despite the disasters; one can only wonder where the Ebola virus came from and why it did not spread as expected.

The West also stepped up the amount of money used in population reduction services and applied new pressures on the legalization of abortion. Posters hung in rural areas usually show two types of families. The first one is the European type, made up of two children who are depicted as being deliriously happy. This family is rich, owning a fine house and car. The second one is an African type family, as revealed by the dress mode. The several children are depicted as being poor, untidy, wearing torn clothes and no shoes, looking miserable and living in a mud slum. The message is clear; what is European is "better" than what is African. However, the campaign to make parents "family plan" has been a failure. It is enough to note here that the contradictions within the neocolonial structure in Africa prevent the complete success of neocolonialism, and that will cause its eventual downfall. The level of poverty in rural areas is desperate and this is the result of neocolonial exploitation. It is this poverty that frustrates all efforts to cut down the population. Apart from racism as a motivator, the richer states fear that if the African population reaches a certain level while still in desperate poverty then the sheer pressure will cause people to question this system more, and even overthrow it, as is happening in Nigeria — where ethnic militias have begun to redirect their anger at foreign companies and are plundering the oil supplies rather than attacking other ethnic groups. If neocolonialism did not so ruthlessly exploit Africans, the level of poverty would not be so dire and population control campaigns would be successful, thus protecting the neocolonial system.

2) That exports in primary products be increased.

This policy is not intended to help Africans; it is not they who determine the price of exports. It is aimed at helping the rich North avail themselves of African products at little cost. It is also intended to reinforce the colonial economic structure. For example, the minerals in DR Congo do not benefit Africa. The rich countries are the principle beneficiaries. Congo's uranium went into the construction of the first atomic bombs, which America dropped on Japan. The Belgians had extracted it. Africa gained nothing. South African gold went to make up the gold reserves of the rich countries. All the mineral wealth of Angola, Congo, South Africa and others has not lifted the living standards of the indigenous peoples.

The export of raw materials as encouraged by the IMF is meant to ensure that industrialized nations always have enough cheap raw materials available and to ensure that no advanced industries ever develop in Africa. It also reduces the integration of African economies; additionally, different sectors within that economy fail to react beneficially on each other as they would in a normal economy. The export of raw materials, if pursued incorrectly, does not and cannot lead to "export-led growth"; it simply retards industrialization, increasing the neocolony's dependency on others for manufactures.

This leads to exploitation through trade. The terms of trade are constantly deteriorating against African countries, which have to export more and more to buy the same amount of manufactures. Many manufactured commodities are made by relatively few giant corporations. Once the prices begin to fall, these companies cut back production, thus pushing prices back up. But in Africa, mineral production and other raw materials such as "cash crops" are for the most part controlled by companies in whose interest it is to keep prices low, through overproduction. Where foreign companies do not control production, a few foreign companies usually have a monopsony, that is, they are the only buyer(s) for a certain product, and act in concert to keep the prices as low as possible. This is why African exports always fetch low prices. In other words, the unlimited export of raw materials offer no advantage and export-led growth as designed by the IMF is a fallacy.

3) That Structural Adjustment Programs (SAPs) be implemented.

These programs were intended to alter the economic setup to allow free movement of goods, services and money between nations, ideally to promote trade and boost prosperity among participating countries. However, they resulted in the increased exploitation of Africa, the reinforcement of neocolonialism, and to the securing of markets and raw materials for Western companies through the elimination of any possible competition within Africa. These policies begun to be implemented in the early 1980s and according to the WB, they were meant to increase foreign investment in Africa by making Africa a pleasant place for foreigners to do business in. SAPs were actually designed to encourage wrong economic policies: import liberalization and unrestricted foreign investment. These programs allow full repatriation of profits by foreign companies, easing of foreign exchange controls, the taking over of parastatals by foreigners and the simplification of the foreign investment approval process. Foreign investment institutions have been established to solicit foreigners to come and seize the opportunity; these are the Investments Promotion Center and Capital Market Authority. In addition, currencies in Africa were devalued and floated.

These programs were designed by the EU, Japan and US to destroy those African economies whose growth rates were threatening to overturn their neo-colonial structures. They have claimed that unregulated foreign investment is beneficial to the recipient country. But, have SAPs increased foreign investment in Africa? No; they have failed. Figures released by the WB revealed that despite a total of Kshs 13,860 billion ($231 billion) invested in poor nations in the whole of 1995, Africa got less than 1% of this amount — less than $1 billion[60]. In 2003, total foreign direct investment was a mere 2% of the global amount[61]. Foreign investment in Africa is marked by a nearly total absence of portfolio equity investment. This is mainly because more money can be made more quickly through loans with high interest rates, and by extracting oil and mineral resources, than through any form of capital investment.

As is well known, foreign investment is discriminative and concentrates in some countries and in some sectors. More than in 90% of the total amount of investment inflows to Africa go to the oil and mineral producers. The most favored countries are Nigeria, Congo and South Africa. An exception to this is Liberia, which also receives high investment inflows. This is mainly because of the Japanese flag-of-convenience investment in shipping, from which Liberia derives little benefit. In Botswana, all foreign direct investment (FDI) is confined to mineral extraction, especially diamonds. Less than 10% of FDI goes to productive investment such as manufacturing or essential services.

The WB and IMF have cut loans to Africans numerous times, causing a funds crunch in order to increase the pace of SAP implementation. But the reason they deny further funds, according to the former WB vice president for Africa, is because "Africa lacks the absorptive capacity for funds"[62]. In effect, this means that indigent Africans have no use for money!

Have the SAPs worked in any sense? In a way, they have been completely successful. Africans have not benefited and in fact have lost a great deal, since the

---

60. Samboma, "Economist downplays foreign investment."
61. UN Department of Economic and Social Affairs, *Economic Report on Africa 2004*, New York.
62. Umoren, "SAP's pill working, says Jaycox."

principle beneficiaries are foreigners. It has worked for them and not for the Africans. The consequences of these policies have left Africans poor, politically and economically, as they were a century ago. The burden of the "adjustment" has been heaped upon the poor and vulnerable in the form of reduced health and education services, elimination of food subsidies, reduction in wages, increases in taxes and cost of services, abolition of price controls, increased unemployment and poverty.

General and specific examples prove that SAPs were deliberately pursued with the aim of wrecking African economies.

Industry expanded at a 14.6% annually during the 1965-75 period in Africa (more than twice as fast as GDP). During the 1980s, after the introduction of SAPs, manufacturing value added (MVA) grew at only 0.5% annually. Now, according to the World Bank, economic growth in Africa averaged 0.02% between 1990 and 2002[63]. The following table shows the economic growth record of several countries before and after the implementation of IMF and WB policies.

Country	Growth Rates %	
	Before SAPs [1970-80]	After SAPs [1980-89]
Cameroon	9.2	2.5
Cote d'Ivoire	6.3	0.3
Ethiopia	7.6	1.5
Kenya	8.5	3.5
Nigeria	11.7	-5.0
Tanzania	6.7	-5.0
Zambia	7.7	-1.0
Zimbabwe	6.4	-3.5

Source: The Royal African Society, *Africa: 30 Years On*, Heinemann Educational Books Inc., London, 1991.

After the introduction of SAPs, Botswana appears to have experienced de-industrialization with the share of manufacturing falling from 12% in 1966 to 6% in 1989[64]. In Nigeria, the government announced that economic restructuring was being undertaken to diversify the country's oil dominated economy, to liberalize trade and promote foreign investment, and to strengthen local industry and develop a strong rural agricultural base. The effects of the adjustment were just the opposite. Wages fell and inflation trebled, causing earnings of workers to

---

63. World Development Indicators online, http;//devdata.worldbank.org/dataonline/
64. The Royal African Society, *Africa: 30 years On*, Heinemann Educational Books, London, 1991.

decrease to between 800 and 1000% below the actual living cost[65]. This directly resulted in widespread hunger and malnutrition. Healthcare services, education and other welfare expenditures were cut, resulting in increased illiteracy and increased deaths from easily preventable diseases. In fact, the World Bank came up with guidelines on how the government could recover money from the sick and dying patients in state hospitals: patients who do not pay up front are to be denied treatment or if treatment has been already been given, then the non-paying patient is to be held hostage until all the bills are paid[66]. This is now very common in Kenya. At one hospital in Nairobi, a pregnant woman had to give birth in the ladies' room after the hospital denied her use of their facilities because she could not pay Kshs 200 ($2.50) for the midwife's gloves. In other hospitals in Kenya, accident victims have been left to die on operating tables if the good Samaritan who took them in failed to pay up front a quarter of the bill and guaranteed to pay the rest later. Back to Nigeria, restructuring has caused local industries to collapse due to cheap imports becoming available through liberalization of imports and also because local firms lack access to foreign exchange — often, materials necessary to production must be imported. It has also been noted that political interference in African countries has increased ever since the adoption of SAPs.

In the 1970s, Kenya was beginning to be viewed as a newly industrializing African country. The WB at the time said, "Kenya has a distinctly more favorable economic structure and better incentives and institutions than most other countries in Africa."[67] Gross Domestic Product (GDP) growth rates surpassed 6.6% per year during the first decade of independence. Agriculture grew at a comfortable 5% annually. In the second decade of flag independence, savings and investment grew at about 20% per annum[68].

The tax/revenue ratio according to WB had increased from 12% in 1966-67 to 21% in 1979-80, and the current fiscal account had produced a *surplus* of 2.5% to 4% of the GDP annually. Fertility figures had increased from 6.8% to 7.9% during the same period in the 1980s. After the implementation of the SAPs, the figures fell to 7.7% and 6.7% by the later 1980s[69].

---

65. "Are SAP's an American ploy?" *Daily Nation.* July 30 1994.

66. *Ibid.*

67. Reuben Nasibi, "Studies by World Bank, SAP's and Africa's mess," *Daily Nation,* April 7 1994, p. 6.

68. *Ibid.*

69. *Ibid.*

When the Kenya Government agreed to implement the SAPs, the economy simply collapsed. When the WB and IMF ordered Kenya to devalue the shilling, the Government went ahead, increasing Kenya's external debt by a whopping 43%[70]. This in turn forced up imports, increasing the profits of importers; it also increased food prices; all of which provided more profit for the West, selling their surplus to Africa. All this led to inflation, reducing the real income of workers, increasing poverty and finally bringing the downward trend that has led to the collapse of the once vibrant Kenyan economy. The SAPs in effect have made Kenya a good place for foreigners to make money while at the same time inhibiting Africans from deriving any benefit. They have created an unequal playing field which gives unfair advantage to the foreign companies.

There is a disparity in the cost of capital, as determined by real interest rates, that Kenyans and foreigners can borrow. This disparity ensures that Kenyan-owned businesses are driven into bankruptcy while foreign-owned businesses thrive and secure a position in the country. A British company, for instance, can borrow money in British pounds at, say, 5% interest per annum. With British inflation rate at only 2–4%, the British firm actually pays about 3% as its real cost of capital. A Kenyan competitor company has to pay more than 20% interest on its loans per annum and sometimes, with double digit inflation, the company in effect ends up getting less money than it borrowed since the real cost of money (capital) is about 17%[71]. This severe handicap has brought the downfall of many indigenous firms and prevented the expansion of others. This situation prevails in World Bank dominated countries, and the success of Western-owned companies in the same countries also adds to the mental colonization and brainwashing as Africans see it as additional evidence of European superiority. This then compounds the self hatred and self mutilation.

When Kenyan scholars started opposing these SAPs, the Kenyan Government was ordered by the IMF and WB to quiet them. In the universities censorship became the norm. Lecturers who spoke against the IMF- and WB-sponsored SAPs were either sacked, detained or driven into exile[72]. The ones who remained were coerced into silence and so the SAPs destroyed Kenya's economy without anyone saying a word about it. Patriotism is now disdainfully regarded as embarrassing.

---

70. *Ibid.*

71. Diana Patel, "SAP's against Kenyan businesses," *Daily Nation*, April 18 1994, p. 7.

72. H. Ochwada, "Why African scholars do not respond to the continent's woes," *Sunday Nation*, September 14 1997, p. 12.

Ethiopia also followed the advice of WB and IMF. This led the Ethiopian unit of currency, the birr, to depreciate by more than 150%[73]. When the sixteen Francophone countries followed IMF and WB advice to devalue, they effectively became bankrupt[74].

Uganda, as a result of a decade of structural reforms, had by 1997 an external debt of Kshs 216 billion ($3.6 billion)[75] which has now (2004) risen to $4.4 billion, a staggering 58.8% of GDP[76]. In the 1996-97 fiscal year inflation was 10.5%, and the current account deficit 0.9% of the GDP[77]. By, 2002/3 the overall fiscal deficit had reached 11.5% of GDP[78]. Unemployment has risen and so has poverty. Local companies have collapsed under the weight of cheap imports and the Uganda shilling has depreciated in value to almost war time levels, while the economy is in the process of being swallowed up by foreign companies. Despite this reality the IMF praised the reforms and asked the Uganda Government to "step up ..... the programs on track."[79] Neighboring Africans are effusive in their praise for Uganda because it is alleged that its economy is growing at more than 2%; they seem not realize that growth does not necessarily mean development. For example, opening up many supermarkets and petrol stations may cause growth, but the society does not increase its capacity to deal with the environment and such investments do not create any wealth, as they do not turn raw materials into finished products.

It should be noted that the USA floated its currency in 1973, long after it had developed[80]. But African governments floated currencies even with the knowledge that their financial structures are underdeveloped and that they lack external reserves to support the effects of the flotation of their individual currencies. In several African countries, after the introduction of SAPs the per capita income fell by 20%, inflation rose from 30% to 160%, unemployment increased, wages were dropped, and meanwhile taxes were hiked. The result: child malnutrition increased and affected 70% of the population, real wages fell by 50%, drop out rates from schools skyrocketed and so did incidence of disease; levels of

---

73. Umoren, "SAP's pill working, says Jaycox."
74. *Ibid.*
75. Reuters, "IMF lauds Ugandan economic reforms," *E. A. Standard,* June 1998.
76. IMF, *Sub-Saharan Africa Regional Economic Outlook,* October 2004.
77. Reuters, "IMF lauds Ugandan economic reforms."
78. IMF, *Memorandum of Economic and Financial Policies of the Government of Uganda for 2003-04.*
79. *Ibid.*
80. Reuters, "IMF lauds Ugandan economic reforms."

poverty were deepened and the number of poor increased both in absolute terms as well as the proportion of the population affected. The UN stood by and cheered this unprecedented mass impoverishment, and at the end of the decade showed up with "millennium goals" such as reduction of maternal mortality by 75% by 2015, to paper over reality with attractive words.

Japan provides a stark contrast to the "solutions" presently being pursued in Africa. After being destroyed during the second world war and having no massive aid inflows, Japan encouraged domestic savings. Taxes were raised and government deficit eliminated. Unlike Africa, Japan relied on its domestic savings to productively invest within its borders, reducing its cost of capital to less than half of that available to foreign investors. All financial resources were mobilized for productive investment. Its leaders did not siphon off funds for personal profit and remove capital to Europe. There was no massive capital flight due to policies such as import liberalization. And, Japan was free of the mentally retarding influence of the IMF and World Bank.

The former WB vice-president for Africa E. Jaycox claimed during an interview that the SAPs had "worked"[81]. This is true, but only if one considers that they were intended to wreck African economies. Two decades after the introduction of the devastating programs, a smiling Jaycox announced the results of the IMF's and WB's efforts, triumphantly stating that African countries would need forty years to reach the level they had attained in 1975[82]. He also calculated that it would take most of Africa 2000 years to close the gap between it and the West. With the advent of SAPs, liberalization, and MAI, the West now has a free hand in Africa, just as in colonial times, and is now growing much faster as a result of this parasitic relationship, while Africa has stagnated and is now regressing. Where there were tarmac roads, there are now none; where food security had been attained, it has now been lost; where the life expectancy was 72, it is now 35. The gap between the developed countries and Africa must be more like 6000 years, by now.

The economic policies propagated by the two Bretton Woods institutions represent imperialist interests and aid in the re-colonization. One is forced to recall the IMF's role in the overthrow and murder of Chilean President Salvadore Allende in 1973, because Allende had the audacity to reject the IMF's destructive policies and advice. Because these two organizations are under fire for their role

---

81. Reuters, "IMF lauds Ugandan economic reforms."
82. Nasibi, "Studies by World Bank, SAP's and Africa's mess".

in the collapse of Southeast Asian economies, they have increased the propaganda in their favor. Recently, with the cooperation of the Kenya Government, the World Bank established a "virtual university" at the Kenyatta University fed by direct satellite link from the USA to help entrench its economic views in Kenya's highest institutions of learning. This means that IMF's and WB policies will continue to be followed by future leaders as long as these institutions have direct educational access to Africa's future leaders.

It is interesting to scan various countries which have followed the IMF's and WB's prescriptions, which have resulted in their economic and sometimes political collapse.

Ever since the early 1980s, Mexico meticulously followed all the economic conditions and policies supplied by the IMF and WB. According to the World Bank, Mexico had "opened its economy to world trade, reduced regulation, privatized much of its state sector, reduced the fiscal deficit to less than 2% of GDP and made the Central Bank autonomous."[83] The first policy introduced was the SAPs. Mexico undertook to implement these adjustments for a decade at a cost of Kshs 46 billion ($767 million) in loans from the WB and much suffering to the people. The adjustments, as in Kenya, involved suppressing wages, sacking government employees, and reducing state spending on health, education and other vital social services by more than half; and to top it all, import liberalization was adopted. In that decade of adjustments, deaths from easily preventable diseases and mass hunger increased by 300%. Illiteracy rose by more than 30% as more and more students were forced out of school. All the money saved through these measures did not become available for productive investment, however, but went to pay off the large external debt and finance importation of unnecessary luxury goods.

The second policy the IMF and WB imposed on Mexico was the encouragement of unrestricted foreign investment. Mexico was advised to relax foreign exchange controls to allow full repatriation profits by foreign investors and certain other conditions that led to a massive inflow of money and foreign investors. These investors concentrated in the stock market and government bonds. To increase "investor confidence", the Mexican government with the prodding of the IMF and WB pegged the Mexican peso to the United States dollar in order to keep it steady, and the foreign investors poured in. Parastatals

---

83. The following observations and data on Mexico come from Mutuma Mathiu, "Banks path leads to assured failure," *Sunday Nation*, August 17 1997, p. 12.

were also privatized and taken over by foreigners. At this point, the domination of Mexico's economy by foreigners was complete. A quarter of the stock market and half of Mexican government bonds were controlled foreign investors. The Central Bank, having been wrested from government control, was acting on the advice of the World Bank. In effect, it was the WB that was running Mexico's economy.

The IMF and WB had also called for the complete opening up of the domestic market to foreign products. Other policies already adopted by Mexico came together and wreaked havoc on the economy. With a strong peso, pegged to the dollar, imports were cheap; importation rose by several hundred per cent. Like today's Kenya, Mexico stopped producing and started consuming what it had not produced. This is what stimulated the first rounds in a downward spiral that ruined the Mexican economy. The cheap cost of imports created a powerful illusion that blinded many to what was actually happening. In Kenya, cheap imports have enabled many people to afford consumer durables, which create false signs of growth and development. This is what happened in Mexico. Between 1983 and 1994, growth was a low 2.4% on average. But importation in the same period averaged over 200%.

To make matters worse, the Mexican government agreed to a proposal to join a preferential trade area with the US and Canada. In 1994, Mexico entered the North American Free Trade Area (NAFTA). Theoretically, this meant that Mexicans could sell their goods to the US and Canada, which would also be allowed to sell their products in Mexico without hindrance. This would have been beneficial if the three countries had been at a similar level of economic development, so Mexico lost more than it gained. The result of Mexico's entry into NAFTA was increased importation of North American products, which led to increased capital flight. Mexico also lost because it was able to sell very little to the US and Canada, due to stiff competition, and because its industries had collapsed either due to the deluge of imports or the repatriation of industry profits. The strong peso also made US products cheap in Mexico.

Massive loss of capital as a result of repatriation of profits by foreign investors and unrestricted importation meant that there was no capital for productive investment, hence little job creation. The collapse of local industries and companies, the retrenchment of government workers as demanded by the SAPs, all increased poverty and unemployment levels. The people, already poor, were subjected to untold suffering when the government cut spending on healthcare, while foreign investors and the local elite continued to mint money. Billionaires multiplied from two in the late 1980s to 25 by 1993. The wealthiest fifth of the population held 50% of the national income in 1980. A decade later their share had increased to about 60%.

As the control of Mexico's economy by foreigners increased, its vulnerability to forces outside its control also increased. After the Mexican economy collapsed in 1994, it was accepted that up to 80% of the cause of the financial meltdown was linked to events across the globe, such as the rise of interest rates in London and Tokyo.

The downward spiral that finally destroyed the Mexican economy also had political repercussions. The downward trend started when the foreign investors begun to liquidate their peso investments in favor of other currencies and begun to repatriate the money to their own countries. This happened when the investors realized that the peso was overvalued. The low worth of the peso was a result of a greatly reduced capacity to produce (since Mexico was concentrating on consuming imports rather than producing). Foreign investors scrambled to disinvest and left Mexico, which they were able to do since the reforms allowed unrestricted repatriation of profits and foreign currency. This massive outflow of capital knocked down the Mexican economy.

The only viable option available to the government would have been to devalue the peso to reflect its real value. Anything else would lead to hyperinflation, which would increase the cost of imports, thus reducing importation, particularly from Mexican trading partners in NAFTA. That would have made the North American exporters lose money. This appears to have been the main factor that the IMF and WB considered as they concocted a "solution" for Mexico's problem. Under the first phase of implementing the SAPs the Central Bank of Mexico had been made independent of the government. The IMF and WB exerted pressure to influence the subsequent economic policies pursued by Mexico. The government was advised to do everything in its power to shore up foreign investor confidence; in other words to prop the peso, which was not supported by real production.

Following the World Bank's advice, the government borrowed more hard currency to buy the peso at the artificially high exchange rates. Now, the foreign investors still stuck with peso investments could sell to the government and not lose money when the peso was devalued. In just a few weeks this policy cost the Mexican government $9 billion, but still the WB encouraged it not to devalue. In fact, the government was advised to step up its buying campaign. Mexico borrowed more and more to buy up the peso, causing the external debt to increase from $23 billion to $120 billion. This fueled the predictable cycle of cuts in government domestic spending, more inflation, unemployment and so on.

At this point, Mexico as a nation begun to unravel. Living in desperate poverty, suffering, and offended by the wasteful lifestyles of the rich, people in the Chiapas region revolted and a ragtag army, the Zapatistas, started to attack government outposts. Beleaguered on all sides, the government collapsed and by December 1994 a new government was in office. This new government devalued the peso by 15% and floated it[84]. The peso lost 70% of its value and Mexico was bankrupt. The peso became almost valueless, an inflation rate of 50%, interest rates around 80%, 70% growth of the external debt, and 60% unemployment (up to 2 million Mexicans lost their jobs). The main beneficiaries of Mexico's collapse were the IMF and WB, as the loans to Mexico had to be repaid at high interest rates, and of course the foreign investors who had arrived in Mexico millionaires and left as billionaires.

The tragic story of Mexico was repeated in mid-1998 in Russia. The Russians, perhaps through the cultural colonization of their elite, started "reforms" in their economy to transform it from a centrally planned one to a capitalist one. Naturally, they followed policies promulgated by the IMF. These reforms had destroyed the Russian economy by 1998. After the reforms began in 1992, inflation increased by 520%, within the first three months, increasing unemployment, poverty and all the effects of poverty.

In Southeast Asia this also happened in late 1997. Collapsed economies brought down some governments. In Indonesia, Asia's former longest ruler, Suharto, was forced out of power by weeks of riots caused by economic collapse.

China is the only low income country that has recently transformed itself into an industrial powerhouse that has avoided the perilous policies by the IMF and World Bank. During its transformation from a centrally planned to a free market economy, it did not suffer from economic collapse, rather, it recorded one of the highest rates of growth ever attained. While all the other countries that followed IMF's and WB's advice and adjustments ended up in economic decline and eventual ruin, experiencing negative "growth" rates. China's economy supposedly has the opposite problem: overheating, which means growth that is "too fast." It is averaging a rather high 9%[85].

---

84. Mathiu, "Banks path leads to assured failure."
85. UN Department of Economic and Social Affairs, *World Economic and Social Survey 2004*, New York, 2004.

"AID"

The word "aid" is supposed to mean "help". However, in relations between unequal partners, it often means something quite different and in the case of Africa and the rich countries, it means "help yourself". The "donor" states help themselves to the recipients' resources.

Aid programs may consist of a wide assortment of "gifts" and loans. There are several types of aid which are equal in importance and are designed for a common purpose. The first type is military, whereby entire African armies are trained and armed by the West. This gives foreigners enormous influence in local politics and enables them to control the ruler. When the ruler refuses to obey Western orders, this army is used to topple him or to coerce him through threats. In this way, armies in Africa administer and enforce the neocolonial order. "Aid" in the social spheres such as education and health is equally sinister. External assistance has financed projects like the construction of schools, provision of scholarships and textbooks. This ends up meaning that outsiders control the curriculum, enrollment, and other aspects. In healthcare, Africa is the world's largest pool of human guinea pigs. The health sector has become modeled on the Western one; there are more large hospitals in cities and very few clinics in rural areas where majority of the population lives. Therefore, the majority of people have little or no access to proper medical care. The West uses "aid" in the health sector as an instrument of population reduction: most health "aid packages" are conditioned on a fixed percentage of the funding being used for population control services and products such as contraceptives, even in cases where medicinal drugs are desperately needed.

Agricultural foreign "assistance" is used to strengthen the externally responsive agriculture-based economies with the aim of retarding industrialization. This is accomplished when agricultural assistance is directed towards the production of "cash crops," which compromise the capacity of the recipient country to attain self sufficiency in food and places emphasis on production of raw materials rather than finished products. For instance, Kenya has committed vast acreage to the cultivation of pyrethrum, from which pyrethrin, the main ingredient in insect repellent, is extracted. This is exported in a nearly raw state to Germany. Kenya then imports insect repellent as a finished product, which even has the instruction labels printed in Swahili, from Germany. Foreign "assistance" will be provided to encourage further export of unprocessed pyrethrum, rather than to develop the local value-adding capacity.

We shall concentrate on financial "assistance". Monetary aid ties African economies to the West's. The more Africa relies upon producing only primary products, the more it becomes economically dependent on the West. The West sets the prices of Africa's exports and subjects them to cuts, resulting into wild fluctuations in income which cause deficits that force African countries to borrow from the West — at interest rates determined (and sometimes jacked up) by the West. Debt servicing requires mortgaging a segment of future exports to pay back the debt.

President John F. Kennedy himself said, "Foreign aid is a method by which the US maintains a position of influence and control."[86] It serves to reinforce neocolonialism both as an economic and political system. This is accomplished in various ways.

In all cases, the acceptance of foreign investment is a precondition for receiving aid. The Foreign Assistance Act of 1963 in the US decreed that "no assistance shall be provided under this Act as of December 31 1965 to the government of any less developed country which has failed to enter into agreement with the president to institute the investment guaranty program...."[87] In this way, aid is used to obtain economic benefits for Western companies. Neocolonialism is greatly strengthened when African countries are forced to implement economic and political policies which result in an economic model totally unsuitable to Africa's needs. The alien economic system ensures that Africa borrows to eliminate the shortfall between exports and expenditure, and goes into debt.

Aid is used to enforce the "open door" policy so that Western companies have guaranteed access to Africa's raw materials, trade and investment opportunities. Concerning Africa, a high ranking US official once said that the US grants aid because "their respect for our interests is illustrated by their special facilities and rights made available to us, by our exploitation of Africa's important mineral and other resources."[88]

Africa's markets are kept open by the West by retarding and opposing innovations and scientific development. When Kenya came up with the disease resistant Ruiru II coffee, the West launched an international campaign to discredit this achievement[89]. Its success would have meant closing down the

---

86. Harry Magdoff, *Age of Imperialism: The Economics of US foreign policy*, Monthly Review Press, New York, 1969.

87. *Ibid.*

88. *Ibid.*

lucrative agrochemical market for coffee which is dominated by Western companies.

Foreign aid strengthens neocolonialism by distorting and weakening economies. All products from Africa face stiff tariff charges in the West while all manufacturing in Africa has been re-colonized by Western companies, which hamper the growth of exports because they have no interest in competing with themselves. Even when manufactured products are exported, Africans do not benefit because profits are quickly repatriated. This has been the main cause of the stagnation of African economies.

Aid also distorts the recipients' economy and economic activity. As one US official boasted, "our foreign aid programs constitute a distinct benefit to American business. It provides a substantial and immediate market for US goods and services. It orients national economies to [neocolonialism] in which US companies can prosper."[90] Apart from this, African businessmen and potential industrialists rank industrial projects not according to their viability, but on eligibility for aid. The dependency mentality has become so ingrained that the most important economic activity is chasing donor money. This is very important in retarding economic growth because the people best placed to invest are busy using their ingenuity to plead with Westerners for money, which goes into non-industrial ventures that add nothing to the productive capacity of the economy.

Foreign aid is also used to reinforce political colonialism because it is used to prop up Westward-looking rulers and is withdrawn from leaders with a nationalist or regionalist vision. Mobutu was given considerable amounts of aid to maintain him in power while a progressive leader such as al-Qathafi has been consistently denied support, as a way of toppling him.

The aid industry at first aimed at reinforcing neocolonialism and fighting communism but later on, it became an end in itself when the West discovered how lucrative it could be. Even food aid given to Africa is sold like any other commodity, but the income ends up with the "donor" government while the ordinary African (and ordinary American) is given to imagine that the food was donated out of generosity.

Lending and trade are, of course, most beneficial to those who set the terms. More than 80% of all funds provided by the West are in fact spent there,

---

89. Otula Oduor, "Why Africa must enter technological fray," *Daily Nation,* June 16 1994, p. 4.

90. Magdoff, *Age of Imperialism.*

and on commodities that were sold at 40% above their market price. This is why the official American aid agency USAID was able to boast that "thousands of jobs are created right here at home."[91] The recipients have to repay all the money, at a usurious interest rate, despite the fact that they actually received less than 20% of total funds. Most financial assistance goes to repay previous debts. The West has designed the aid program as the best way to trap nations into debt.

Most of the money, if spent on economically viable projects, would have brought Africa forward and enabled the complete repayment of the loan. But this is not what happens. Most aid never leaves the donor country, which decides what it shall be spent upon, and at what prices; and an industrialized Africa is the last thing the West wants. Over 80% of foreign funded projects fail. This is by design, as viability is not a factor in selecting projects. The intention at all times is to weaken Africa.

The total financial outflow from Africa is far more than the inflow. Once a country is caught in the vicious cycle of borrowing, it necessarily ends up a neo-colony. Today, most African countries are in this trap and have to borrow to pay past debts, rather than to invest. The debt has grown so big that exports are insufficient for repayment — because no money is being invested in the export of manufactured goods. Borrowing continues to such a degree that most countries repay the West up to three times the amount allegedly received, due to the interest charged. Every year Africa spends $14.5 billion to repay debts. Nigeria, for example, borrowed $5 billion and out of this amount, has already paid back $16 billion and still owes $32 billion[92]. When the country defaults, the creditors quickly move in to reschedule the repayment — provided the recipient country accepts conditions specifically designed to further erode its sovereignty and reduce it into a neocolony. The poor South's transfer of finance to the rich North is $ 30,000,000,000 annually[93].

A special type of aid is channeled through the UN. When Western countries finance the UN, they benefit from it more. They win lucrative contracts which are worth more than the amount they initially contributed. Westerners also gain employment opportunities; in fact in most of Africa, the term UN is synonymous with Caucasians. Africans are rarely employed by the UN in serious positions. Westerners imported into Africa by the UN are maintained at great

91. Magdoff, *Age of Imperialism.*
92. http://www.keepamericaspromise.net/whyafrica/issuedebt.php also IMF, *Sub-Saharan Africa Regional Economic Outlook 2004.*
93. Mathiu, "Have Kenyans lost their business sense?"

cost even if they are inefficient or are unable to work with Africans because of climatic or racist reasons. When employed, Africans are paid up to 20 times less than the Westerner doing the same job. Foreign companies are also contracted even if there are local companies capable of doing the same work and at a cheaper cost. In fact, a percentage of all financial "assistance" funds is always allocated to secure lucrative contracts which are denied to African companies. For example, a European company was given a Kshs 6 billion ($100 million) contract to build a road. Half a year later, the road had collapsed because it was constructed using substandard materials and techniques[94]. But that African country still had to repay the loan plus interest accruing.

Foreign aid is also used to harm fragile African economies through import dumping. This is common in the agricultural sector. The results, as described in the chapter dealing with under population, is food aid dependency. Meanwhile, publicity campaigns make Africans feel grateful to the West for all their help and encourage them to imagine that they cannot survive without it. The first misstatement peddled is that Africa is "given help". Ninety per cent of the aid is in the form of loans. The second is that such aid is needed. It isn't. The amount of aid provided is usually insignificant, for instance, in 2004 it averaged at a mere 1.2% of GDP[95]. African governments want loans to cover up their errors and to establish patronage systems to guarantee their political survival. The West is more than willing to lend; they make money, and they know that a high level of corruption weakens countries and makes the corrupt ruler more pliant to Western demands.

People are also led to believe that the amounts of money involved are huge. Between 1945 and 1951, Europe was aided by the US through the Marshall Plan by $4 billion annually[96]. Most of that was in grants. This aid was a mere 2% of USA's GDP. Since 1950, the Western economy has doubled several times over but money in Africa is *lent* and not given, and only a tiny 0.3% of the GDP[97]. During the 1970s this figure increased to 0.52% of the West's GDP[98] but by 1997, it had fallen to 0.21% and the richest nation of them all — the USA — generously provided a mere 0.1%[99]. Even these tiny amounts are offered largely for propa-

---

94. Hancock, *Lords of Poverty.*
95. IMF, *Sub-Saharan Regional Economic Outlook 2004.*
96. Magdoff, *Age of Imperialism.*
97. World Bank, *Global Development Finance*, Washington DC, 1998.
98. *Ibid.*
99. *Ibid.*

ganda purposes. Glorifications of Western "help" are common in Kenyan news-papers. In one, Africans were made to feel indebted to the Japanese who, it was claimed, are "our friends and partners". This message was promoted through headlines like "Japan comes to KBC's rescue"; "college owes success to JICA"; "Japan uplifts Kenya's economy" and "Japan helps horticulture industry to grow"[100].

The Repercussions of Aid

The greatest irony about aid to Africa is that it hampers rather than encourages development. Projects are usually determined by the donors, who also have a direct interest in seeing Africa fail to develop. The debt repayment has its own contradictions, but above all, it ensures that Africa is perpetually broke. This is why Africa even as received more "assistance" the GDP fell by an average of 3.4% annually. In the case of Kenya, the public debt increased by Kshs 20.7 billion ($258 million) in 2004 as a result of borrowing from the domestic market to repay the external debt but mainly because the shilling depreciated as a result of the emphasis on importation rather than production. As of July 2004 Kenya's public debt is a staggering 61% of GDP[101].

Servicing the large debts directly causes underdevelopment in Africa. All monies meant for health, education, food subsidies, productive investment and so on are taken by the West. The SAPs are responsible for the large debt and all money is directed at servicing the loans; African governments have no funds to invest locally, to expand and industrialize their economies.

Tanzania is a good example of how aid is used to weaken and reduce the population of African countries. By the end of the 1990s, Tanzania was using 35% of its budget to repay its debt.[102] Due to poverty, lack of food and medical care, 165 children per thousand were dying before the age of 5 while 33% of the population was dying before the age of 40[103]. The debt servicing repayments were more than nine times what was spent on health and four times the edu-cation expenditure. In addition, today Tanzanians pay 20% VAT on all products in order to raise more money for debt servicing[104].

---

100. "Kenya/Japan relations special," *The Standard*, September 24 1992, pp. 1-16.

101. Central Bank of Kenya, *Monthly Economic Review*, July 2004.

102. Kipkoech Tanui, "UK body steps up campaign for debt relief," Business Week Magazine, *Daily Nation*, April 21 1998, pp. 6-7.

103. *Ibid.*

Most African countries sinking under the weight of debt have external trade deficits averaging at 7% of GDP and inflation at around 15%[105]. This increases the cost of goods, aggravating the already extreme poverty. African countries had, in 2004, a combined debt of Kshs 220,000,000,000,000,000 or $275 billion; which costs Kshs 2,144 billion or $26.8 billion to service in annual repayments[106]. And every dollar received is repaid twice or thrice over.

The Solution

There are two possible ways to actually get out of the debt problem: "can't pay — won't pay", or paying through the development of manufactured exports.

However, all profitable spheres of manufacturing have been re-colonized by Western companies with multinational interests. This cripples Africa in two ways. These companies are not interested in competing with themselves by exporting to countries where they have operations. Africa loses whether these companies choose to export or not. The profits end up in the West anyway, so that a growth in exports does not mean a growth in income for the African countries.

Africa does not need foreign aid. Africa can develop faster and better on its own. It is a wealthy continent, 85% of which is underutilized and unoccupied. The poverty stems not from the lack of resources or "overpopulation" but mainly from bad policy.

Let us look at some examples showing that aid is not a precondition to development but is a constraining factor. After Nicaragua ousted the US-backed Somoza, the Americans and Europeans cut off all aid with the intent of causing the new anti-neocolonial government to collapse. But the progressive government did not fall. Food production increased by 8%. As a result of increased investment in education and health, literacy shot up (illiteracy among adults was reduced from 53 to 13%[107]) and there was a staggering 98% reduction in malaria cases[108]. Three-quarters of the population were provided with adequate healthcare. In other words, in the absence of aid and with a bloody destabili-

---

104. Evans Ombiro, "Debt must go, media talks conclude." *Daily Nation*, November 24 1998, p. 23.

105. Mishael Ondieki, "Africa victim of restrictive trade blocs, says paper," Business Week Magazine, *Daily Nation*, September 8 1998, p. 8.

106. IMF, *Statistical Appendix 2004*.

107. Pilger, *Heroes*.

108. *Ibid.*

zation campaign by the US under the Reagan regime, this tiny country's population begun to live longer and enjoy a higher quality of life. Cuba has also managed to give its citizens political stability, and a higher quality life with free education and healthcare, in the absence of aid. Russia was a superpower until it began to receive aid, and now, according to the mainstream view, it is not. The USA has grown increasingly powerful because of giving — and not receiving — aid.

Thus, we can only conclude that "aid" is not aid but is a means of transferring wealth from the least developed to the most developed countries through legalized financial means.

CHAPTER 6. UNDERPOPULATION

Africa is the least populated continent today. Yet, most Africans (and many others) strongly believe it is overpopulated. This is the result of a successful "information" campaign aimed at masking and distorting the truth.

The UN, IMF, World Bank and Western governments have joined forces to convince Africans to reduce their population. Their propaganda claims that problems caused by neocolonialism are caused by "overpopulation". The repercussions of African alleged overpopulation are food shortages, famines, civil wars, unemployment and poverty. The US, EU and Japan have higher population densities than any African country, yet they are largely free from the problems that they claim are caused by overpopulation. This contradiction itself is enough to prove that the economic problems in Africa have nothing to do with overpopulation.

The UNFPA in its 2004 State of the World Population report claims that the sub-Saharan African population is 869 million. The truth of the matter, however, is that today Africa has a population of less than 400 million and it is quickly falling. It has been predicted that at the present rate of depopulation, by 2025 Africa shall be virtually empty[109]. To mask this, the UN has published figures that claim Africa's population by 2050 shall be 1.8 billion. It also claims that the average population growth rate of Africa is 2.2%. This figure is questionable when one considers the short life expectancy, high infant mortality and maternal mortality and the continuing wars. In fact projections by UNFPA

---

109. *New African*, 1996.

forecast that by 2025 the populations of several African countries with adult HIV prevalence of 20% or more, will be 35% lower than it would have been in the absence of Aids[110].

Let us examine this "overpopulation" myth. Overpopulation is not a factor that slows down economic growth. The problems of economic stagnation, unemployment, poverty, political instability and mass hunger have roots in the neo-colonial nature of African economies. Because Western economies are free and not colonized, the industrial states have fewer economic problems despite the fact that they are relatively overpopulated. For example, Botswana is about the same geographical size as Germany and has a population of 1.8 million, while Germany has 82.5 million[111]. One may argue that Botswana has more desert land, hence the low population. But Angola has fertile land and is about the size of Germany. Angola has a small population of 14 million living in desperate poverty, while Germany has 82 million living in considerable wealth and comfort.

The second largest country in Africa is the former Zaire, with a land area of 2,345,409 sq kms. Austria, Belgium, France, Germany, Ireland, Italy, Netherlands, Portugal, Spain, Switzerland and UK have a total land area of 2,327,079 sq kms, more or less equal to the area of DR Congo. Yet the combined populations of these European states is about 356 million, while DR Congo has only some 54.4 million[112]. Still, the Congolese are pressured to establish "family planning" services to reduce their numbers because they are "overpopulated". And they believe it.

If we compare the population and land area of two industrial countries that derive some of their wealth from Africa, with equivalent African territories. The combined populations of Japan and Germany total some 210 million, occupying an area of 729,556 sq kms. To aggregate so much population in Africa, we would have to combine Mozambique, Tanzania, Madagascar, Angola, Chad, D.R. Congo, Botswana, Guinea Bissau, Mauritania, Namibia, South Africa, Mali and Niger. In this case, a combined population of 210 million is spread over nearly twenty times the area, 13,410,793 sq kms[113]. This would appear to suggest that Africa is dangerously under populated.

If 210 million people can live in wealth and comfort in a land area of only 0.73 million sq kms, then the same number of people should be able to live in

---

110. UNFPA, State of the World population 2004, *UNFPA*, 2004, p 15.
111. *Ibid.* p. 106.
112. *Ibid.* pp. 106-108.
113. UNFPA, State of the World Population 2004, pp. 106-108.

even greater wealth and comfort in a land area of 13.4 million sq kms. The African countries named above have more resources than Japan and Germany and indeed Western Europe combined, but the population is desperately poor.

Most Africans do not realize the fact that, due to its small population, "poor" Africa has the most resources per person in the world. It is only logical to ask, where do these resources go? African wealth goes out to the most developed countries through the economic policies discussed above; and these policies cause congestion in rural and urban areas, giving the impression of overpopulation.

The city of Nairobi has a population of less than 3 million and 70% live in slums and shanties. This situation, coupled with ignorance, has led many to believe the UN mantra that the congestion is due to "overpopulation". Few have noted the fact that the populations of cities in industrial countries outstrip the entire populations of African countries. For example, the cities of Tokyo and New York each have more people than the entire populations of Kenya, Botswana, Namibia, Guinea Bissau and Gabon. But there is minimal congestion in New York and Tokyo and very few live in "slums".

The African race is the least numerous race on earth. The population of India alone is far greater than the entire race of Africans. The populations on other continents are growing crowded, and the largely vacant African continent is the target of many a covetous gaze. Still, Africans have been convinced that they are "overpopulated" and must therefore reduce their numbers.

This view has received official recognition in Kenya, and the Government has agreed to disseminate false information concerning population. An important avenue are public schools. The Sessional Paper No. 1 of 1997 on National Population Policy for Sustainable Development proposed the teaching of Family Life Education in all schools. In essence, the FLE program erodes family values by pushing for the acceptance of promiscuity and alternative lifestyles which traditionally were considered sinful and immoral, such as lesbianism and homosexuality. University students in Kenya are taught that "overpopulation" must be overcome; a typical student's notes read:

> The natural resources available cannot support the population and there is pressure applied on our environment. Due to population explosion, there are food shortages. 3rd World countries should try and minimize the number of children from each woman, hence the growth of family planning [*sic*].

The true causes of food shortages lie elsewhere, but the IMF and UN will never admit it. The causes are:

- Civil wars: These displace farming communities and destroy farmland through the laying of landmines.
- Poor farming methods: African farmers are mostly uneducated and practice traditional agricultural methods; and the overall economic structure has no connection between agriculture and industry.
- Food prices: These are so low that there is no incentive for farmers to produce more. African governments cannot afford to subsidize farmers to increase production.
- The neocolonial economic system also wreaks havoc on food production. The best land is allocated to cash crops such that African countries are then forced to import food despite the fact that they could attain self-sufficiency in food.

All these factors drive down food production and in cases of emergency, such as famine, the country is unable to send relief food from one region to another because stocks are too low; hence, mass hunger becomes common.

INTERNATIONAL POLICY ON AFRICAN POPULATION

In summary, the industrialized nations look on Africans as a "resource" to be exploited rather than as their equals. The newly industrialized Asian countries have a population problem. Increasing population is threatening to reduce their prosperity and bring down their economies through unemployment and rising social unrest. They are unwilling to reduce own their population and, in fact, encourage immigration due to a problem in their own demographics. While the populations of many Western countries are ageing much faster than the population of Africa and family planning would only accelerate this undesirable process. The following are two examples that compare a typical African country and a European country typical of the industrialized nations.

	Kenya	Sweden
Over 65	24%	27%
Workforce 15 – 64	30%	52%
Under 15	46%	21%

Looking at the two examples, over the next three decades Sweden should have lost the 27% in the over-65 group by death through old age, plus enough of the working contingent to affect its overall economic performance. The West knows that a small population is unable to support the industrial economy which is needed to create the wealth to maintain a population, never mind actually producing further wealth. The populations of Western Europe, Japan and North America are not sufficient to maintain their high living standards in the long run. Africa is being drawn into colonialism again to support their economies.

The implications of an ageing population are interesting. As more and more people retire and stop producing, the market for certain products diminishes. Commodities such as expensive fashionable clothing, contraceptives, alcoholic drinks, vehicles, tools and a whole range of other products lose market. The younger smaller segment of the population does not need to buy many of the most expensive items because either they are too young, and they already own many of the other products.

In the Scandinavian countries, where this pattern has emerged clearly, people of twenty to forty-five years of age are a poor market because they own most of what they need. Through inheritance, this group already owns vehicles, houses and other durables, hence that market is effectively closed; in much of the so-called Third World, the population is expanding and more people are moving into the work force and providing an eager market for houses, cars and other products. In the West, as the "baby-boomers" approach retirement age, most of the population is actually moving out of the workforce and the effect on the economy is disastrous. In most European countries, the population is not sustaining itself as it is growing at an average of -0.1%[114]— too few to replace their own parents' generation. This trend began in the late 1970s and is a product of their culture. Most Westerners set a high premium on personal enjoyment of life and are wary of the responsibilities and restrictions brought on by parenthood.

Excessive materialism has shifted their priorities, inclining parents to have fewer children and contributing to the tolerance of abortion. The Scandinavian countries are experiencing depopulation; the culture focuses on individual gratification at the expense of family, as exemplified by their liberal approach to sexuality, including pornography. Their governments are trying to reverse this trend and are actively encouraging their citizens to have larger families, but with little success. Adults in Scandinavian countries are given many incentives to bear children — within or without marriage. Among the incentives are free healthcare, free education to university level, tax reduction, cash payments, and free baby supplies. However, all these incentives have failed. As a result of the waning population, hospitals, schools, local councils and other institutions have

---

114. UNFPA, State of the World population 2004, p. 108.

been closed down. Large developed areas are being abandoned wholesale — there are ghost towns, and empty farms.

When the population of retirees increases as a proportion of the total population and the proportion of people in the lower age brackets decreases, the economy is strained. Large numbers of older, unproductive people consume large amounts of services, healthcare and other forms of social welfare. A society benefits when it has a larger proportion of younger, working people to support a relatively small group of older people.

The West sees a solution to this problem when it looks abroad. As the ageing population and depopulation of Europe both in terms of current population and falling birth rates started to affect their economies in the late 1970s, African countries begun to be pressured to accept Structural Adjustment Programs, which opened up African markets and new investment opportunities for outsiders. The diminished markets and investment opportunities in the West were compensated for by the increased exploitation of Africa.

However, this was not enough, and more debilitating economic policies were forced on Africa in the late 1980s. African markets were totally opened as dictated by trade liberalization; foreign companies have been allowed to re-colonize the land and were given the right to repatriate all profits; previously, a fixed percentage was to be repatriated with the remainder of profits to be reinvested within the country.

The demographic trend in the West is not about to end; rather, it is accelerating and Africa will have to bear the consequences. The ageing of the population of the industrialized countries has another implication. In two to three decades, barring any novel solution, their over all populations will decline precipitously as the older, more numerous generations expire. Massive depopulation would mean that industries, schools, hospitals, and towns will be emptied. With diminished power, the rich countries fear that the poor countries may be ascendant.

The US, for example, fears that the South American countries it has been dominating for the last hundred years may band together and resist it, while Europe fears Africa, especially an Africa with 1.5 billion people all seeking to migrate to the halcyon Europe. In the East, Japan and Australia fear the growing population and power of China — another country that was terrorized by the West and Japan for most of a century.

The industrialized countries are in a bind. The shifting demographics of Europe and America has forced them to hire foreign labor. The massive recruitment of foreigners has both political advantages and disadvantages. Having a large proportion of foreigners can be very advantageous if they do not have to be given rights, if they are pliable and willing to make sacrifices in order to continue living in that country. But accepting a large number of foreign nationals can be politically dangerous, and expensive, too. For example, a large Egyptian population lived and worked in pre-revolution Libya; the then ruler, King Idris, feared a pro-Nasser social revolution engineered by the Egyptians. And he was correct; when he was overthrown, the new rulers were strongly pro-Nasser. This was also the case in 869 AD, in Arabia, when African slaves became so numerous that they were able to overthrow the Abbasid hegemony and form an independent kingdom that survived for 14 years[115]. This also happened in Haiti in the 1800s.

So, Europe needs more people but is fearful of the rapid increase in African immigrants. In fact, Europe is estimated to needs a large number of immigrants every year to maintain its existing level of development. The US needs and fears its South American immigrants. Africa might just end up colonizing Europe. The West's campaign to reduce the already tiny population of Africa is aimed at forestalling such an eventuality.

Africans have long been imported into Europe and the Americas to perform menial and difficult tasks. Most Africans wish to leave Africa because of the desperate poverty which is caused by the West's efforts to save themselves; on top of that, the success of cultural imperialism has enabled the West to convince millions of Africans that the US and Western Europe are havens of peace and plenty. Africans even have the advantage of speaking various European tongues.

Nations with overpopulation problems are now seeking new areas for settlement. This is their best option as it would help them ease congestion, reduce unemployment, increase productivity by cutting the amount spent on welfare and for nationalistic reasons. Africa has been chosen as the continent where the surplus populations of other nations are to be dumped. Our continent Africa is being targeted by the West for specific reasons.

- Africa is underpopulated, unlike Asia and South America, and its small population is dying off through "civil" wars, disease and hunger.

---

115. Jonathan Burrack, How Textbooks Obscure and Distort the History of Slavery, *The Textbook Letter*, November — December 1992.

• Africa has extensive undeveloped resources including a wealth of mineral deposits.

• The West knows that Africans will welcome and accept them and allow them to live in luxury at their expense. After suffering 300 years of slavery, after taking power the Blacks of South Africa still serve the Caucasian oppressors and allow them to live off the fat of their land.

• Africa also has a stable climate. It is warm enough so that Europeans with rheumatism and other diseases caused by the cold will be comfortable. It is a beautiful, unspoilt continent. Pollution in most areas is non-existent. There is an abundance of wild life and there are large uninhabited tracts of land. The continent also has clean energy sources, and is a good candidate for solar energy solutions.

In 1986, the USA, Canada, the EU, Japan, China and even India held a meeting whose theme was 'the devastation and decimation of Africa by AIDS." The topic was, "How to seriously carve up Africa in the light of this new development"[116]. Since that time the destruction wrought by AIDS, a disease whose origin remains mysterious to this day, has decimated the indigenous populace.

Other important shifts are also under way, which anecdotally suggest that East Africa (that is Kenya, Uganda and Tanzania) have been informally allocated to India and China. The Ugandan president was pressured to allow Indians to return after their expulsion by Idi Amin; in Kenya, Chinese clinics and restaurants have proliferated. In fact, the Chinese have become so numerous that there are reports of a lucrative business in dog meat — supposed to be a Chinese delicacy. South Africa, it would seem, was allocated to the US and Britain. Members of the British royalty and the US elite have been migrating there in large numbers[117].

Several factors hinder massive European and Chinese immigration into Africa. Note that none of the obstacles to immigration is raised by African governments or people.

• There is political instability and uncertainty in many African countries.

• Most of Africa is quite undeveloped, and so represents a less appealing place to live.

• The high level of deep poverty is unappealing to potential immigrants.

---

116. This story was carried in the magazine *New African* in 1996. It indicates that the spread of Aids in Africa serves the interests of other nations and fuels suspicion in Africa that the disease is hardly coincidental.

117. "In Capetown, an invasion of sorts, by the rich and famous", Lifestyle Magazine, *Sunday Nation*, February 4 1996, p. 2.

The depopulation of Africa is currently being achieved in several ways:

- family planning
- disease
- reduced food availability
- tainted water and food supplies, and
- poverty.

FAMILY PLANNING

The notion of "family planning" originated with Margaret Sanger of the US. She herself said her reasons for inventing it was that, "my family on both sides were early colonial and pioneer stock, and I have worked with the American Coalition for Patriotic Societies, to prevent the [European] type people from being replaced by Negro stock"[118]. From the outset, family planning was anti-African. When the Planned Parenthood Federation was started, all it efforts were directed at the Afro-American population. For example, in Pittsburgh, the US government established a Planned Parenthood Clinic in the slum section of the city where the "negroes" lived. No such clinics were to be found in "white" areas. Birth control pills were also distributed to Afro-Americans girls as young as twelve[119].

In many "black" communities, birth control services and free contraceptives are provided when basic medical facilities are not[120]. In the US Congress, bills were introduced for allowing the provision of cash incentives to Afro-American women who agreed to be sterilized. In some cases poor Blacks are forcibly sterilized. The Relf family, illiterate Southern "Blacks", were evicted from the farm where they used to live and drifted into the city in search of work. They lived for a while off the municipal garbage dump. Only after a newspaper publicized their plight was the family helped to apply for welfare and moved into a public housing facility. One day, two nurses from the local family planning agency took the two daughters in. Their mother was told they were being taken for birth control shots, so she marked a consent document; the hospital sterilized both her daughters by tubal ligation. This kind of deception is common[121].

---

118. Quoted from Thomas B. Littlewood, *The Politics of Birth Control*, University of Notre Dame Press, p. 16.

119. *Ibid.*, p. 76.

120. *Ibid.*, p. 76.

121. Littlewood, *The Politics of Birth Control*, pp. 107-110.

In addition, the youth are encouraged to be promiscuous by the ghetto culture. This has resulted in the increase of the number of Aids victims among "Blacks" and today, a majority of all Aids cases in the US occur among Afro-Americans. This campaign is being pursued globally. In the US, "Black" women are tricked into sterilization campaigns while the same occurs in Africa. Family planning is promoted by the West in many ways, from the distribution of contraceptives to the legalization and official encouragement of abortion. In fact, the US government provides the equivalent of Kshs 23,100 million ($385 million) worth of condoms, IUDs and birth control pills every year. CNN owner Ted Turner and Microsoft chairman Bill Gates have each offered the UN Kshs 120 billion ($2 billion), 90% of it to be used to reduce the population of Africa. In Kenya, one may recall the 1986 school milk scandal in which milk supplied to students was discovered to have been laced with "family planning" agents[122]. In fact, the US has distributed chemical pellets that cause irreversible sterilization. These pellets, called Quinacrine, are banned in the US because they are not safe and may cause cancer. For many women in Africa who have been tricked into using these poisons, the side effects include abnormal menstrual bleeding, back aches, lower abdominal pain and headaches. On using this drug, the pain is so intense that many women faint.

Foreign investors are already cashing in on the contraceptive market. This is part of the larger scheme to promote family planning through the provision of contraceptives. The first grants of contraceptives from the West were aimed at "want development". This was successful because once the want for contraceptives was created in Africa using the original grant, foreign companies immediately invested in manufacturing these contraceptives. In Kenya, "Trust" condoms are manufactured by a US company which uses widespread advertisements to create more demand for condoms.

The last and most effective way of achieving the sustained use of contraceptives in Africa is by demolishing the value system and culture and, in the vacuum created, implant decadent notions. In Africa, children were always regarded as socially prestigious and were highly valued. The "modern" view seeks to make Africans see children as irritants and agents of economic waste.

---

122. This is a news article quoted from the *Wall Street Journal*. "America's scheme to curb Third World population?" Lifestyle Magazine, *Sunday Nation* June 21, 1998. p. 6. See also Information Project for Africa, *'Excessive Force: Power politics and population control'*, Washington DC, 1995.

The large, traditional African family is held up to scorn. To Africans, a family was formed by a man and woman (or several women). Today, this concept is being destroyed and Western governments are trying to force African governments to accept the Western family, in which all traditional standards are abrogated. Even the promulgation of women's rights and gender equality are weapons to destroy society as they create rifts and misunderstanding.

Lastly, Western governments are pressuring African governments to adopt Family Life Education (FLE). Where FLE is taught, sexual promiscuity has increased, and so has teenage pregnancy, abortion, and STDs[123]. This precisely is the reason why the West wants Africa to adopt FLE. Once moral order collapses among the youth, promiscuity increases. This situation has direct advantages to the West. They stand to make more profit from the sale of contraceptives; and more unwanted pregnancies would eventually force governments to legalize abortion. Then Western hospitals would quickly cash in by opening abortion clinics all over the continent since they have the capital and experience — generating more profit for the West. And finally and most important, AIDS would spread faster and large segments of the population would die off.

It has been noticed that the availability of contraception leads to an increase in the abortion rate[124]. Apart from causing infertility, abortion when widespread results in moral collapse and disorder. When the West dumps contraceptives in Africa and then start manufacturing contraceptives there, they are creating a chain reaction.

When the West began forcing African governments to adopt "family planning" and the distribution of contraceptives, national governments adamantly refused. Then, the West destroyed African economies through the SAPs and later the MAI and TRIM. Today, economies all across the continent are effectively dead, which ensures that Africa will remain a cheap source of raw materials and a market for finished products. No competition will emerge from Africa, politically, economically or militarily. And the African population can be controlled.

When African economies collapsed, the governments became vulnerable to outside pressures. These pressures took the form of conditions set by the donors in exchange for aid. The conditions include balancing the budget through

123. Wangeci Kahara, "Dangers of family life education", *The Family*, (August/December, 1997), p. 4.

124. Dr. Raphael Wanjohi, "The Catholic Church's view on provision of contraception and family life education to adolescents", in *The Family* (August/December, 1997), p. 6.

cuts in social services such as healthcare and education, increase in taxation, hikes in services charges such as water, electricity etc., elimination of food subsidies, and the deregulation and state control of food prices. All these measures were aimed at increasing the cost of living for the ordinary African. School fees were introduced and the farming of cash crops caused the importation of food, hence shortages and high food prices. The ordinary African today is too poor to send his children to school or even to provide a daily meal, or decent housing. In other words, he cannot support many children. And so Africans are forced to reduce their families and use contraceptives, which opened a market for the West but destroyed the moral fabric of the society.

Today, African populations are being reduced by Aids, and the fact is that families are not having as many children as they would like. That is just fine with the West.

DISEASES

The rate of disease occurrence in Africa is the highest in the world. The rate of mortality is also the highest. The introduction of diseases but also their control, and factors that affect disease control, are exploited by the West to encourage the spread of diseases in Africa. While many factors increase the rate of disease occurrence, the main ones are poverty and ignorance.

The principal means by which the West is encouraging the spread of diseases is through the intensification of poverty. Most Africans have little or no access to basic health services and proper nutrition. In the slums, overcrowding is common. It is usual to find families of eight or more living in a single room[125]. Any disease that is picked up quickly spreads, throughout the family and the neighborhood, causing epidemics[126]. Whooping cough and tuberculosis are common, and the prolonged use of firewood with inadequate ventilation eventually causes lung and eye problems.

Poverty also means that families cannot afford adequate clothing. In slums and rural areas children generally have to go naked or at best wear torn clothes. In cold weather or at night, these unfortunate children are vulnerable to respiratory diseases such as pneumonia or whooping cough, which then spread to

---

125. I have witnessed this. Also for a deeper analysis consider Harrison, *Inside the Third World*, p. 280.

126. *Ibid.*

other family members; this further drives them into poverty as funerals cost money, and eventually it is the breadwinner who is incapacitated. The lack of shoes also poses a health risk. In the mud floors all manner of parasites are found, and outside the home the risk increases, especially near pathways and water points where people relieve themselves. Anyone without shoes risks penetration of the feet by parasites like bilharzia or hookworms, and tetanus.

Many Africans also live in constant hunger. Even when they get food, they can only cook it partially because they lack fuel. In urban areas, many live off food scavenged from garbage dumps. Incomplete cooking and the consumption of food in garbage dumps increases the chances of parasitic infections. In addition, obviously, they lack balanced nutrition and they have to work hard physically while eating less. This large deficit in body energy is malnutrition[127]. Malnutrition lowers resistance to disease and the illness aggravates malnutrition. Poor nutrition leads to diseases like kwashiorkor, marasmus, and bowlegs. A mother's malnourishment during pregnancy may cause chronic diseases in the child later in life, including diabetes, cardiovascular disease, pulmonary and liver diseases.

Many people are also affected by lack of adequate clean water. Poor people cannot even boil water meant for drinking. Kerosene is unaffordable; firewood is hard to come by and so is reserved for cooking. Polluted water therefore transmits cholera, typhoid and dysentery[128]. The chronic shortage of water means that children and adults all go to bed unwashed and spend the day in dirty clothes. This in itself fosters disease, and once a person is infected it aggravates terrible illnesses such as leprosy, meningitis, and trachoma which leads to blindness. The poor also lack proper sewage disposal facilities.

The easiest way to reduce illness among the poor would be to provide cheap, clean water in adequate quantities, and sewage facilities[129]. Also important is public education in health as a way of encouraging hygienic living even in cases of limited financial resources. Healthcare facilities should be increased in poor areas and made free. But the best solution is poverty alleviation.

The effects of the intense poverty in Africa have been a large factor in depopulation. Many children die within the first five years. Families living in

---

127. Harrison, *Inside the Third World*, p. 267.
128. *Ibid.*, p. 290.
129. Harrison, *Inside the Third World*, p. 290.

poverty commonly lose more than three children to preventable diseases. Those who survive may suffer from various infections and nutritionary diseases such as kwashiorkor, marasmus, and rickets, and worm infestation — for example, hookworms, roundworms, bilharzia, filariasis, tapeworms, threadworms — and leprosy, measles, bronchitis, sleeping sickness, anaemia, trachoma and so on. All these are preventable but they have reduced the average African's life expectancy to only 54 years. The average mortality rate during birth, in Africa, is 830 per 100,000, while under 5 mortality is 148 per thousand, while in Europe under-5 mortality is 18[130].

It comes as a surprise to many that 90% of all Aids cases in the world are in Africa. This is because Aids is regarded as a disease linked to immorality while in reality Aids is, for the most part, a disease of poverty. Africa is the poorest continent and has the highest unemployment levels; dire poverty obliges people to engage in prostitution. In slums, up to 90% of the women, some as young as 12, prostitute for a living. That is why Aids spreads so rapidly in Africa.

As for the men, chronic unemployment or underemployment leads to hopelessness, so that the victim lives for the day only. Idleness also inclines the underemployed to go to prostitutes. Hopelessness contributes to alcoholism and drug abuse, which lower inhibitions, and promiscuity increases. Furthermore, at the bottom of the social ladder alcoholism and drug abuse can lead to quick death because the intoxicants sold may be tainted with dangerous chemicals which kill, blind or cause liver disease, lung cancer or insanity. Young women become prostitutes as a means of survival, and young men patronize them because they see no future and because they are always under the influence of drugs and alcohol and cannot afford to marry.

In areas of extreme poverty, pressures on the family increase[131]. When the fathers leave the family, the mothers have to provide for the children and many are driven into prostitution. Such women end up being alcoholics to avoid facing the facts of their lives, and they end up mistreating their children. The girls may be encouraged to join their mothers in prostituting and boys become street children, always hungry and drugged — leading to premature death in both cases. In this scenario, everyone eventually becomes promiscuous and Aids runs rampant. There are about 35 other STDs, too, which are fatal if left untreated.

---

130. UNFPA, *State of the World Population 2004,UNFPA*, 2004 p. 106.
131. Harrison, *Inside the Third World*, p. 157.

Other ways in which the spread of Aids is promoted is through national economic collapse. Migration occurs when one country is in economic decline and unemployed people move to a neighboring country whose economy is growing. In West Africa, there are more than 6 million migrant workers, mostly male[132]. A similar situation prevails in South Africa. When large numbers of unmarried men are living in one location, poor women from surrounding areas are bound to move to the men's area — especially when the men have jobs. Conversely, where large pools of women are living together, men go there looking for sex. For example, most of the population in refugee camps are women, and they are, of course, in desperate need of cash. In both these cases, the spread of Aids is rapid.

Superficially, poverty affects reproduction in a positive way (because poor people tend to have many children), but the wealthy West intensifies African poverty for several reasons. Studies have revealed that menopause occurs earlier in women who have lived in poverty. Infant mortality and child mortality are also higher in poor than in rich areas. It is therefore in the interests of the West to sustain intense poverty as a method of population control and reduction.

Cuts in healthcare expenditure have directly increased the rate of disease occurrence and death. For example, in Kenya's North Eastern province, one doctor is shared by 120,000 people[133]. African countries now allocate only 2.1% of their GNP to public health[134]. During the 1960s and 1970s, the population of Africa was growing at a comfortable rate and it was estimated by the UN that by the year 2000 there would be one billion Africans. The main cause of the population rise was improved public health. When the SAPs and other policies encouraged unemployment, malnutrition and political instability, these factors eventually took their toll on the African population, which is said by UNFPA (1998 figures) to stand at about 600 million, 400 million short of the projected one billion[135].

In other words, the projected population of Africa has been reduced by 400 million in a short period of 20 years as the projected growth was lost. Western companies have been the main beneficiaries of the ill health of Africans.

---

132. *Ibid.*, p. 142.

133. Society for International Development (SID), *Pulling Apart; Facts and Figures on Inequality in Kenya*, Nairobi, 2004, p. 25.

134. UNFPA, *State of the World Population 2004*, pp. 106-7.

135. UNFPA 1998, "Healthy ageing through the lifecycle", UNFPA, *State of the World Population 1998; The New Generations*, (September 1998).

Because African governments have cut expenditure on public health, available resources for healthcare facilities and trained personnel have drastically reduced. Therefore disease outbreaks recur, creating a big a market for imported medicines, usually paid for by additional aid packages which have to be repaid. The breakdown of health administrations and veterinary services (either through poverty or so-called civil wars) has contributed to the spread of once controllable diseases and the reappearance of others (including those which affect livestock, such as rinderpest).

Another problem is the mis-education of African doctors. The African doctor is trained to handle Western medical problems, the kind of problems the Europeanized African elite also suffer from[136]. The affluent are afflicted by heart disease, cancer, and obesity, while ordinary Africans suffer from infectious parasitic, respiratory and nutritional diseases. Most refuse to work in the rural areas, where they are most needed. Once the town's upper class areas are saturated with doctors, they migrate to Europe and North America[137]. African doctors should be trained to treat the majority of their people; they need skills that are not in demand in the West, and there should be incentives to keep them where they are needed.

Furthermore, while there is little verifiable evidence, many highly-educated Africans believe that Africa is the testing ground for biological warfare weapons. Anthrax is a disease invented or at least "weaponized" by the West. It is found throughout Africa and is rare in the West. It is very costly to cattle farmers; it attacks all farm animals and its main symptom is sudden death. It can also be transmitted from animals to human beings. It is a notifiable disease, meaning that the authorities have to be informed to quarantine an area at the first sign of it, because it can cause high economic losses. It is therefore not surprising that the world's largest outbreak of anthrax occurred in Africa in 1978-80, when with American and British help, the White Southern Rhodesian (now Zimbabwe) regime launched biological warfare on Africans resisting colonialism. Lieutenant-General Niels Knobel, the Surgeon-General (1988-97) of the South African Defense Force — which was working in close cooperation with the white Southern Rhodesian dictatorship — admitted that in obtaining cholera and anthrax, they received "tacit under-the-counter help from Britain and the United States."[138]

---

136. Harrison, *Inside the Third World*, p. 299.
137. *Ibid.*

This resulted in the infection with anthrax of 10,738 people; 182 of them died. According to Dr. Meryl Nass, in the 29 years prior to the Zimbabwe outbreak, only 7,000 cases had been recorded worldwide and of these only 334 in Zimbabwe[139]. In addition, the British Broadcasting Corporation (BBC), in a 1998 television documentary aptly titled "Plague Wars: Apocalypse Delayed", dealt with the deliberate spread of cholera and anthrax, by the West, in Africa[140].

Some also suspect that the West has deliberately introduced AIDS into Africa, although again, needless to say, hard proof cannot be found. However, a Special Virus Paper by Dr. Robert Gallo (1971) shows that the US was seeking a virus particle that would destroy the body's immune system. In April 1984, Dr. Gallo filed a US patent application (patent number: 46 477 73) for his invention, HIV. It appears that HIV was developed from the Visna virus found in sheep. In 2001, Dr. Gallo admitted that he had been the project officer for the 1962-78 Federal Virus Development Program. According to Aids researcher Dr. Boyd Graves, the US government designed Aids as a biological weapon against people of African descent. He suggests that the Aids virus was added by vaccine manufacturer Merck to smallpox vaccines distributed as humanitarian aid in central Africa in the late 1970s and early 1980s[141].

If experiments in biological warfare aim to invent diseases that spread and kill quickly, Ebola looks like an ideal product. Its mode of transmission is through any contact, such as handshakes, brushing of shoulders on the street, and even breathing the same air. When it broke out in Central Africa it seemed unstoppable but, astonishingly, it failed to destroy a large proportion of the population. This disease first surfaced near the rainforest and the West proclaimed that it was caused by contact between wild animals and humans. Africans suspect that Ebola came from a laboratory outside Africa; they note that when it failed to spread, the Americans quickly flew in to investigate.

In early 1998, a new disease-causing organism cropped up in northeastern Kenya[142]. Several hundred Africans died before it mysteriously vanished. It was

---

138. David Martin, "Traditional medical practitioners seek international recognition," *Southern African News Features*, November 2001.

139. Dr. Meryl Nass, "Anthrax epizootic in Zimbabwe, 1978-80: Due to deliberate spread?" *Physicians for Social Change*, December 1992.

140. BBC TV, Panorama, "Plague Wars: The Secret Killings," July 1998.

141. Matt Woods, "Lawyer sues US government over the true origin of the Aids virus", *Daily Nation*, October 29, 2004. This article also states that Dr. Graves will present his case on June 27, 2005 in a San Diego Court. Also, "Smallpox vaccine triggered AIDS virus" *The London Times*, May 11 1987.

later dubbed "Rift Valley Fever". Africans fear that this disease looks like an improved version of Ebola because of the characteristic bleeding from mucous membranes and body orifices.

Another method of encouraging the rapid spread of disease in Africa is through the sale of expired or untested medicines that either kill the patient or fail to cure the illness[143]. Drugs not authorized for sale in the West, or that were withdrawn from the market for reasons of safety or lack of efficacy, are dumped on Africa. Africa has now become the testing ground for dangerous medical experimentation. For example, beginning in 1989, the Edmonston-Zagreb (E-Z) vaccine was tested in Senegal and Guinea-Bissau as an experimental drug. But, it resulted in such a high rate of infant deaths that the WHO intervened to stop further tests[144]. In September 1997, in the *New England Journal of Medicine*, Dr. Marcia Angelle wrote an editorial strongly critical of US-funded Aids tests in poor countries. These tests involved the use of placebos where desperate patients were deceived and given fake medicine[145]. A precedent in the US was the Alabama experiment in which Afro-American men infected with syphilis were denied treatment for forty years so that Caucasian scientists could study the painful and terrible effects as the disease progressed. In 1932, the US government promised free treatment to 400 men for "bad blood", a euphemism for syphilis. The Tuskegee Study of Untreated Syphilis in the Negro Male lasted 40 years until 1972. This has the dubious distinction of being the "longest non-therapeutic experiment on human beings in medical history"[146].

Medicinal products not meeting quality requirements of the exporting Western country, including products beyond their expiry date, are repackaged and given a new false expiration date and sold to Africa[147]. Twiga Chemicals was taken to court in Nairobi for exactly that[148].

More broadly, the spread of life threatening diseases is encouraged in Africa through cultural imperialism in the form of increased promiscuity,

---

142. "Killer disease wipes out 143," *Daily Nation,* December 23 1997 p. 1 and "Mystery disease claims 28 more", *Daily Nation* December 24 1997. p. 1.

143. Harrison, *Inside the Third World*, p. 300.

144. http;//www.thetalkingdrum.com.

145. Jon Elliston, "US AIDS tests denounced" *Dossier*, 1997.

146. http;//www.thetalkingdrum.com/tusk/html. The quote is taken from James Jones, *Bad Blood: The Tuskegee Syphilis Experiment*, 1992.

147. Harrison, *Inside the Third World*, p. 301.

148. *Daily Nation*, 27 October 1998.

smoking and alcoholism, all of which have been popularized through association with "sophisticated" Western culture.

Neocolonialism has meant that the Western model of development has been imitated even in healthcare. African countries have concentrated on constructing prestigious and expensive hospitals using imported equipment and drugs, focusing on heart ailments and other diseases of the wealthy, and manned by expensively trained personnel[149]. These large hospitals are concentrated in urban centers which also have many doctors in private practice. They are geographically accessible to less than 20% of the national population and are hopelessly out of reach financially and culturally — only European languages are used. A more logical arrangement would be to construct small clinics throughout the country to deal specifically with the diseases of poverty. The cost of a single Western-style hospital would cover construction of more than one thousand health centers in rural and slum areas[150].

REDUCING FOOD AVAILABILITY

Mass starvation is a major drag on population growth in Africa. Famines are not as the result of overpopulation, as Western pamphlets claim; they are the result of misguided policies in food production and distribution, under the advice of the West. Even as the projected increase in population falls, the incidence of famines and mass starvation is actually increasing. Two decades ago, most Africans had food in abundance. But today, 70% of all Africans live in constant hunger. Of this group, 20% will die of starvation.

There are several causes of food shortages and are all linked to neocolonialism. These are:
- Over emphasis on cash crop farming
- Poor farming methods
- Political instability and civil strife.
- Climatic factors and desertization
- Colonial economic system that forces food imports.

In Africa today, the best land has been allocated to cash crops at the expense of food crops, a distortion of priorities that cannot be claimed to be in the interests of a starving population. In 1980, a meeting held by the OAU

---

149. Harrison, *Inside the Third World*, p. 295.
150. *Ibid.*, p. 296.

stressed that self sufficiency in food was of utmost importance. Plans were made to achieve this goal[151]. Soon afterwards, the IMF and World Bank moved to introduce SAPs. These programs sabotaged food production and distribution in Africa such that by 1985, Africa was importing two fifths of its food[152]. In other words, the move towards self-sufficiency in food production was halted and the opposite process of food dependency was accelerated.

This was achieved through the heavy emphasis on the farming of cash crops on a large scale, which had the effect of strengthening neo-colonialism as an economic system. If they do generate cash, it is not for Africa.

Low productivity is one of the most obvious characteristics of African agriculture. Poor farming methods such as monocropping, continuous cropping and burning fields lead to the loss of soil fertility through the reduction oxidation process, change of soil pH, exhaustion of nutrients and the accumulation of salts. Very little land used for food production is mechanized. The usage of fertilizers is also minimal. Developed countries use more than 100 kg of fertilizer per hectare while African countries average 6 kg. Most African farmers cannot afford the use of pesticides, fungicides and other chemicals that protect crops. In fact, more than 40% of the crop is lost in the fields while an equally vast amount is lost during storage.

Apart from this, most land in Africa is unused. For example, 75% of Kenya's land lies idle while people die of hunger. Most of it is arid or semi-arid, but with irrigation it could boost food production. Neocolonial interests have seen to it that this land remains idle. The Government constructed an oil pipeline from Mombasa to Eldoret because Western oil companies wished to outflank the ordinary Kenyans who were distributing oil outside those companies' control — they were earning an honest living, but at no profit to the Western companies. It would have made more sense to build a pipeline to carry water from Lake Victoria to northern Kenya for irrigation.

Of the little land that is under cultivation in Africa, most of it is under inedible cash crops. Of the little of this land that is under food crops, nearly all of that is wasted on subsistence production. In Africa, 80% of the population is engaged in agriculture. Nearly all of these are small holders with plots of land too small to maintain a family above subsistence level. This means that most of the national agricultural output is produced for not the market but for self con-

---

151. Ogova Ondego, "Hunger Warning sounded" *Daily Nation*, 1998.
152. E. Ombiro, "Food for thought for Africa", *Daily Nation*, January 12 1996, p. 16.

sumption. Because they are limited by shortage of capital and the fact that the holdings are so tiny, peasants are unable to use irrigation, machines, fertilizers and other essential inputs. Productivity would be increased many times over if this rural population was moved to urban areas in order to aggregate the land into more viable tracts that could be more efficiently farmed using modern methods.

The lack of mechanization also means that productivity is limited by the debilitating effects of disease, high heat and weakness due to hunger. All these, after they take their toll, may reduce the productivity of farm laborers by more than 70%. Inefficiency, due to all these factors, is thus to blame for low productivity, not "overpopulation". The developed countries are far more "overpopulated". Europe, excluding Russia, has 1.4 million sq miles of cultivable land. In this area live some 700 million people who obtain some 95% of their food supplies from European agricultural production[28]. Up to one billion people would be able to obtain their food supplies from this area alone. Today, the EU is paying farmers to take their land out of production because too much food is produced. North America has 2.3 million sq miles of cultivable land with about 300 million people living on it. This land can provide food for up to three times the amount of people it provides for currently[153].

Africa has a massive 6 million sq miles of cultivable land with a population of less than 500 million people. This land can support more than 1.5 billion people[154]. Yet despite this massive potential for food production, two out of three Africans are constantly hungry and a large number will starve to death.

In Africa, increased total production of various crops is almost entirely due to extensions of cultivated land and to not increased productivity from the land already under cultivation. This clearing of land for crop production has led to desertization and environmental degradation. As if this was not enough, the West sells Africa substandard seeds. In Kenya, these seeds were sold to farmers in Trans-Nzoia and Uasin Gishu districts, which are the country's most productive in food crops[155]. Improved planting material, mechanization, urbanization, better farm and soil management, and control of pests and diseases could raise the output of food by more than 100% without any extension of the cultivated land.

---

153. UNFPA, *The New Generations*, 1998.
154. UNFPA, *The New Generations*, 1998.
155. Ondego, "Hunger warning sounded."

Food availability is also sabotaged through the instigation and fueling of political instability and civil wars. During the two decades of the US-sponsored war in Angola[156], millions of Africans were starving because of the destruction of agriculture through the displacement of farmers and the mining of farmland. Also during the short war in 1997 in Congo (Brazzaville), thousands of Africans went hungry for weeks in the capital because the French invasion had cut food supplies. But the best examples in this area are the recurring famines of southern Sudan. After 15 years of war in Sudan, the southern Sudanese people have been substantially reduced.

These wars affect agriculture and food production even many years later. This is because of landmines. For example, in Angola there are over 15 million US landmines planted in the most productive land. Mozambique, also a victim of US-Apartheid terrorism, has millions of landmines dotted around the country. These mines were provided by the USA to its mini-terrorist armies in poor countries, over a period of 20 years, free of charge. The US has refused to help in the eradication of its mines on African farmlands, or even to ratify the anti-landmine treaty.

Environmental factors and desertization also affect food production and distribution, hence availability. The most important environmental factors influencing agriculture in Africa are heat and rain. Let us first look at heat.

The high temperatures common throughout Africa tend to affect crops negatively. Plants transpire more during hot weather. High temperatures plus high winds and drought cause massive crop failures. Heat and wind both increase the rate of evapo-transpiration. High temperatures also cause all manner of crop pests and disease agents such as fungi to thrive. These affect the crops in the field and the stored food as well. There is no money to buy insecticides or fungicides.

The industrialized nations drive up temperatures — they are responsible for the largest share of accumulated greenhouse gases[157]. But Africa bears much of the brunt of the weather changes caused by large scale pollution. Global warming may reduce food production in Africa while boosting it in the West.

The other factor which greatly influences agriculture in Africa is rain. The total amount, distribution and reliability of rain determine the type, distribution

---

156. http://www.socialistaction.org/news/200204/Angola and also John Stockwell, *In Search of Enemies: A CIA Story*, Andre Deutsch, London, 1978.

157. Patricia Glick, "Global warming: The high cost of inaction", a report by the Sierra Club, 1997. See also Harrison, *Inside the Third World*, p 474.

and performance of crops and animals in a given area. Most of Africa suffers from a cycle of drought and flood. Even within this pattern of alternating very dry and very wet seasons, the rainfall is unreliable from year to year and even within one season. During the short rainy spell, torrential downpours may cause more damage than benefit. The heavy rain can destroy crops in the fields, washing them downstream. It also causes massive soil erosion. Torrential rainfall reduces soil fertility by leaching out nutrients and minerals essential to proper plant growth and high yields. This causes the deserts to spread, and more land becomes unavailable for agriculture. In Africa today, there are two factors which encourage desertization. These are cash crop farming and poverty.

Very few areas in Africa have fertile soils, moderate temperature and rainfall equally distributed throughout the year. Yet all these areas are entirely devoted to cash crop growing rather than food production. As more and more fertile land is brought under crops meant for export, more people are prevented from farming it for food and end up landless. The destruction of African forms of land tenure meant the discarding of egalitarian incomes and land ownership since each family was given as much as its members needed. The emergence of private ownership as the dominant form of land tenure creates gross inequalities and increases the number of landless families even if the population is not growing.

To add to the effects of landlessness is land fragmentation. When a father dies, his land is inherited by his sons. This means that farms are constantly being fragmented into smaller and smaller holdings. In many cases a family of eight will be found trying to survive on half an acre. Eventually, landless people are created through this process. All these people, without land or employment, migrate. When populations expand, as when the arable land contracts, the amount of land available for each person shrinks. These people too, migrate. These migrants end up in the cities or on marginal land. This creates a problem which disguises itself as overpopulation.

The neocolonial economy only requires a few people at any one time. In Kenya, it requires only 30% of the national population, most of whom enjoy high living standards. The remaining 70% are effectively outside the alien economy and end up poor, unemployed and landless, creating an illusion of overpopulation.

Since most of the population has no place in the alien economy, they are the most exploited and derive no benefits. Most of the landless go to the city imagining that they will also enter the alien economy (through employment).

They end up in the slums and shanties, poor and unemployed. Others migrate to marginally productive areas or forested areas. Where they settle in semi-arid and arid areas, quick soil degradation and desertization follow. All types of pastoralism, i.e. nomadism, transhumance and sedentary pastoralism, are practiced in semi-arid and arid areas. In all cases, overstocking and overgrazing are common and this, too, increases the aridity of the land.

When the landless settle into forests and water catchment areas, the environmental damage is worse. The lush vegetation and proliferation of plant species give the impression that the soil in rainforests is fertile. That fertility depends on the constant replacement of the rich humus cover. High equatorial temperatures accelerate the rate of decomposition of fallen leaves and other of vegetable matter. Temperatures of up to $20°C$ make humus form quickly, enriching the soil with plant nutrients and giving it a good structure that is both porous and retains moisture. The temperature rarely exceeds $20°C$, because the tree canopy shades the ground below, regulating heat. The rich topsoil is constantly replenished by falling plant matter. The tree have very shallow roots, enabling them feed on the shallow nutrient-rich layer[158]. But, when temperatures increase to more than $20°C$, humus is formed faster than the plant matter is supplied. Above $25°C$, humus is broken down much faster than it forms, reducing nutrient supply.

Once human beings enter the scene, this well-balanced ecosystem is shattered. When the forest is cleared, the trees' shade disappears and the temperature rises, and the supply of plant material that forms humus on the ground is reduced drastically. With every drenching rainfall humus is lost, along with plant nutrients. Degradation follows and the land loses all fertility. Deforestation is followed by erosion. If the forest was part of a water catchment area, once it is deforested the amount of rain is reduced, causing drought in many lower-lying areas. If reforestation is not undertaken quickly, then a semi-arid area forms. It may later degenerate and finally become a desert.

The final way in which food availability is affected is through the importation of food. To support the cash crop economy the West has to either sell food to Africa or provide food aid[159]. The first time the West gives food to any African country, the effect is to start the downward spiral that leads to food aid dependency. After the poor country gets caught in the food aid trap, it is not given any

---

158. Harrison, *Inside the Third World*, p. 24.
159. Hancock, *Lords of Poverty*, p. 168.

more food; rather, it has to purchase the food. This effectively retards industrialization in Africa.

Once food aid dependency[160] is achieved, it is used to further the aims of neocolonialism. Once large amounts of food are dumped on a poor country that could grow its own food, the prices for food crops automatically fall as a result of oversupply. The fall in prices discourages local farmers from investing more in food production. In any case, the original imports will have already ruined them, and not many would be willing to even consider growing food crops for market. Naturally, the next season there is a food shortage, probably a famine, creating the need for more food imports which are quickly availed by the West — but this time, as purchases and not grants. This increased importation serves as a disincentive to local farmers to grow food. The importation of sugar into Kenya has, apart from lowering sugar prices, caused the collapse of the local sugar industry that is the livelihood of thousands of families.

The IMF, WB and Western governments then move in. They "advise" the government to pressure its farmers to begin growing cash crops on the land that had grown food crops before the first food aid was dumped. Logically, local farmers would be more than willing to grow cash crops which offer more prices than food crops. In this way, large areas of the most productive land are drawn into the cash crop economy. The growing of permanent cash crops like tea or coffee leads to a permanent need for imported food and creates a large guaranteed market for Western farmers.

At this point, a country is caught in the food aid dependency trap. Cash crop farming leads to landlessness, increasing the level of degradation on already marginal land, adding more pressure on the environment through overgrazing and monocropping. This leads to infertility of the soil, and desertization — hence, less land for growing food crops, thus more food imports.

Food aid and dependence enables the West to acquire more leverage over African countries. The influence over the recipient country is best exemplified by Chile. When President Salvadore Allende started to reject neocolonialism in the early 1970s, the West cut off food supplies. This was part of what caused the chaos that eventually brought down the Chilean government. The same tactic of cutting food supplies was used to weaken the Iraqi government of Saddam Hussein.

---

160. Hancock, *Lords of Poverty*, p. 168.

When food importation fuses with domestic corruption, the country is severely weakened politically as well as economically. The business is lucrative, so local government officials and other well-connected people begin to import food.

Food aid, when it is needed, is also provided or withheld to support or undermine the country's ruler. It can be used to ward off or to induce revolutions. Food sold or dumped in Africa also keeps food prices artificially high in the West and so encourages those farmers to over produce, eliminating the possibility of famine and political instability at home while keeping Africa weak and at the mercy of the donors.

The West also gives or sells food to Africa as a way of disposing excess production. When the population of the West began to fall relative to its farming output, large surpluses were generated. They are too costly to store and they threaten to bring down prices. Due to the promotion of cash crop farming, Africa is forced to buy up this surplus.

Africa has also been directed to open up its markets to imported agricultural produce as a "way of boosting [Africa's] own productivity through competition," on the premise that Western farmers enjoy high profits because they are "competitive"[161]. This only increased the trade imbalance and Western profits. What the theory ignores is that Western farmers are not so competitive; they are heavily subsidized by their own governments.

Imported food is sold at prices lower than the cost of locally-produced food. The transportation costs, tariffs and other costs reveal that this is import dumping. In the West, about 40% of the farmers' cost of production is met by their governments; the farmers are also assured of a minimum base price for their produce when market prices are low. In fact, at one time the US, Japan and EU provided equivalent of Kshs 1,620,000 million ($27 billion) to prop up their agricultural sectors and prevent unemployment due to overproduction.

The fact that the West is willing to sell large amounts of food at artificially low prices to Africa, when it could simply cut down production, raises several questions. They appear unconcerned by the destruction of local farming; they also appear to have a desire to control the main supply of food to Africa. Some believe this gives them the opportunity to control what is in the food Africans' consume.

---

161. Alex Whitling, "Farm subsidies yield bad blood", *The Financial Standard*, June 11, 2002 p. 7.

Finally, food aid is given for propaganda purposes. This is meant to entrench the image of the selfless *mzungu* volunteer giving food and saving the lives of skeletal African — victims of never ending "tribal" wars, drought and famine. This image has been promoted so successfully that whenever disaster strikes, Africans expect the soft-spoken British, American or French volunteers to come to their aid (it is never the Chinese, Japanese, Russian, Arabs or other Africans). In fact, whenever the UN is mentioned, an African always sees a *mzungu*.

All these factors have prevented the establishment of an agricultural surplus in Africa, and without that political independence cannot be sustained or guaranteed. As of 2004, out of 53 countries, only 7 African countries were not dependent on food aid[162] and at least 17.6 million Africans were totally dependent on food assistance to avert starvation,[163] while more than half of Africans have trouble obtaining three meals per day.

TAINTED WATER AND FOOD SUPPLIES

Africans also suspect that the population of Africa is being kept in check through mass sterilization campaigns. In 2004, several state governments in Nigeria refused to participate in an anti-polio campaign conducted by the WHO on the suspicion that the vaccine supplied had been laced with sterilizing agents and AIDS[164]. In 1996, a New York-based company, Pfizer Inc., was sued in a US court by 20 disabled Africans for testing a risky experimental meningitis drug which resulted in many being infected. Typically, the case was thrown out[165]. Mainstream newspapers in Kenya report that during famines and other disasters, the aid which the West rushes to the victims is often contaminated by similar sterilizing or disease agents[166].

After the Chernobyl nuclear plant explosion in Ukraine in 1986, extensive areas of Western Europe were irradiated. The crops harvested from the radiated fields were banned in Europe as poison. It has been suggested that this toxic

---

162. FAO, *Food supply situation and crop prospects in Sub-Saharan Africa*, FAO/GIEWS Africa Report, December 2004, p. 12.
163. *Ibid.*
164. BBC News, Nigeria Polio Vaccine Passes Test, http://news.bbc.co.uk
165. CNN.com
166. Woods, "Lawyer sues US government over the true origin of the Aids virus".

food was given or sold to Africa as food aid[167]. Indeed, immediately afterwards in many regions of Africa, including Kenya, strange new diseases or medical conditions were reported. The New York Times has run stories about bad meat, experiments in genetic modification, being introduced into Africa[168]. And when food stored in European and US silos passes its time limit it is not destroyed; it is sent to Africa. A consignment of food donated to Djibouti was found to be unfit for human consumption and the government rejected it. This consignment was returned to Europe. Two years later, it seems, this same food was supplied to Zaire[169].

When British cattle developed mad cow disease, the European Union immediately banned British beef and recommend that all the affected cattle be incinerated. The British government protested that the ban would cause a Kshs 1.2 trillion ($20 billion) loss. A British MP then suggested in Parliament that this infected meat be *sold* to the Third World (Africa) since the Africans were "dying anyway"[170]. Shortly afterwards, the first consignment of tainted meat arrived in Kenya[171]. Consumption of this meat causes debilitating and sometimes fatal diseases in human beings. Quick action by the Government blocked this meat from being sold on the open market; but Kenyans still look to Great Britain as one of their main supports.

On October, 30 1998, the Government issued a warning to Kenyans to avoid eating any maize or maize meal, when it was discovered that 65,000 tons of maize from the West had been deliberately poisoned with chemical agents and dumped in Kenya[172]. On November 21, 1998, thousands of liters of expired Guinness beer were dumped in Mombasa to the joy of local Africans who drank it and sold it on the open market. The beer was not destroyed but deliberately made available in a public place[173]. Even imported sugar and wheat are of dubious quality and safety.

---

167. Hancock, *Lords of Poverty*, p. 13.

168. *New York Times*, June 8, 1990.

169. Hancock, *Lords of Poverty*, p. 14.

170. Mark Kimutai, "British MP's talk insulting," *Daily Nation*, April 1996 and also Anthony Barnett, "Feed banned in Britain dumped on Third World," *The Observer*, October 29, 2000.

171. Additional details may be found in all daily newspapers in Kenya during the period August/September 1996 or specifically in the *EastAfrican* of September 23 1996.

172. J. Otieno and K. Waihenya, "Residents scramble for toxic maize" *Daily Nation*, August 1997, p. 1 and also look at the *Daily Nation*, October 30 1998.

173. *Daily Nation*, November 21 1998.

POVERTY

Poverty is being used as a method of population control. This especially is clear in government spending on health. The first demands made by the "donors" at the start of the SAPs was that public spending on healthcare be slashed. The following facts concerning poverty's toll on African life were published by the UN in 2004. The main problem in Africa is not overpopulation, but poverty, and poverty is an effective killer of Africans.

Country	Infant mortality per 1000	Average life expectancy	Maternal mortality ratio
Kenya	69	45	1000
Guinea-Bissau	120	45	1100
Sierra Leone	177	34	2000
Japan	3	81	10
Sweden	3	80	2

Country	% births with trained attendants	Per capita G N I $PP	Under 5 mortality M / F
Guinea Bissau	35	750	221 / 198
Angola	45	1,730	259 / 234
Luxembourg	100	51,060	7 / 7

Continent	Ave. Pop. Growth rate %	Total fertility rate	% birth with trained attendants	Under 5 mortality M / F	Projected population (2050) (millions)
Africa	2.6	5.31	51	152 /138	1803.3
Europe	0.0	1.38	98	12 / 10	631.9

Source: UNFPA, 2004.

POPULATION AND ECONOMY

The coercion of African governments to adopt SAPs and trade liberalization is the main cause of economic collapse. Kenya loses 100,000 jobs annually. The SAPs have also led to high taxation, rising prices, inflation, low pay, unemployment and intense poverty. The Western-induced problems push skilled Africans to the West where they find lower taxation, lower prices, little inflation, high pay, employment and extreme wealth.

Most economists agree that, in most cases, a large population is better than a small one as far as the economy is concerned. In addition, a country with a large population has more political and economic power; Nigeria, the ninth largest population in the world, is the most powerful country on the continent. The smaller the country, the weaker and, often, the poorer a country is. A small population has a far higher per capita cost for running industries and government services. Countries such as Botswana, Gambia, Mauritius, Gabon, Namibia, Guinea-Bissau have populations of less than 2 million; they still have to maintain governments with several ministries, a parliament, armed forces and services. In most of these countries, the government employs 90% of the labor force in one way or another.

The result is obvious. Governments are consumers and not producers, and where there are more civil servants than workers, then who is taxed to run the government? National and individual poverty is greatly increased through high taxation of the few producers of wealth and the national debt increases rapidly. Then, the West moves in to re-colonize the country. For example, Italy finances about 70% of the Djibouti budget and therefore literally runs the country. For all practical purposes, Djibouti is a colony. As opposed to popular Western mythology, the high poverty levels occur in African countries often hit those with the smallest populations. Therefore, it is economically disadvantageous for Kenya to adopt Majimboism (Federalism) and create a prime minister's office as a section of the Kenyan elite is demanding; that would mean the creation of several more state governments, each consuming more income than its subjects or citizens are able to produce.

A large population encourages economic growth and industrialization as much as a small population discourages both. Most industries are benefited by increasing population, as they work under the law of increasing returns. Industrialization is inefficient and uneconomical with small populations. An increase in population (and, therefore, market), allows productivity per head to increase. It is widely accepted that without the large populations of the US and Western Europe, industries there would be working under great difficulties and they most likely would never have come into existence at all. It is under population and not overpopulation that reinforces African poverty and economic stagnation.

As the population increases, so does the move to industrialize increase in pace. A large population creates a natural tendency to industrialize and urbanize. This is because as numbers increase, land per head decreases, hence economic development cannot be pursued by extending the agricultural sector; industrialization becomes the best and only option.

Even with a large population industrialization is not guaranteed, especially if a large proportion of the populace is hungry, sick and uneducated. These are the very conditions that were created when the SAPs and import liberalization were inaugurated. Even for those who are more fortunate, neocolonial education in Africa today mainly involves pro-West content and the sending of the most promising students to the West for further studies. Now, every African who has been so educated has a natural desire to migrate to Europe or North America; that is brain drain. By luring all the highly trained African personnel to its own side, the West has ensured that economic development in Africa is permanently stagnated. No need to fear that any homegrown competition will crop up. Without skilled labor and guaranteed markets, industrialization in Africa has been halted and de-industrialization proceeds apace. The first phase was the body drain that started in the 16th century and lasted for 300 years. This is slavery, whereby the strongest, healthiest and most active individuals were kidnapped and taken to the Americas as slave labor — building the foundation for the US economy to become the richest in the world. The next phase began in the 20th century and lasted for 70 years. In this second phase, Europeans invaded the continent and enslaved Africans on their own land. Here also, Africans were forced to toil, building up Europe's economy into the developed state it is today. Today, the third phase is more subtle. In this phase, Africans are being mentally kidnapped and taken to Europe and America to work there willingly. Africa is still working hard at building and maintaining the developed economies of the West.

The West benefits immeasurably when it absorbs migrants from the rest of the world. The first direct gain is through payments by all those seeking to immigrate, the visa seekers. There are numerous Western companies operating in Africa, whose work is to lure Africans abroad.

Their governments also make money. The US government has a program called the Green Card Lottery, whereby anyone may apply in the hope of obtaining a visa and a work permit. When an African is declared the lucky winner of a Green Card by the US State Department, he is requested to provide several documents, including his tax return and proof of income level for the previous years[174]. This is important in filtering out the ones thought to be poor. The would-be immigrant is then required to pay several fees to the embassy: first, for the visa, Kshs 20,000 ($333). The visa seeker is then asked to pay about Kshs 1,500 ($25) per injection for several required inoculations. The embassy doctor

---

174. Wanja Githinji, "Pitfalls of magic green card", *Sunday Nation*, May 16, 1999. See also Mutuma Mathiu, "Going to America: Is it worth the hassle?" *Sunday Nation* July 12 1998 pp. 12 – 13.

performs a medical examination, which costs the hopeful immigrant another Kshs 4000 ($66) and several other tests that eventually add up to about Kshs 32,000 ($533). There is still no guarantee that one will receive the visa[175]. In fact, most Africans who go through this process end up without visas. A few are allowed to pass in order to give credibility to the system and induce others to apply.

Of all people from the Third World, Africans are the ones who most would like to migrate to the West. But the reality is that it is easier for any other race to be allowed into the West than Africans. Even with the exorbitant fees demanded for just applying for a visa, many Africans still try to obtain visas. The intensification of cultural imperialism ever since 1990 has induced more and more Africans to try to migrate to the West. This has in turn created a market for imported books and magazines which claim to show how to go about obtaining a visa.

The West also benefits economically when the immigrants arrive. This immigration is deliberately encouraged to help boost even greater rates in output and economic activity. This is achieved both in population increase and from the fact that all those allowed to settle as citizens are highly skilled. The West is able to dampen the effects of its own dwindling population. In fact, the West has to import migrant labor to maintain its existing level of development. In addition, in the Third World, business opportunities for Westerners are created. Take the example of doctors. When they are lured away to the West, disease shoots up wherever the shortage of doctors is acute. This boosts sales in medicines for Western drug companies because medicines take up to 40% of health budgets in African countries[176].

Apart from providing these countries with their skills without the social costs of raising and educating them, immigrants bring in hard currency. Many Western countries demand that those who wish to settle must have a minimum amount of money to invest. The following notice has appeared in Kenyan newspapers on many occasions:

Please note the Kshs 50.6 million ($633,000) minimum required from entrepreneurs. If only one thousand entrepreneurs were to migrate from Africa to Canada every month, each having a minimum net worth of Kshs 50.6 million, we would lose at least Kshs 607 billion ($7.6 billion) to Canada every year.

---

175. Rajen Shah, "The green card visa lootery" *Sunday Nation*, July 19 1998, p. 16.
176. Harrison, *Inside the Third World*, p. 299.

However, the figures involved are much higher: More than 50,000 highly skilled and rich Africans are lured into Europe and North America every year. One can only imagine the amount of money Africa loses directly and indirectly. All these skilled people are educated in Africa at great cost (we all know of entire villages holding fund raising meetings just to take a single student to school). The return on all the capital invested as education is lost, as well as the skills[177]. In the 1960s, the West absorbed 30,000 skilled personnel annually. As Africa slowly industrialized the West quickly moved to block this industrialization by stepping up its efforts at "grabbing" all the highly skilled labor, and so the human traffic increased. By the early 1970s the West was sponging almost half a million immigrants each year. For example, the USA managed to get 90,000, the UK 84,000 and Canada 56,000. UNCTAD calculated that this human traffic was worth a total of Kshs 3.06 trillion ($51 billion)[178]. The large outflow of skilled labor from Africa creates the need for expatriates, thereby providing jobs for Europeans and Americans. In fact, today, Africa has more Western expatriates than it ever had during colonialism.

The claim that overpopulation is the cause of economic backwardness and poverty in Africa is belied by the West's efforts to increase its own population density. The question is, why has Africa not been able to increase productivity to match the increase in population while the West has managed to increase its living standards on top of huge increases in population?

Today, 500 years after the first Africans were forcibly migrated to the US, their descendants are being used by the US for political gain through propaganda. This propaganda induces Africans to admire the US and blind them to the effects of US-led policy. It has worked marvelously. Africans identify with Afro-Americans on a racial basis. In addition, Afro-American music is exported wholesale to Africa to reinforce cultural imperialism. When Africans are aping Afro-Americans, they are actually being manipulated to love the West, because the Afro-Americans are *wazungus* in everything except race. The US government also uses Afro-American emissaries like Rev. Jesse Jackson to increase its influence and hegemony over Africa.

In sports, music, and the arts, Africans who have migrated bring the West international recognition and prestige. We have all seen the Afro-American runners and other athletes win numerous gold medals at sports meetings for the

---

177. Harrison, *Inside the Third World*, p. 361.
178. *Ibid.*, 361.

USA. In fact, Afro-Americans are responsible for 80% of all US Olympics medals. In music, the world knows Michael Jackson and others. It is unfortunate that most Africans do not know that 90% of all internationally acclaimed music and dance forms originate from Africa. The *Samba*, the national dance of Brazil, was derived from *Quizomba* and the *Batuque* from Angola and Congo. There is also the *Rhumba* from Cuba, which came from Congo. From the Caribbean, Jamaican *Reggae* music is derived from several African dances. Closer to home, there is the music and dance form called *Sega*, which emerged from African slaves in Mauritius. There is also the *Calypso*. Several music forms also emerged from the Africans who were kidnapped and taken to North America. These include *jazz, rhythm and blues*, and more recently *rap* and *break dancing*.

In all these music forms, a clear African pattern is found: the infectious rhythm of motion, sound and especially the intricate beatings of drums. Also, most of the instruments used in these music forms are percussion instruments derived from the drum, which is Bantu in origin. Where Africans did not resettle or find themselves forcibly resettled *en masse*, there are no globally popular music and dance forms. Britain, France, Germany and Japan have contributed few "hits" to the world audience.

Today, all these cultural forms are used by the West to gain political mileage in Africa. Most Africans who have heard of *Sega, Samba,* and *Rhumba* think that these are Spanish or Portuguese music and dances, so if they love the music, they extend this positive feeling to the Spaniards or Portuguese and by extension to the West. During the 1998 World Cup, in the last two decisive matches that saw the French win, all but one of the goals scored by the French side were scored by players of African extraction. Brazil has also consistently won the World Cup because of the Negro players. Pele scored an amazing 12 goals in the 1958 World Cup and is considered the greatest footballer of all time, but whenever African migrants cause victory, the prestige and honor accrue not to Africa but to the West. And this prestige is redirected for political gain. Africans are being used against themselves.

Africa has lost in many ways as a result of large outflows of population and skilled personnel. Social capital is lost when those who are trained and educated leave Africa. The means of economic recovery and development are also lost. All educational development and potential are automatically nullified when the educated few migrate. It is more expensive to produce a doctor or a simple electrician or computer analyst in Africa than it is anywhere else. It has been calculated that it costs Kshs 1.44 million ($24,000) to produce a single medical graduate in Kenya, while in the US, it is less than half a million shillings. The poorer a country is, the more expensive education becomes. In the poorest African countries, it costs more than Kshs 5 million ($83,333) to produce one medical graduate. When this graduate is lured to the West, then the cost to the African country is great. When expensively trained technicians, architects and others leave in large numbers, economic development is cut off.

There are several factors which make a skilled African to want to work to develop the West rather than Africa. Cultural imperialism is one of the strongest mechanisms at work. Many Africans are fervent believers in the slogan, "America — land of the free." This belief reflects a state of historical amnesia which is the result of prolonged exposure to cultural imperialism. The West dominates the TV, radio, newspapers, magazines, and religion in Africa.

Western movies and television programs show highly efficient police forces: whenever a robbery is reported, thousands of police cars arrive at the crime scene within seconds, tires screeching and sirens blaring. The comparison to Africa's bungling police forces leaves many a viewer wishing to see an adequate police response, for once. These movies also show that anyone aggrieved by any other person, or government, or corporation, can sue and win — easily. In Kenya, suing is the preserve of the rich and the patient — as it can take many years before the case is even mentioned. The African television viewer has to concede that it is easier to get justice in the West than in Africa.

Many Africans who have never gone to the West are unable to separate facts from myth. They cannot appreciate by how wide a margin these movies and programs exaggerate the facts. They come to believe that everyone lives in a beautiful house with a green grass lawn, and that all the roads are free of potholes. Even if some people there do live in slums, and conditions are not quite as good as they are portrayed, things are still far better than in Africa. This negative comparison engenders a sense of inferiority among Africans, which easily slips into a racist notion that Africa suffers from a useless police force, corrupt judiciary, and poverty *because* they are Africans. This is a powerful form of propaganda because the negative effects of neocolonialism are translated not as part of a larger scheme by the West to harm Africans but as a result of the inherent inferiority of Africans. This drives mentally-colonized Africans try to deny and destroy their Africanness, whether in culture or physically.

In effect, cultural imperialism tells Africans that their culture is bad, their language is primitive, their clothes are bad and their skin color and hair are even worse; that, in fact, there is something inherently wrong with Africans and that is the reason that they are poor, hungry and suffering. If an African wants a good life, he should emulate the Westerners. With the beautiful visions provided by television acting as a "pull" and the poverty in Africa acting as a push factor, it is no wonder so many take the bait and only find out through experience that no heaven exists on earth.

Education is also used to lure Africans into the West. All schools in Africa use European languages, and therefore the students are automatically tied to and trained to identify with a Western country. Further, the curriculum focuses disproportionately on European content, especially in history. Then, via scholarships, the brightest African students are induced to migrate to Europe or the US for further studies. If they excel, the governments are quick to offer inducements that keep them from returning to Africa. The SAPs have simply added to the brain and monetary drain. African governments were forced to cut expenditure on education, reducing the number of already scarce universities and other higher institutions of learning. In Kenya, the universities and polytechnics are too few to absorb all the students graduating from secondary schools. This has led to many students to pay their own way to seek higher learning in the West, thus diverting more money to those who already have the most. Even worse, many stay on and so, in effect, Africa is providing Western students with free primary and secondary education.

At the same time, Africans are pushed from Africa by the widespread poverty, anarchy, hunger, and suffering. The West has a direct hand in causing political instability and insecurity in many African countries. For example, when the pro-US Siad Barre of Somalia was overthrown, the cream of Somali society fled to the West. Zaire's pro-US Mobutu kept most of his Kshs 600 billion ($10 billion) wealth in the West and when he was overthrown, his henchmen fled with more money.

The enforced poverty in Africa is the main cause of high level corruption, bad governance and oppression, all of which fuels a cycle of uncertainty and insecurity which in turn impels the rich to stash money in the West, where they feel it is more secure, and the few with skills saleable in the West to migrate, to be more secure.

Having set the stage for encouraging immigration, the West then opened up the way through which skilled Africans can leave the continent. One way is through notices in magazines and newspapers which encourage educated or skilled Africans to migrate to the West, to the benefit of their own economies and to the cost of Africa's. These notices sometimes appear three or four in the

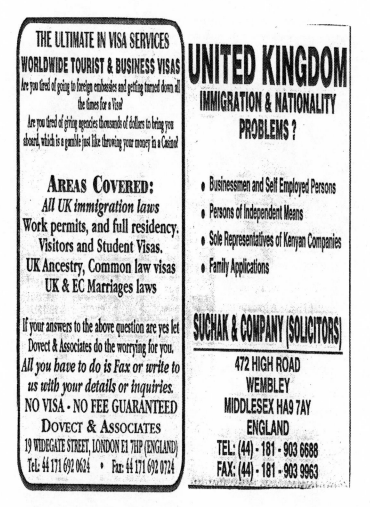

Source: *Daily Nation* 1997–2000.

same newspaper, meaning that the West feels increased pressure to recruit migrants. Here are few of them; (All newspaper adverts are acquired from the *Daily Nation*, 1997-2000)

Once a *mzungu*-worshiping African enters the West, he soon discovers that for "niggers" America is not the land of the free and the American dream is just that — a dream. If he is in Europe, he finds out that it is not utopia. Many Africans are shocked when they first experience anti-African racism in the West. There are two types of racism: official and unofficial. Official racism mainly involves the police, politicians and government workers. When a British

Source: *Saturday Nation*, January 1, 2005.

parliamentarian suggested that beef infected by the mad cow disease should be sold to Africans, the British government implemented his suggestion. A Finnish member of the European parliament and former mayor of Helsinki, Raimo Ilaskivi, in his campaign against Africans said that "they...compete and snatch Finnish jobs, souring the unemployment situation. They [also] sponge off our social welfare system." In France, the government ordered heavily armed police to attack African migrants who sought refuge in a church building. They were brutalized and kicked out[179]. Yet Europeans are retained in Africa, where they compete and snatch jobs even at higher levels.

In Europe, the media constantly attacks migrant Africans. In Britain the *Sun* reported under large headlines that "blacks....pose the most dangerous threat to Britain since Hitler"; others promote anti-African propaganda. At one time, the *Daily Mail* produced headlines claiming, "Black crime: the alarming figures"[180], while the *Sun* trumpeted, "Black Crime Shock". This biased reporting led to increased racist attacks on Africans and Afro-Caribbean migrants, both by the public and police[181].

In the West, the police are particularly hostile to migrant Africans and descendants of slaves, and incidents of police brutality are common. In September 1998, the Belgian Minister for the Interior was forced to resign when Belgian police killed a Nigerian woman while trying to deport her. The victim, Sumira Adami, was suffocated to death. In 1997, a Kenyan student was killed by gang of Americans in what the police there described as a racist attack. A year later the federal police closed the file without arresting anyone and told the parents of the deceased to stop "bothering" them[182]. The beating or killing of Blacks in the West is rarely investigated fully.

There is also unofficial racism. Taxis refuse to stop for Blacks; they are treated last in hospitals if non-Blacks are in line; supermarket cashiers, bank tellers and other service personnel ignore them. Africans who visit their heaven in Europe and America have also been victims of assault. In fact, the situation has deteriorated so much that Africans are advised not to walk about, at least not alone, day or night[183]. Today, Africans visiting the West may be killed not only

179. Report by Reuters, "Africans face deportation", *Sunday Nation*, August 25 1996, p. 11.

180. Pilger, *Heroes.*

181. Pilger, *Heroes* p. 532

182. Wednesday Magazine, *Daily Nation*, March 4 1998 p. 1.

183. Elias Makori, "Skinheads cause terror in Moscow" Wednesday Magazine, *Daily Nation*, June 17 1998, p. 8.

for racist reasons but also for monetary gain. No fewer than 300 murders of African-type people are reported in the West annually, while fewer than 10 *wazungus* are killed in Africa, mainly in accidents or armed robberies. Ku Klux Klan (terrorist) methods have now been adopted throughout Europe. In 1993, in Stuttgart, Germany, two Africans were killed when their neighbors burned down their house[184]. In December 1993, a Kenyan was shot dead in Texas. A year later, another Kenyan student was murdered in a similar racist attack. In August 1998, a 20-year-old Kenyan girl was murdered in what appeared to be a rape homicide. It has appeared as a new factor that many Africans who are murdered have their body parts, such as kidneys, robbed.

Many Africans fail to realize that Afro-Americans and Afro-Britons live in poor, underprivileged conditions just as Africans do who have remained on the continent. In the US, most of them lack quality healthcare, employment, decent housing, education and in some cases adequate food. One out of three Afro-American males is or will be in prison, and Blacks were 6 times more likely than whites to be murdered in 2002[185]. There are more than 700,000 Afro-Americans in jail and less that 50,000 in higher institutions learning. Despite the fact that less than 15% of criminals involved in illegal drug trade are Afro-Americans, more than half of those who are tracked and arrested by the police are Black[186].

In the UK, for every racial attack on a Caucasian, there are 36 on Blacks[187]. In employment, it is far worse. In competition with a European with exactly the same qualifications, the chances of the Black getting the job are less than half. Throughout the West, migrant Africans and native Blacks are employed as underpaid day laborers, night watchmen, street venders, low level civil servants and so on, or are homeless, or prostitutes.

Some of the organizations or agencies that help Africans migrate to Europe and America are facades, in that their objective is not to enable students to get to universities or workers to find jobs, but to provide prostitutes for brothels and pornography rings. Even students, once in the West, are economically exploited. Most of them drop out of school to work for survival. The employers pay them as little as possible because they know they are desperate.

---

184. *Daily Nation*, 1993.

185. US Department of Justice, Bureau of Justice Statistics. http://www.ojp.usdoj.gov/bjs/welcome.html

186. Jamsheed Sande Jnr., "Racism increasing in America", *Daily Nation*, December 31 1997, p. 7.

187. Pilger, *Heroes*.

Some former students end up dead, or as drug addicts or prostitutes, morally destroyed. Even if they return to Africa they have been totally Westernized and they unwittingly become agents of neocolonialism.

In contrast to the brutality and racism that greets the African in the West, the European in Africa is feted and treated with great respect. They are preferred candidates for the best jobs, the best land, the best of everything and without even a finger being raised against them. In Kenya, at Nairobi's Wilson Airport, the Caucasian-owned aircraft companies have an open policy of not employing African pilots[188].

URBANIZATION AND ECONOMIC DEVELOPMENT

Urbanization is the growth and spread of urban centers. It is fed by rural-to-urban migration. Many people in nations making the transition from agrarian to industrial (or nations that need to make that transition) migrate to urban centers to escape the extreme deprivation prevalent in rural areas. Few peasants work anything approaching a full year whether on large or small holdings. Many are unemployed for four to seven months a year; then they drift to towns in search of work. High poverty levels and landlessness also encourage rural people to migrate. Modern conveniences and facilities denied to people living in the countryside (electricity, piped water, health centers and schools) also lure them to urban centers.

But rural to urban migration does not guarantee a step up on the ladder; most African migrants are forced to live in slums and shanty towns in even worse conditions than they faced in the rural areas. Crime and family collapse are common.

However, urbanization has politically significant advantages to Africa.

1. Urbanization is a precondition to the transition from an agricultural economy to an industrial one.

When large numbers of people move from rural to urban areas, the resulting unemployment/underemployment means that former agricultural workers are freed for industrial jobs. It also frees the land for mechanization and commercial agriculture which boosts food production, leading to self sufficiency.

---

188. Mutegi Njau, "Wilson airport: Colonial outpost in a free Kenya?", *Daily Nation* February 23 1994, p. 6.

When a country is self sufficient in food, it escapes the food aid trap, with the political handicaps that implies.

Rural to urban migration helps to create excess labor supply in the urban areas. This pushes down wages, decreasing the amount of capital needed to invest in industry. It also enables the shift from capital-intensive technology to labor-intensive methods, creating employment.

Urbanization provides a large centralized market for numerous goods and services which are not saleable in rural areas. This helps in capital accumulation and industrialization. Living in urban areas creates several needs and wants that do not exist in rural areas. For example, in towns, there are entertainment centers, restaurants, daily transport to workplaces. People who live in cities have to buy food, water, light bulbs and other electrical gadgets. In fact, urban areas create almost infinite business and employment opportunities that are totally absent in rural areas. Urbanization is the greatest single factor that aggressively promotes industrialization, which is a pre-requisite to escaping neocolonialism and its attendant poverty.

Without urbanization, Europe would never have developed industries. England became the first country to industrialize because, and only because, it was the first nation to undergo the Agrarian Revolution which, in effect, brutally encouraged rural to urban migration when small land holders were evicted from their land. They had little choice but to go to towns, where their labor became a commodity. Their land was then consolidated and fenced off, paving the way for scientific agriculture.

The advantages that Britain acquired by being the first country to industrialize can be seen to this day. England was able to conquer the world, and today, half the planet speaks English. Western Europe also industrialized before the rest of the world did, and this gave Europeans the power to invade and occupy territories all across the earth. When the United States industrialized, it extended its control over much of the world. Urbanization and industrialization can turn insignificant nations into powerful countries. After industrializing, Japan was able to defeat both China and czarist Russia. Russia was perhaps the most backward country of Europe until it industrialized, in the early 20th century, and through bold and crushing efforts became a superpower.

It was industrialization which enabled the USSR to repel Germany's 1941 invasion. The Soviet Union became so strong that between 1942 and 1945, it was able to conquer half of Europe and maintain hegemony for 45 years. It is a historical fact that Stalin forced the USSR to make up for centuries of lagging behind by industrializing rapidly. He did this by inducing rural to urban migration. In fact, it was official government policy in the Soviet Union to construct entire cities where none existed before, and then populate them with rural people. In just 40 years and with a devastating war in between, Russia was able to move from being the most underdeveloped and backward country in Europe to being the first nation to send a man into space. They accomplished this without taking resources from other nations, that is, colonies, and without external help like the Marshall Plan. How did they do it? They allowed no foreign investment, no trade liberalization, no brain drain and no cultural imperialism.

It is the eventual emergence of a powerful, industrialized Africa that the West fears most. Not only will they lose a source of raw material and cheap labor, and a market for their goods, but Africa on the ascendant would owe the West very little quarter. This is why they shall *never* allow Africa to industrialize.

2. The political consequences of urbanization.

The other very significant political advantage that rural to urban migration offers Africa is the urban mob. It is this mob, which consists of the urban poor, that demanded the end of colonialism, especially in Ghana. In the late 1940s and early 1950s in Ghana, the schools were producing very many graduates. Their colonial education all led them to despise the rural way of life in favor of the urban, Western lifestyle. They migrated to urban centers where, typically, the colonial economy was unable to absorb them. Therefore most were unemployed, had nowhere to live, and were destitute without the protection of their extended families. When they recognized that they were suffering poverty and deprivation because of colonialism, they demanded decolonization. This was called the "school leavers bottleneck crisis" and it was a significant factor in determining when the British withdrew their colonial servants from Ghana, as early as 1952.

It was the urban mob which demanded the end of one-party rule in Kenya and the end of dictatorships throughout Africa in the late 1980s and early 1990s. And it shall be the urban mob which shall end neocolonialism by demanding employment opportunities and a better quality, dignified life, both of which can only be achieved through industrialization, which will only happen when the IMF and WB-controlled economies of Africa are dismantled.

Urban mobs are dangerous to all political systems and have been responsible for many internal revolutions. Roman emperors were brought down by the crowds of Rome. The French Revolution of 1789 was executed by mobs and so was the Bolshevik Revolution of 1917 in Russia. Urbanization breaks many bonds, breaking up the extended family, clan and tribe. It weakens traditions, stable beliefs and values. People become more susceptible to the appeals of nationalistic movements especially when the majority of them are hopelessly poor[189].

To forestall the development of a poor mob which was strongly anti-European and anti-American, the West stepped up cultural imperialism. But even more important, they encouraged African governments to block rural to urban migration, which would also retard industrialization as a logical consequence of urbanization. In Kenya, this took the form of the District Focus for Rural Development (DFRD). It went hand-in-hand with a campaign promoting the notion that migration to the cities had to be arrested to prevent the growth and spread of slums so that people do not suffer, to ensure that there was employment for everyone, and various other seemingly humanitarian reasons.

Kenyan schools promoted this line. One secondary school textbook claims that DFRD was started to "bring development to rural areas" and so prevent the people from migrating to urban areas, and also "to ensure that there is enough manpower to work the land for increased food production". Experience has shown, however, that in this age of mechanization the more people who live in rural areas the less food is produced. In the West, less than 12% of the population lives in rural areas and yet they overproduce food. In Africa over 80% of the population live in rural areas, yet most Africans have trouble obtaining enough to eat. Thankfully, such machinations to stop the logical migration into urban areas have largely failed.

If it cannot be stopped, rural to urban migration may yet be to the advantage of the West. Programs like the District Focus for Rural Development were either scrapped or abandoned at about the time when it was discovered that Aids is more prevalent and spreads faster in urban slums than in rural areas. Today, the "donor" community is encouraging rural to urban migration by funding projects aimed at building and upgrading the slums.

---

189. Harrison, *Inside the Third World*, p. 402. Additional reference: Ben Wattenber and Richard Whalen, *The Wealth Weapon*, Transaction Books, London, 1980.

CHAPTER 7. CHARACTERISTICS AND CONSEQUENCES OF UNDERDEVELOPMENT

Economic underdevelopment is characterized by several intertwining factors. At the first level is the adoption of self-destructive economic policies such as structural adjustment programs, foreign investment and import liberalization.

These policies are the principal cause of capital flight, inflation, unemployment, general poverty and human suffering. The two most egregious effects are the massive capital outflows caused by SAPs, import liberalization and foreign investment, and the large external debt that is accumulated as a result of faulty economic policies.

Massive capital flight and other factors stop local production, increase unemployment and poverty, and reduce economic activity, cutting government revenue and creating a need for borrowing which leads to a large external debt. This is the aid trap

The results of economic exploitation are political and military weakness, economic weakness and mass poverty.

POLITICAL AND MILITARY WEAKNESS

African countries are weak militarily and politically. In most of these countries a tiny, weak army is maintained at high cost. Its main functions are to keep the ruler in power and to stage parades. Any determined invasion of Africa militarily by a foreign power would meet very little resistance from these armies. All through the 1960-2000 post-independence period, European and American armies have launched or sponsored military invasions of African nations A topic which is dealt with in the last chapter. In each case organized resistance collapsed once the foreign army made contact with African troops. This is because from the bottom up, African army personnel share a common mindset and the very thought of fighting their "superiors" defeats and demoralizes them. These armies are also weak because of lack of equipment and proper training, and because much of their training is done by military personnel from Europe and the US. They are the only nations that repeatedly invade African countries, and any tactics deployed by African armies are already known.

Countries whose ruler is pro-Western are effectively colonized since they cannot determine their own policies. This applies equally where the ruler is installed by the imperialist powers, where the country is deep in debt and where the ruler is mentally colonized. In all these cases the very concept of sovereignty is sabotaged. By these criteria most African countries neocolonial states. African rulers are either willing or unwilling accomplices of imperialism and colonialism.

Neocolonialism is an advanced state of colonialism. Colonialism was the originator of dictatorship in Africa and because it was survived by neocolonialism, dictatorships will be a permanent feature of the African political landscape until neocolonialism is dismantled. Most of them are unpopular and are not in power by the wish of their people but because outside forces put them there. Take the Congo (Brazzaville) ruler Sassou Nguesso as an example. He was installed through a French-led coup, was replaced by Lissouba in a popular election, and managed to return to the presidency when the French helped mastermind Lissouba's downfall after only several months. Nguesso did not return to the presidency through the will of the Congolese, and he did not originally attain that position through popular vote. He does not represent the people. He is president because France keeps him in power through the force of arms. This means he is a dictator. The Congolese government workers, whose attitude had positively changed after serving under Lissouba, reverted to their apathy, inefficiency, corruption and incompetence upon Nguesso's return.

In Kenya of late, poor people are being driven from every inch of land that they occupy. The land upon which Kigali market was built for small-scale traders in Nairobi had been occupied by curio sellers for the best part of two decades. On the night of July 26, 1998, the Nairobi City Council demolished all the kiosks and everything in them, destroying goods, vital documents and liveli-hoods. The people have no rights, and what is in their interests is not a concern to the State.

Corruption — which includes bribery, tribalism, nepotism and all manner of vices, is inherent in neocolonialism. Corruption is worse in neocolonial coun-tries because the people are unable to demand transparency, accountability and efficiency from their rulers. Types of high level corruption that are relatively rare in the rich countries are rampant in Africa. Rich countries use democracy to control high level corruption.

There is a connection between underdevelopment and colonialism. Africa's contribution to the development of Europe is equal to the extent by which Europe caused Africa's underdevelopment. There is a relationship between bad governance and neocolonialism, since corruption in high places is linked to underdevelopment which is caused by colonialism and neocolonialism.

Corruption permeates the whole society and becomes incorporated into a country's culture only when it originates from the political rulers who avoid arrest by accumulating power. When the leaders are above the law, this makes a mockery of government and the citizenry have no resources to combat it. The result of this increased power is tyranny and dictatorship. Corruption, unlike wealth, does trickle down and the government's ranks become increasingly incompetent and inefficient until things come to a standstill. Government employees demand bribes to perform their basic duties. When this point is reached, tyranny and anarchy paradoxically exist simultaneously. Hard eco-nomic times cause crime, banditry, robbery, and even lynching becomes common. Land grabbing and open plunder of state corporations increase along with murder and mini civil wars between different ethnic groups. Government inefficiency limits education, health, and services such as street cleaning; anarchy becomes an accepted state of affairs.

Official high level corruption in Kenya increased at the same rate that poverty increased and the economy collapsed. This means that corruption is not the original cause of poverty in Africa, but poverty is a cause of corruption — corruption only perpetuates poverty, therefore perpetuating itself. Ever since the introduction of SAPs in the early 1980s, poverty has increased both in the absolute number of people affected and also in proportion of the population. It is widely accepted that Kenyans began to become poor in 1980. As poverty increased as a result of SAPs so did corruption. In 1985, reports of large scale cor-ruption were rare. In 1988, when the SAPs were beginning to destroy the Kenyan economy and poverty had increased, incidents of massive theft of state resources by top officials became common. By 1994, when foreign investment was being officially encouraged and liberalization pursued, three-quarters of Africans in Kenya were living below the poverty line and also by this time Kenyans had become used to massive official corruption. Reports that the Kenya Government had wasted Kshs 107 billion ($1.78 billion) through questionable spending are no longer surprising to Kenyans[190]. Also during this period (1980–1994) the power of the state and the executive increased to such an extent that the president became unassailable.

High level corruption requires a corrupter. In most cases the corrupters are those who are in the dominant position in any transaction. Multinationals and other big companies use bribery for several reasons. They pay government officials because the goods or services that they provide are substandard or over-priced and would never be chosen in fair competition. The company reduces the quality of its products to increase profits by maintaining the same price. Buyers end up purchasing low quality stuff for the price of high quality commodities. They also pay to keep a lock on monopolies. In 1990, British Airways paid the equivalent of Kshs 100 million ($1.67 million) into the bank account of a paper company owned by an Antiguan minister in order to preserve its monopoly of the London–Antigua air route[191]. Bribery is also used to persuade officials to buy goods and services that their countries do not need. This is commonly a factor in unnecessary purchases of hi-tech military equipment by African countries.

In Kenya, a clear example of international corruption occurred in 1986 at a great cost to the country. The contract for the Turkwell Gorge dam was awarded to French contractors without international competitive bidding. The price of Kshs 16.2 billion ($270 million) was more than double the sum that would have been expected from competitive bids. The installed turbines cost Kenyans Kshs 16.62 million ($277,000) while their actual cost was Kshs 8.4 million ($ 140,000) each[192]. The huge difference was divided between the officials responsible for the project and the French contractors.

A large number of projects and supply contracts are funded by the IMF and WB, and those institutions could stop this kind of corruption. But donor agencies finance projects whether corruption is involved or not, because high

---

190. "Government wastes 107 billion", *Daily Nation*, June 22 1998, p. 1.
191. *The Observer*, January 21, 1991.
192. Blaine Harden, *Dispatches from a Fragile Continent*, Houghton Mifflin Co., 1991.

level corruption is a prop of neocolonialism — a corrupt government is politically weak. In international relations, the West uses its political power to extract an economic contribution from poor nations. Thus it is these rich countries who perform the role of the corrupter, because it is they who stand to benefit from corruption; and the donor agencies always act in the interest of the rich countries[193].

Recently, the United States and its partners agreed on a plan to criminalize business graft of foreign government officials as a way of curbing international bribery. They also admitted that "bribery is a major distortion of international trade and has a corrosive effect on economic and political development". France and Germany were most reluctant to ratify this agreement[194]. The US appears to have backed this anti-bribery agreement in view of the invention of the Multilateral Agreement on Investment (MAI). Bribery is a costly way to win contracts. Rather than bribe ministers in order to win the contracts, the MAI proposes that foreign companies move into African countries and take over parastatals, infrastructure and everything else. This would eliminate the need for bribery because, for example, once a foreign company takes over the national rail network it can give contracts to other foreign companies for the supply of steel rails, by-passing the respective African government, which would cease being an active player in the running of the country and would be demoted to the role of a spectator while the foreigners run the country.

ECONOMIC WEAKNESS

Having a small production capacity due to non-industrialization of an economy is a major factor in a nation's economic weakness. It also means government has a constant shortage of funds, which can only be aggravated by debt servicing and implementation of wrong-headed economic policies such that government is unable to deliver services. The Kenya Government's failure to provide accessible education has more than tripled illiteracy in the country. Statistics show that more than 50% of primary school pupils drop out before they take the national exams. Of those who take the exams, less than half are admitted into secondary schools. Of this group, more than 30% drop out as a result of preg-

---

193. George Moody Stuart, *Grand Corruption*, Worldview Publications, Oxford, 1997.
194. "Industrial States to criminalize business graft", *Sunday Nation*, May 25 1997, p. 8.

nancy or lack of school fees. Of the tiny group that remains to sit for the K C S E exams, less than 20% make it into higher institutions of learning, and most of them will be unable to secure relevant employment within two years of their graduation. Where the majority of people are ignorant and illiterate, quality of life is obviously going to be low. They have no chance of securing well paying jobs, their ability to create wealth is compromised and most important, they become susceptible to manipulation by the foreign states and companies. Most Kenyans and indeed most Africans have no idea how the Multilateral Agreement on Investment is likely to affect their lives.

When the governments of Africa were told to cut spending on healthcare, the death rate in Africa increased by 70%. More Africans in Kenya die of easily curable diseases than any other cause. In July 1998 the health minister admitted that 85% of deaths in Kenya were caused by preventable diseases caused by lack of healthcare facilities and lack of drugs. This is the result of a budgetary cut in the health ministry by almost Kshs 2 billion ($3.33 million)[195]. There has also been a marked increase of disease occurrence and epidemics. In western Kenya, hundreds have died of malaria because all the hospitals and clinics ran out of anti-malarial drugs.

Most wealthy people in Kenya who run the government do not believe that currently there is widespread hunger. Poor people are surviving on scarcely-cooked food and many can manage only one meal daily. To the middle and upper classes, the main concern is not food but the type of food — reducing cholesterol and enjoying the fashionable restaurants. Famines in Africa are caused by (apart from civil wars instigated by outsiders) a combination the allocation of the best land to cash crops and the importation of food, which causes a drop in prices and discourages local production of food crops. These are part of the IMF and WB's policies for Africa, as a result of which any hard currency gained through increased exports will have to be spent paying interest on debt and buying unnecessary imports as allowed by trade liberalization. In fact, Africa is so economically weak that it produces only 1% of world GDP.

It has been estimated that as of December 2005 there shall be some 11 million Kenyans unemployed or employed in economically insignificant jobs

---

195. *Daily Nation*, July 1998.

such as roasting maize[196]. This means that several million people are idle and perhaps this helps explain the rapid increase of violent robbery and sex offences.

MASS POVERTY

The causes of widespread poverty are the same as the causes of economic weakness and unemployment. More than 220 million Africans or a quarter of all Africans live in absolute poverty[197]. These people have no access to health services or formal education and have no control over their lives. For many, the prospects of a better life are getting worse as the exploitation of Africa is intensified in new ways. 70% of the poor are women.

In the 1980s after the implementation of SAPs in Africa, poverty also increased, not just in the number of people living in desperate poverty but in the proportion as well[198]. In 1992, the WB took $370 as its poverty line and found that the number of poor in Africa had increased by 215 million in just seven years (during the SAPs) from 1985 to 1992. The proportion of Africans who were malnourished and constantly hungry had also increased, from 101 to 168 million in the same period[199]. In 1980, 77% of primary age children attended school; ten years later only 67% did[200]. Total spending on education in Africa in real terms fell by a third, from Kshs 660 billion ($11 billion) in 1980 to only Kshs 420 billion ($7 billion) a decade later.

The poverty of most Africans imposes limits on the growth of industries. Given the limited internal demand (since no one can afford to consume much), African companies started selling goods in the wealthy markets of the West to boost export-led growth. The West immediately imposed tariffs and other barriers on African commodities. Neocolonialism sustains itself by ensuring its victims remain in poverty, and industrialization shall never be achieved in Africa so long as neocolonialism is in place.

According to the findings to the of a survey in 1994, 29% of Kenyans in rural areas and 11% of those who live in urban areas are so poor that they would

196. Report by the International Centre for Economic Growth (ICEG) in its debut publication, *Micro-enterprise Development* as used in the *Daily Nation*, December 1998.

197. UNFPA, *The New Generations* and Harrison, *Inside the Third World.*

198. World Development Report 1992, World Bank, Washington, 1992.

199. Alexandros Nikos (ed), *Agriculture: Toward 2000*, Belhaven Press, London. 1988 and World Bank, World Development Report.

200. World Education Report 1991, UNESCO, Paris, 1991.

be unable to meet their food needs even if they channeled all their efforts and resources only into food. About a third of Africans in Kenya, even in the absence of drought, are always hungry, malnourished and lacking basic necessities[201]. Weakened by malnourishment, they are more prone to disease. Resources are so tight that the poor are unable to provide for two essential needs simultaneously. For instance, for a child to be taken to hospital or sent to school, the entire family has to forfeit food or other basic necessities[202].

In 1996, the Central Bureau of Statistics embarked on a study to assess poverty in Kenya. The study covered the districts of Kajiado, Kisumu, Makueni, Mombasa, Nyeri, Nakuru and Taita Taveta. The method used was designed to include the views of various communities in the study areas. The five main forms in which poverty manifested are[203]:

1. Begging and dependency on external assistance, mainly in food.
2. Poor health.
3. Unemployment or employment in informal, economically meaningless jobs such as street peddling.
4. Lack of basic facilities, like proper shelter and clothing.
5. Child labor, homelessness or street children.

When the communities surveyed were asked what they thought was the cause of their poverty, their answers were very significant[204]:

1. Unemployment.
2. Droughts leading to a reduction in the farm production capacity.
3. Landlessness.
4. Having many children per family that are too expensive to maintain.
5. Collapse of families and the loss of breadwinners.

The respondents seemed to be quite oblivious to the fact that neocolonialism stands behind their poverty as the upstream cause of the immediate problems they recognize.

Roughly 80% of those interviewed felt that poverty had worsened in the previous five years. This is remarkable because over that five-year period, the

---

201. National Welfare Monitoring Survey, Nairobi, 1994.
202. *Ibid.*
203. Central Bureau of Statistics, Nairobi, 1996.
204. *Ibid.*

government had liberalized the economy, relaxed exchange controls and the Kenyan economy had collapsed. The communities surveyed also referred to the provision of essential service by the government, with reference to that past five year period. This was in terms of quality, availability, affordability of the services provided where provided.

Education services were not available according 21% of interviewees; 80% felt that education was not affordable; 25% felt that the quality of education was low and had not improved.

Medical services were unavailable according to some 40% respondents; 75% felt that healthcare was unaffordable; about 65% said that the quality of health services provided were low and falling in standard.

Agricultural services were unavailable to some 65% of the interviewees. These extension services are essential to increased food production and their unavailability is also a contributing factor to low production and mass hunger in Kenya. To 80%, these services — where available — were not affordable[205].

On a bus in rural Kenya, one might see a woman with several children and a crying baby. After the baby cries for a long time, the woman might open a handkerchief and carefully count the few coins tucked in it, ponder her options, and finally decide that she can afford to buy one banana to keep the baby quiet. But, no sooner does she buy the banana than the other children will demand the same. Now she has the whole family upset and no way to quiet them at all. Or, one may meet a young man whose wage, like millions of others, is very low. Having tired of being harassed and hustled from one street to another while working as an informal peddler, he may manage to get a job as a sweeper. Despite his 12 years in school, he has no hope of sending his two children to secondary school because the fees for one child for one year are more than his four months' wage.

Market stalls in Nairobi overflow with all types of fruits and vegetables most of which rot because most Kenyans cannot afford to buy them. In rural areas, *hundreds* of people die of malaria each week for lack of 20 shillings (25¢) to buy chloroquin tablets, and many more go hungry every day. While in the cities the rich flaunt their big cars, buy dieting pills, go to aerobic classes and night-clubs where they dance the night away to foreign music.

---

205. *Ibid.*

As neocolonial exploitation intensifies, the disparity between rich and poor also increases, engendering political instability. The spread of poverty has reduced the middle class in Africa to insignificance. Most African countries are polarized with a small, rich, Westward-looking elite and a mass of poor people. The rich are firm supporters of neocolonialism because it is their source of wealth. The poor have failed to rebel, to unite and call for the demolition of neo-colonialism, because class differences are less important in Africa than other social ties that cut through class stratification. People are more conscious of ethnic background, language, and religion than class. These are factors which confuse the central issue of privilege and poverty and the role of neocolonialism in condemning the majority of the people to desperate poverty. But below the seemingly peaceful surface, lies the potential for rebellion and anarchy. This tension is created by extreme deprivation, injustice and constant hunger and occasionally erupts in killings famous as "mob justice".

The poverty is so desperate in many regions of Africa that it is too much for the people to bear. This desperation is manifested as psychological trauma and violence, especially in the family. In the slums, the pressures leading to family breakdown increase as fathers, unable to support their children, abandon their families, and mothers who work as prostitutes abandon the children or are killed by Aids; and the number of street children increases, as well as overall home-lessness. Suicide has also become common, especially as parents find they cannot provide for their children. All these are the result of economic collapse.

In fact, the slum problem is a tragic monument of neocolonialism and not overpopulation. Most people realize that they do not have any future in the current economy of Kenya. Many are therefore seeking to migrate. Those con-demned to remain in Kenya are unable to find proper employment, and this is why today there are armies of peddlers, hawkers and acres of squalid kiosks, bat-talions of beggars, street children, prostitutes and Aids sufferers all over.

TRIBALISM

A tribe, according to the Oxford Advanced Learners Dictionary, is a racial group (especially in a primitive or nomadic culture) united by language, religion, and customs, living as a community under one or more chiefs. "Zulu Tribes" are prominently given as an example. According to this definition, in Kenya there are no tribes. In these terms, tribalism does not exist. People sometimes favor their kith and kin in getting jobs, tenders, contracts, and places in schools, but this can hardly be described as tribalism. A more appropriate description would be "nepotism," except under the wider umbrella of a language group.

As people spread all over the continent, contact between them diminished and the original language fragmented, eventually forming totally different languages but with very close relationship. The three main language groups are Nilotic, Cushitic and Bantu. In Kenya, the Kalenjin tribe has smaller sub-tribes with very similar languages. The Mt. Kenya peoples' languages are also very similar. To a greater or lesser extent a Kamba, Kikuyu, Embu, and Meru can communicate. Many languages of Central Africa are similar with Bantu languages of East Africa.

In contemporary society, the term "tribe" carries less and less meaning as people from different language groups have come together and share a common religion, language, and customs, which have reduced ethnic groups to mere language groups.

Kenyans have been convinced by non-Kenyans that they are divided into 42 tribes, while in actual fact they are no more divided than say, Japan or Britain. There is nothing like a tribe. This notion of tribalism has been so drilled into the Kenyan mind that the term has formed a new meaning: the unfair favoring of people who belong to one's language group. Political rulers worldwide pack their governments and armed forces with their supporters to consolidate their power. In Africa, the only difference is that the ruler gets his supporters from the people whose language he shares, crystallizing enmity among different language groups. Loyalty to the ethnic group in Africa comes before loyalty to the state.

Whenever people of different cultures come into prolonged and effective contact, living together but leading different and separate ways of life, misunderstanding and suspicion are likely to emerge. In due course one group is likely to dominate the other, as the Tutsi who dominated the Hutu in both Rwanda and Burundi; or, the two cultures merge and form a new culture, as the Swahili culture and language emerged from Arabic and coastal Bantu cultures. Swahili culture is strong because it took the best aspects of Arabic culture, such as organized trade, coinage and other technological advancements, while from the Bantu it took social organization, a strong family unit, and language among other things. This combined strength has helped the spread of the Swahili language throughout Eastern and Central Africa.

The forced contact between different ethnic groups in Africa by colonialism led to the rise of many misconceptions. The colonizers heightened ethnic animosity and misconceptions where they existed and introduced them where none existed. Colonial policies were deliberately aimed at increasing "tribalism" because a divided populace is easier to rule.

In the colonial era, some communities and regions were excluded from any form of technological advancement because the colonialists did not find anything to take from them. The most exploited community in Kenya was the Kikuyu. This was because of their proximity to the colonial capital and the fact that they occupied fertile land in cool areas that the colonizers coveted. They were absorbed into the money economy much earlier and more completely than any other ethnic group. This gave the Kikuyu a head start; hence, they were the first to form political parties, independent schools and churches. The people of northeastern Kenya were never absorbed into the colonial, money, economy because the colonialists saw less of value in that region and left them more or less alone.

After independence, it became popular for other communities to say that they were being fleeced by the Kikuyu and the seeds of suspicion and animosity were sown. At the height of the Mau Mau war for land and freedom between 1952-58, the colonialists incited other ethnic groups against the Kikuyu to prevent nationalism from spreading throughout the colony. This is the origin of anti-Kikuyuism in Kenya. President Kenyatta did not help things by favoring his Kiambu kin.

Owing to the Kikuyu-dominated government that was formed immediately after the attainment of independence, a popular myth about the "thieving" Kikuyu started. It later escalated until all the ethnic groups fashioned their own myths about the others. Kambas were allegedly witches, Luhyas were gluttons, Luos were filthy, and so on. The Maasai are portrayed as prehistoric fools. This kind of ethnic stereotyping has been entrenched by jokes that have been popularized and promoted by the media. Kids in city suburbs tell one another that Kikuyus love money so much that in a mortuary one can identify a dead Kikuyu by simply dropping a coin. The Kikuyu bodies will try to retrieve it. Although these youth grow up mingling with people of other ethnic groups, they end up marrying into their own ethnic group because the ethnic prejudices they were exposed to at an early age solidify with the passing of time. When inter-ethnic marriages do occur, in many cases the parents of the both the bride and groom are vehemently opposed to the marriage. Most inter-ethnic marriages are from communities that are "close", either linguistically or physically, or from communities with no previous contact so that no harmful stereotypes have been promoted.

Cultural integration of various language groups, or at least the establishment of smooth relations, is made more difficult by certain cultural practices and values held by one group but unacceptable to other ethnic groups, such as wife inheritance, and conflicts over burial rights. These differences need to be addressed.

It is often assumed that tribal differences are responsible for civil wars in Africa. This is false. Conflict arises either from external influence or economic reasons. The "tribal" clashes that erupted after multipartyism was introduced in Kenya were not a result of ethnic or linguistic differences. Throughout history, human beings and human groups have fought for the control of resources necessary for their survival, or their happiness. This is part of the reason why Europeans invaded Africa, and it is the reason why the Mau Mau fought to recover control of their lives and land. The Mau Mau asked for political independence to guarantee their right to the use of land. In the Rift Valley, the clashes were the result of poverty complicated by destructive politics — political power is used to guarantee easy access to economic resources. Thus, economic competition becomes political competition, provoking armed conflict.

In Europe, people are divided by religious, political and social affiliation, all of these groups compete with each other. If we exclude the Mongol incursions, and perhaps the Persians, it is only the Europeans and people who originated from Europe that have, as a race, gone out of their own territory to attack other human groups (as distinguished by racial differences) in order to take their resources.

The Somalia tragedy has nothing to do with a civil war between tribes. They are the only sub-Saharan African nation having a common language, religion and culture. Even without "tribes", the Somali still massacre each other on a clan basis.

Most Africans have reason to believe that wars in Africa have nothing to do with tribal animosity; they are a product of external machinations. Economic collapse often entails government collapse and the collapse of law and order, too. It is interesting to compare the collapse of governments and civil wars and upheavals in Europe in the years during and immediately after the economic depression following World War I. In Germany, the Nazis attempted to overthrow a state government during the 1924 Munich Putsch and later came to power because the post-war tribulations had left the people desperate for a change. Spain underwent a civil war in the 1930s. In Italy, Mussolini and his fascists took over the government by force. All this instability was brought on by economic collapse and all the resulting governments were dictatorial. Not much different from today's Africa. History shows that a country does not need to have tribal rivalries in order to fight a civil war; economic collapse is the major ingredient in civil wars and political instability.

Today racism is also manifested in movies, made in Europe and America. Africans are depicted in the colonialist image of the "unspoiled African savage", divided into numerous, ever warring tribes that still marvel at European skin and hair. In reality, many African communities never had an autocratic ruler. They had councils of elders and pure democracy. These communities did not have any idea of state violence or government coercion and exploitation. But according to the European invaders, who have known democracy for less than 100 years, the Africans were not civilized. Where there were highly organized political states, such as in the inter-lacustrine zone around the Great Lakes region, the Europeans declared that their size was too small and so did not represent "civilization." The idea that the political state is an index for measuring civilization stems from ancient Greek thought. The Greeks believed that civilization was political organization. Loyalty to the state and obedience to laws made by the state were more important than morality, or the principle of fairness. To precolonial African, civilization was first and foremost morality, which included obedience to elders, chastity, selflessness, humility, decency, and so on. Today, Africans often confuse the term "modern" with "European" or "Western", and elements of Western culture, including pornography, are often described as "modern" while elements of African culture aimed at promoting chastity and decency, including clitoridectomy, are considered negatives.

It is true that in "civilized" Britain, not all people are English. Due to tribal differences the English had no compunctions over exploiting the Irish and taking their resources. Ireland was invaded and colonized by the English centuries ago. The racist "jokes" and other expressions of "hate" merely mask the fact that they are rivals fighting over resources.

At most, the varied ethnic groups in Africa share a language and a common geographical location. Since the invention of political states, governments have been used as a tool by one class to control the rest of society in its own interest. In Africa today, this class has taken the form of a wealthy elite within one or several language groups. The individuals who make up this ruling elite share nothing with the rest of their ethnic group except names, because this elite despises its own culture and language and opts for a European language. In Kenya, the elite is English speaking. In countries such as Japan and Germany, capitalists form the group that controls the government in its own interests. And this ruling class prides itself on speaking very formally and despises the slang used by the lower classes. In czarist Russia, the nobility spoke French and emulated European ways. All these ruling groups are analogous to tribes, sharing a common language and culture that sets them apart from the rest of society; and they also share the same desire of keeping others who are different from them out of power.

Favoring the policy of "divide and rule", the colonialists took it upon themselves to accentuate any divisions among the colonized. They used one ethnic group to police and oppress another, creating deep bitterness and enmity, as the Rwandese have so clearly displayed. Initially, invading European armies engaged some Africans in fighting units. In Kenya, the Swahili and Maasai were used to attack other African groups. In Uganda, the Toro were subdued and humiliated by the Buganda who fought along the British. Other kingdoms in modern Uganda, after being overrun, were stripped of their laws, customs and culture but the Buganda state retained the Kabakaship (kingship), Lukiko (parliament) and were pampered by the British. After independence, the bitterness and divisions which the British had created threw Uganda into civil war and political instability that still goes on today. Many other countries have collapsed politically as a result of colonial induced divisions.

Although largely underdeveloped, the mass media in Kenya influences public opinion. The mass media has been an accomplice in the entrenchment of ethnic suspicion, misconception and prejudice. Newspapers are generally trusted by the reading public and most innuendos are absorbed uncritically. Thus, an article about a young girl who was abducted in a family feud may be reported by a local newspaper as a "Somali girl kidnapped....". Her being Somali had nothing to do with the abduction, but the emphasis leaves a certain impression on the reader.

In locally produced programs on either TV or radio, the programs overemphasize the characters' ethnic background. A thief will always have the accent of a Kikuyu. Newspapers are open in the entrenching of ethnic stereotypes; they have made it fashionable to be a tribalist. Cartoonists poke fun at the Maasai, painting them as hopelessly inept in the modern world. The promotion of negative stereotypes particularly affects young people's worldviews, and makes detribalization more difficult. One newspaper reported that when a policeman asked a *matatu*[206] tout (conductor) how many passengers had been in the vehicle, he replied that there were fourteen passengers and one Maasai!

This bombardment of misconceptions undermines the very concept of nationhood. Politics, too, have been deliberately ethnicized. This has increased inter-ethnic tension and hostility. Ethnocentrism has deep roots in the Kenyan colonial experience. This so-called tribalism is abetted by biased generalizations which are entrenched by the media.

Tribalism shall only be eliminated by the end of neocolonialism and the end of political competition based on ethnicity that make tribalism possible. Urbanization should also be encouraged as a way of integrating people of different communities. The media must also be more regulated, to stop it fanning and fueling irrelevant ethnic differences.

---

206. Minibus used for public transport.

CHAPTER 8. POSSIBLE SOLUTIONS TO THE ECONOMIC DILEMMA IN AFRICA

Solutions to the economic collapse in African countries are easily identified:

1. End foreign investment and end trade liberalization. In other words, block off the principal avenues of capital outflow.
2. Strengthen the linkages between various sectors of the economy so that they can react beneficially on each other, particularly agriculture and industry.
3. Expand local productive capacity. Local entrepreneurial capacity plus local scientific and technological capacity should be developed to construct an industrial society.
4. Underwrite social overhead costs and initial investment, and later privatize the investments by a public issue of shares with the exclusion of foreign investors.
5. Encourage local investment with local capital. Income leakages abroad have always been limitations on development. To rectify this, inflation and protection may be used. Deliberate inflation may increase the level of money demand as the money supply increases. It also stimulates local investment by raising profit expectations and is a means of extracting forced savings to match the investment made with bank credit. However, real income and not money will offer the best incentive to local investors.
6. Dismantle the colonial economic systems in all African countries and create linkages between different regions such that they react beneficially to each other. The mineral wealth of DR Congo should be able to

stimulate the growth of industries in East Africa, if the two regions were economically integrated.

7. Liquidate the influence and aid of the donors, especially the IMF and WB.

One may observe that, while a few countries broke away from the international capitalist investment system, those which have remained in this system and managed to industrialize did it by using socialist policies. A good example is South Korea, which refused any form of foreign investment until it was faced with an economic crisis in 1997, when the IMF forced it to accept foreign investors as a condition of bailing it out. Another example is India. India has developed a large technological capacity and has more genuine independence than most African countries. This has been achieved by the restriction and regulation of foreign investment, high tariff protection (e.g. no trade liberalization) and other agricultural and economic policies that have restructured the Indian economy so that it is internally responsive and does not contribute agricultural and other raw materials for the industries of the outside world. African countries are unable to emulate these examples because of many complex factors, which all boil down to imperialism and mental colonization.

When the European settlers in Zimbabwe made a Unilateral Declaration of Independence (UDI) in November 1965, the UN imposed comprehensive and mandatory sanctions on the country. This embargo entailed an immediate stoppage of importation and exportation of goods to and from the country. This halted the craze for imports that had been encouraged by trade liberalization, and foreign investment and repatriation of profits also ended. The Zimbabwean/Southern Rhodesian economy grew more than any other African country. Its economy only collapsed when foreign investment, SAPs, and import liberalization were introduced after UDI. During the first nine years of UDI (1965-1974), Southern Rhodesia's manufacturing sector grew by 142% in real terms, while the agricultural output doubled. In this same period, the per capita income increased by 35%. The Gross Domestic Product grew annually by 7%[207]. Although he was a racist, UDI leader Ian Smith employed appropriate economic policies. He stopped all repatriation of profits and dividends by foreign companies, which led to more liquidity within local branches of the foreign companies and forced them to plough back these back these profits in productive investment. Soon, the country had surplus reserves of hard currency[208]. The

---

207. Haron Wachira, Kamau Ngotho, "Going cold turkey," *Executive*, (June 1992), pp. 17-20.

embargo acted as high tariff protection and forced the colonial economy to collapse; it also meant that the wealthy locals could not waste capital on importation of luxuries and pleasure trips to Europe. In the long run an internal
technical base was created and employment opportunities increased, even
though the Africans were not free. Rhodesia as a whole became truly independent and was on its way to becoming an industrialized state. After the collapse of UDI in 1980, the new rulers returned Zimbabwe to neocolonialism and
all the gains made during UDI were lost. Today, Zimbabwe's economy is a smol-
dering ruin.

IDEOLOGIES

Africans have lost confidence in the current system and have come up with
various alternative ideologies to replace neocolonialism; most of them also have
been failures. Even before self government was attained, Pan-Africanism was
invented. It was mainly aimed at achieving the political unity of all African countries. Its best known advocate was Ghanaian president Kwame Nkrumah who,
as a result, was overthrown by his army in league with the British and Americans. That effectively quashed the ideology.

In Tanzania, Mwalimu Nyerere came up with Ujamaa, an ideology of
Brotherhood, which also failed. In most of northern Africa, Islam is the dominant
ideology, while in South Africa apartheid was practiced before neocolonialism
was adopted after 1994. In other regions, people have turned Christianity into an
ideology, while others have moved towards traditionalism as a solution to the
political and economic weakness of Africa.

With the exception of Islam, all of the above-mentioned ideologies have
failed. The main reason is because their adherents failed to make the connection
between the functions that act together to make neocolonialism work. In the
case of Pan-Africanism, its originators knew that political union of all African
countries would create a solid foundation for economic and political freedom.
Kwame Nkrumah became disillusioned as all his efforts came to a naught,
because he failed to make the connection between cultural imperialism and the
lack of vision in the new crop of African rulers who refused to discuss the for-

208. *Ibid.*

mation of a single African state. The following section explores the connection between the various factors that keep neocolonialism in place.

When Europeans first arrived in Africa, they found Africans at various stages of human organization: There were bands of hunters like the Khoikhoi in South Africa; communalism was practiced by the Kikuyu of East Africa; and a type of feudalism was common in the Western Sudan Kingdoms. Although commerce was widespread, capitalism did not exist. It is the Europeans who introduced capitalism as a mode of production. By virtue of its greater economic capacity, European capitalism was the able to establish hegemony over Africa.

When two societies at different states of human organization come into prolonged and effective contact, the weaker of the two (the one with lesser economic capacity) is bound to be effected negatively. The annihilation of the original inhabitants of what are now North America and Tasmania by the Europeans is an extreme example. The African way of thinking and behavior has been destroyed through the obliteration of the culture through which Africans reasoned and based their ideology. In the vacuum thus created, Europeans have filled in their own culture. Africans now fall into various categories; Anglophiles, Francophiles and so on. This is an abnormal situation and has resulted in a psychological crisis in Africans. Having lost their frame of reference, they have come to accept the European version of everything and are proud of becoming "modern". All this is aggravated by self-hatred and self-mutilation. In Kenya, the young people, especially in urban areas, speak with longing about flying out to Europe or the US.

As Africans rushed to abandon their own homegrown ideology in favor of Western culture, they failed to realize that the European/Western culture assigns a very undesirable position to Africans, "modern" or not. As of 2004, there are still numerous reports of Africans being harassed, assaulted and even killed in European countries. This racism is only the most blatant expression of an attitude that keeps Africans down. An entire race of people that has been alienated from their own heritage and despises themselves in favor of another race can hardly expect to maintain their independence from that other race. For any progress to be achieved, Africans most proceed to a higher ideological and cultural level than which currently dominates them.

One approach would be the restoration of the principles of economic equality, as in communalism. This is not communism; communism is a product of the European urban environment and in Africa the aim must be to remove alien European concepts. Communalism is also not traditionalism. It simply aims to hold onto progressive African values while accepting capitalism as the mode of production, except that the principle means of production would not be monopolized by a small number of people. The creation of great disparities in wealth must be avoided.

India represents some useful lessons. They have managed to hold onto much of their culture despite being colonized for a longer period than most of Africa. The "Christian" European Church has served as one arm of cultural imperialism. The Indians rejected the European version of Christianity. To free Africa, Western forms of religion must be eradicated. The current form of "Christianity" in Africa must be Christianized and Africanized for it to be acceptable. Religion can serve useful purposes, but cultural imperialism must be prevented from using foreign religions to retard and warp African minds. It is an aberration for Africans to worship according to instructions from foreigners and their trainees.

It is also necessary to free the mass media from foreign contamination and domination in order to block it as a route of cultural imperialism.

Logically, what is needed is a cultural, political, economic independence and renaissance. Many Africans cannot even see the importance of reestablishing African culture. But, many behavioral problems in society have been directly caused by the spread of Western culture. When earthquakes or other natural disasters strike in the US, shops and buildings are routinely looted. In Japan, no looting occurs after an earthquake even when all the shops are damaged. The US and Japan are both wealthy, at the national level, but the structure of society and the different forms of culture mean that very different conduct can be expected in these two countries.

Chapter 9. The International Community and Africa

The "international community" is very popular within Africa as it is associated with every good thing that foreigners do in Africa, such as (on the surface, at least) providing aid. What many Africans fail to see is the open rejection and isolation which the continent is subjected to internationally. The "international community" is not an aggregation of nations, but of elites within the most influential countries. This means that decisions which control the flow of history and destinies of millions of people are largely in the hands of a few who despise Africa. These elites function as a class that protects its own interests, that is, global finance.

Arguably, the two most important clubs for the North's elites are The Bilderberg Group and the Trilateral Commission. Both of these groups are composed of powerful and influential politicians, tycoons, royalty, academics and others. The Bilderberg Group has an uncanny ability to pick out people who will shortly come to power in their home countries and invite them to join. Ever since it was started in 1952, the Bilderberg has been very powerful in international relations. Neither the Bilderberg Group and the Trilateral Commission invites or accepts Africans to their conferences[209].

The following essay may be a spoof, but it reflects in a very real way the essential direction of these and other international organizations, as the author, Richard Farmer, perceived clearly.

---

209. Baffour Ankomah, "No longer shall they kill our prophets," *New African*, August/September 2004.

MEMO

The following document was in the briefcase of a man flying from Bombay to Paris. He had a heart attack on the plane, and in the confusion, his papers were left behind. The Quatrilateral Commission is composed of powerful and influential people in several states which are interested in world dominion. Three of the groups involved are the US, Western Europe and Japan. It is not clear who the fourth may be.[210]

TOP SECRET

BURN BEFORE READING

TO: Members of the Quatrilateral Commission

FROM: Richard N. Farmer

SUBJECT: The current situation in the Third World.

In the global struggle for domination, the question always arises as to how we are doing. As you know, our plan is a fifty-year effort, it is easy to become confused by short-term fluctuations. But the end we all know. We want to win. You members who are more sophisticated than the usual "send in a gunboat and let them know who's boss" types are well aware that military conquest and occupation are usually dysfunctional, as witness Soviet efforts in Afghanistan or American struggles in Vietnam. No, the long-term effort simply revolves around our abilities to have the Third World destroy itself, or preferably voluntarily render itself impotent. The purpose of this report is to summarize critical Third World developments.

In short, we are succeeding beyond our wildest expectations. Only a few years ago, our situation looked bleak, but now trends are all in our favor. With a bit of luck and proper prodding in the right quarters, total victory should be ours within a decade. To recapitulate our gains, I point to two major developments.

A significant and growing part of the Third World is becoming increasing interested in cultural identity, in maintaining their hallowed traditions. No one asks illiterate peasants what they think of such things, so clearly this movement is led by the world intellectual community, including of course many of our own thinkers in the rich countries. But intellectuals from Third World countries are leading the charge, which is as it should be.

In short, everyone deserves to be what they want, except of course, Third worlders who want to be Western. These poor souls are reviled as misguided tools of neo-imperialism. Moreover, *Development* (a magazine) has given considerable space to the "control of communications" idea that every country has a right to give only that information to the outside world which the controlling government thinks proper. Needless to say, we should back this argument, for reasons to be made clear.

---

210. Richard Farmer, "Memo from the Quatrilateral commission," *Development*, 1982, p. 80.

Country after country is becoming isolationist. This follows from point 1. If you need to protect your culture from foreign contamination, then you must keep the wrong kinds of foreigners out.

At the limit, all foreigners are the wrong kinds, as Iran has demonstrated. The long-term results of the above two points lead to the following results, which give our win well into the 21st century.

Countries in love with their own traditional culture with isolationist Marxist or religious hapless neighbors. They are too busy stamping out Western or Soviet tendencies to pay any attention to anything else. The more such countries there are, the less we have to worry about them. They may do interesting things, but since the world mainstream of development is Western and scientific, all of our competition disappears. No one seriously expects any significant technological innovations from places such as Cuba or Vietnam, and none will emerge, at least until a century or more has passed. Hence we can look forward to steadily growing advantages, in all areas where technology counts.

The brain drain controversy fortunately has quietened down, in part because the isolationist, culture — oriented countries really want to get rid of their dissi-dents, and the major dissidents are those Western trained and oriented scientists, technicians and entrepreneurs. Iran is happy to dump such persons on the West, and we gain the advantage of their brains and skills. We only have to look to the enormous economic contribution made in the US by Vietnamese, Indians, Paki-stanis, Cubans, Mexicans and many others to see the point. Such refugees are seen by the popular press as a major problem and economic drain, where as in fact these persons represent a major capital import from the poorer countries. If those poor countries are happy to give us their best then so much the better. With any luck at all, we can count on large flows of such able people for many years to come.

Even the most isolationist country needs guns, and the more odd the country is, the more guns it needs. Happily, discussions of this point is not considered proper in development circles, so whatever happens goes on outside the purview of intel-lectuals. But those guns must be paid for, since traditional cultures cannot make them, and the usual result is that the traditional culture continues to export what it can, which invariably is the raw materials, minerals and other unprocessed prod-ucts it produced during the colonial period. Since development now is totally non-Western, the possibilities of developing new industries to compete with us are fore-closed. We thus find ourselves approaching a situation exactly like that of 1910, except that the new countries are doing it willingly, not under the guns of the colo-nialist power.

We need only to look at Iran and Angola with oil and Cuba with sugar, to see this point. Occasionally a country will try to build up its heavy industries to develop more armaments capability, but even here we gain by selling them such capital equipment. Fortunately, the western news image of the Third World sug-gest that we sell them many consumer goods, but in fact, these only go the elite. In cynical countries, we will continue to sell such things to the elites, and in moral ones, the previous elite will be living in our countries and buying the stuff locally. Loss of markets will be trivial. One should note the more sophisticated the weapons we sell, the more income we make, and the probability that they will get used declines. Remember that really sophisticated weapons require thousands of highly trained technicians to operate, and this is what the culturally oriented countries will lack. For human reasons, to say nothing of maximizing our sales, we should push the most complex weaponry we can.

Efforts to stress the importance of local cultures will largely be in the West, Since few really care about such things, if the Third World controls its media, so that the only information is government sponsored, then even less attention will be paid. No one believes their own Western government news releases, and they will not believe Third World controlled press reports. The models here are Albania and Burma, which may have many virtues, but which are virtually unknown in the West. More such models are highly desirable.

Education in the new culturally oriented states will be largely along traditional lines. This virtually guarantees that these countries will not be any threat within twenty years. If we can encourage such states to send us their presently educated persons, this timetable will speed up. Perhaps we can prevent countries from living off their current educational capital. In the unexpected event that a Marxist country goes capitalist and opens its doors to the world again, we may win in another way. Marxists are very good at training in basic literacy and simple technical skills. Unfortunately, such states offer little potential for these newly educated people. But if the system changes, or if demands for trained people rise elsewhere, then pools of cheap labor are available. The Indian State of Kherala comes to mind. Here, a communist government really did an excellent job in education. Then, when such persons were needed in the Middle East, they were able to emigrate. The net result, namely higher income for our side, was commendable. Some Western intellectuals are also dangerous. They are beginning to see the game we are playing and raising awkward questions. To date, this has been no problem, since Third Worlders pay little attention to them, but this could change.

Along these same lines, we must make sure that development discussions never, ever include military issues. They must never, ever include military issues. They must never include discussions of third world elites, and what games they play. And they must certainly never raise any sophisticated, real world questions of political power. As long as the simplistic, neocolonial/Marxist vs. capitalist issues are argued, we are safe. Moreover, the more culture is discussed, the better off we are, and the more value judgments intellectuals make about proper development, the safer we are.[*]

PART TWO: HOW NEOCOLONIALISM IS SUSTAINED

INTRODUCTION: SUSTAINING NEOCOLONIALISM

All African economies are externally responsive in structure, aiming only to produce for the "world market" rather than for the people within that economy. The natural tendency of such economies is to gravitate towards being internally responsive. The external states work to prevent this from happening, through cultural imperialism, aid and political and economic threats.

When their former colonies attained independence, the colonial powers set to work to undermine them. They maneuvered to have sympathetic individuals brought into power in the newly independent countries, then provided military support for them and eliminated their political opponents. The US, for example, orchestrated the brutal murder Lumumba[211] to guarantee that Mobutu got a firm hold on power in Congo. Most Africans with a bit of education were not blind to these developments.

It was then necessary to invent an economic theory to favor Western interests. The first time such economic policies were implemented, they faced considerable opposition. To arrest the anti-European and anti-colonialism mentality, the West stepped up efforts to persuade Africans that such recommendations were in their interest. Examples of this cultural and intellectual imperialism are a steady diet in the media, religion and education.

---

211. Mutuma Mathiu, "The story of two giants," *Sunday Nation*, March 23 1997, pp. 16-17. Also, Lisa Pease, "Midnight in the Congo: The Assassination of Lumumba and the mysterious death of Dag Hammarskjold", *Probe*, March – April issue, 1999.

This propaganda campaign has been an astounding success and to date has guaranteed that all the deleterious economic policies invented by the donors for Africa are adopted without question.

Despite African efforts to fight it, neocolonialism it has triumphed. This is due to the concentration of the fight in the economic and political spheres only. Africans have failed to realize that neocolonialism is a complete system with an important cultural aspect. This is revealed in the fact that cultural imperialism is legal in most African countries. In fact, cultural imperialism is the single most powerful factor of neocolonialism. This has resulted in a curious situation. African governments have the duty to protect the people from other nations, but Africans voluntarily accept all elements of Western culture and misguided economic policies. This is what Farmer meant in his memo to the Quatrilateral Commission when he wrote that "the long-term effort simply revolves around our abilities to have the Third World destroy itself or preferably voluntarily render itself impotent". African governments have allowed cultural imperialism to flourish. The rulers have given up on solving their people's problems which are caused by the people's failure to assert their cultural, political and economic independence. Such rulers lose all sense of internal direction and consequently begin to amass personal wealth, giving rise to endemic corruption on which the people then erroneously place blame for their economic problems. In this scenario of national confusion and bewilderment, it becomes very difficult for one to see the real causes of the economic problems.

After independence, African rulers took positive steps which, if they had worked, would have prevented the rise of neocolonialism. They included nationalization of industries, high tariffs, and the formation of the OAU. But the OAU made a misstep by maintaining the artificial borders and foreign languages brought in by Europe. Political independence goes hand-in-hand with economic independence; one cannot be attained without the other.

Neocolonialism is a powerful cycle, which can only be broken at its weakest point — cultural imperialism. Neocolonialism thrives on public attitudes manipulated by the colonial powers; to destroy neocolonialism, public opinion must be brought back home.

Modern Africans sometimes go to ridiculous, uncomfortable and even dangerous lengths to prove how up to date they are. They may wear bell-bottomed trousers, mini-skirts, or heavy coats and woolen hats in an attempt to copy Westerners. Urban African women risk developing skin cancer by applying skin bleaching chemicals; and they are praised for their good looks. The West sets fashion trends and Africans copy them, opening up a ready market for clothes and accessories.

This would be relatively harmless if it was confined to the lower classes. It is unfortunately concentrated in the ruling elite, who adopt Western fashions and policy recommendations with equal fervor. Hence, more land has been allocated to grow cash crops and de-industrialization is now the official policy of most African countries.

By the early 1990s the problems in Africa had come to a head and revolutions were in the offing — revolutions which would have overthrown neocolonialism for once and for all. But the international media undermined any popular nationalist revolution, depicting the West in favorable terms and the African rulers as despots. In Kenya, this was very effective. The then American Ambassador, Smith Hempstone, supported the dissidents in their call for multi-partyism. This fact was widely publicized, and endeared him (and the US) to the African populace. That only made them accept all the more uncritically the Western version of events: that the economic problems in Kenya were caused by Kanu's monopoly on power and, for these problems to be solved, multi-partyism had to be introduced.

One party rule has never been a cause of economic problems. Today, a decade after the introduction of pluralism, the economic problems in Kenya have worsened but the energy that was moving to end neocolonialism is dissipated.

The West's influence is so powerful that even after witnessing their economies stumble and collapse under Western policy, Africans still cannot see that it is those policies that are to blame.

Economic collapse and mass poverty have exacerbated the disparity in the distribution of wealth at all levels. Within a country this has become a factor contributing to ethnic rivalry and hostility. On the global scale, civil wars enrich wealthy foreign states, who make profits by selling arms and ammunitions to the warring factions, unnecessarily prolonging war. Given the weak and confused nature of its African neighbors, a country ruined by a genuine or foreign-orchestrated civil war has only the West to turn to for support. Then, the recipient country gets trapped into dependency and the ruinous cycle that led to the civil war will be repeated. A good example is Rwanda, which fought an internal war in 1959, with Western help; Rwanda was restored but was neo-colonized, leading to economic hardship, ethnic rivalry and conflict, and another civil war in 1994. Today, Rwanda is being "aided" yet again.

Neocolonialism has ensured that the West continues to dominate Africa politically, economically, culturally and militarily. In spite of (nominal) independence, Africans are still tightly bound to the West and have a master-servant relationship. It is only with genuine political independence that other forms of independence can be acquired and guaranteed. In turn, political independence is dependent on economic independence. The rich countries realized this long ago and proceeded to undermine Africa's political independence by ensuring economic underdevelopment and collapse. It is not in their interest to see Africa develop.

In summary, the exploitative system of international foreign investment-based capitalism is manifested in the economies of African countries in various ways. The main ways in which neocolonialism is sustained are:

- religion
- education
- cultural imperialism, and
- military and political threats.

CHAPTER 10. RELIGION

There are several religions competing for converts in Africa. Most Africans are nominally Christians, of various denominations. Catholicism is the largest denomination. The Catholic Church has maintained most of its traditions. There are so many Protestant denominations that it is not possible to study each of them here; we shall therefore consider the general outlook of the protestant Churches.

The main objective in studying the forms of Christianity practiced in Africa is to show how cultural imperialism uses Christianity to shape African minds. Christianity is a tool to neocolonialism.

Christianity arrived in Africa through the Europeans. Over the course of some nineteen centuries, Christianity had undergone major modifications under the corrupt leadership of the European popes, and by the time it reached Africa, it was a fusion of pagan European culture and "Christian" teachings that was far from its roots. The pagan add-ons are what we shall refer to as cultural imperialism.

Cultural imperialism uses Christianity in two ways: (1) pagan European culture is ensconced in the religion brought to the Africans, and (2) the activities of European missionaries increased the amount of cultural imperialism to be found in today's Christianity.

The first Europeans to invade Africa were missionaries. Their work opened the door to their nations to colonize the part of Africa where they were operating. British missionaries always invited the British government to colonize the area that they were trying to establish themselves, and the French missionaries invited the French government. Once colonialism was established, the mission of "civilizing the natives" was a massive exercise in cultural imperialism. In Kenya, to give just one example, the colonial Church and government joined in the oppression of Africans. In 1923, Archbishop Archdeacon Owen was asked by the colonial government to subvert and misdirect the Young Kavirondo Association, which was campaigning for the end of forced labor and other reforms.

The missionaries also took over education. Even the colonial government realized that the detrimental education missionaries were providing to Africans was part of the colonization process, as it created distorted loyalties and aspirations, in some cases creating famous collaborators and traitors. As early as 1919 in Kenya, the colonial government had agreed to finance education for Africans, but under missionary supervision. When John Owallo broke away from the Church Missionary Society (CMS) and formed his own mission and school outside European control, the colonial government intervened directly. The Nyanza Provincial Commissioner Mr. Ainsworth tried to stop Owallo's school and mission. The Churches functioned to preserve the social relations of colonialism. Africans were taught the importance of humility and acceptance, and that they tolerate any abuse in this world because in the next world they would be happy and free.

Apart from claiming to spread the gospel, the missionaries blatantly promoted European cultural practices as "Christian" practices. African practices were condemned as "Pagan". In Kenya they opposed clitoridectomy and polygamy. African music, dance and languages were branded "evil" and banned from being used in religious worship. This is what caused the Kikuyu to reject the foreign missionaries and form their own churches and schools. Since these schools were founded in the 1920s on the prevailing anti-European culture and anti-colonialism mood, both the missionaries and the colonial government fought them. In Tanzania, the Catholic Church in a 1933 report cautioned against Africans being allowed to open their own schools without missionary control because "such schools may easily become hotbeds for sedition"[212]. Hence, the colonial Church was part and parcel of colonialism, just as today's neocolonial Church promotes and sustains neocolonialism.

Independence brought very few changes in the colonial Church. African languages were accepted and Africans became the new local leaders; but the colonial structure was still maintained, with *wazungus* in top leadership posi-

---

212. Rodney, *How Europe Underdeveloped Africa.*

tions. So long as the colonial structure of the Church in Africa remains intact, Christianity will be used as an avenue for mental colonization and control of Africans.

HOW THE EUROPEAN "CHRISTIAN" CHURCH ENTRENCHES NEOCOLONIALISM

The current form of Christianity as practiced by Africans is a tool of neocolonialism because it is designed to idolize and promote the use of pagan European cultural practices. In fact, Christian principles are different from the European pagan traditions that are promoted. This distorted form of Christianity reinforces and sustains neocolonialism through the deliberate confusion and promotion of pagan Western cultural practices as "Christianity", and attacks on African cultural practices in the guise of Christianity and attempts to implant pagan Western cultural practices in Africa.

Other Western religions are being introduced in Africa and they too function in support of neocolonialism. All the Christian denominations in existence were, for the most part, created by the Europeans who had inherited the church intact. For example, the Anglican Church, also known as the Church of England, was formed in about 1530 as a result of a rift between the English monarch Henry VIII and Pope Clement VII. King Henry VIII, famous for marrying women and then having them killed, died of syphilis[213] — but not before destroying papal influence and authority in England and declared himself the "Supreme Head of the English Church and Clergy", a position the monarchs of Britain still hold today. Every African who is a member of this Church accepts the British monarch as his spiritual leader. The Catholics have their Pope, who has always been a European. In Ethiopia, Christianity remained from the Vatican's distortions and did not fragment into different mutually hostile denominations.

The contradictions of Christianity in Europe directly affected Africans when Catholics and Protestants alike begun capturing and selling Africans into slavery. The Catholic Church justified its participation in the slave trade by claiming that it was trying to save African souls by baptizing Africans and removing them from their ungodly environment. Protestants did not even acknowledge that they had souls. But today, Africans are divided along the lines

---

213. Will Durant, *The Reformation*, Fine, 1983.

of different European denominations and these groups are constantly trying to get each other to decamp. Either way, the *mzungu* in Rome or elsewhere still benefits since the proceeds from offerings and other religious ventures are still going to be expatriated.

All denominations that originate from the West have Western leaders. They even have a monopoly on the route to heaven and it seems that an African can only get there through them. Today's Church must be Christianized and Africanized if cultural imperialism is to be prevented from using the Christian religion as a means of strengthening neocolonialism.

The deliberate confusion and promotion of pagan Western cultural practices packaged as Christianity.

We can divide the Western pagan element in today's "Christianity" into its constituent factors, which are the structures of the various Churches, pagan festivals, worship aids and heathen Western behavior.

Church Structure

Most mainstream denominations are controlled by Europeans or Americans. In a 1998 Anglican Church conference held in England, there were more Caucasian bishops than African bishops despite the fact that there are more African Anglicans than European or American Anglicans. In fact, Nigeria has more Anglicans than England, Europe, and North America put together, yet the West had more than 300 bishops at the conference and Nigeria had only 50. The US and England have an estimated 3.5 million Anglicans while Nigeria has 17.5 million[214]. The Caucasian domination of the conference prevents any African from ascending to the top post since it is these bishops who elect the head of the Church — the Archbishop of Canterbury. This situation is common in all Churches of Western origin and although there are more (nominal) Christians in Africa than there are in Europe or North America, no African heads any international church. This is spiritual colonialism.

Pagan Festivals

Several Western festivals are celebrated as "Christian" festivities, which is misleading and costly to Christians everywhere.

---

214. Paul Redfern, "Thorny issues for Lambeth Conference," *Sunday Nation*, July 26 1998, p. 19.

Christmas

Even as a celebration held in commemoration of Christ's birth, Christmas is ahistorical. No one knows the day Jesus was born and he never asked anyone to celebrate his birthday. The words Christmas and Boxing do not occur anywhere in the Christian bible. In AD 354, the Bishop of Rome, Liberius, told the (nominal) Christians to establish a festival on December 25[215]. At that time of year, it should be noted, it is cold and rainy in Palestine and the shepherds would not have been sleeping in the rain. The date of December 25 cannot be linked to the biblical tale of the birth of Jesus. However, the date corresponded with several pagan festivals that take place around the time of the winter solstice, when the days begin to lengthen as winter ends. Northern European tribes celebrated their chief festival of *Yule* to commemorate the sun's "rebirth"; the Romans had a festival called the *Saturnalia*, which was a celebration of the sun's birthday[216]. This day was also the birthday of the god Mithra. The "merry" component of these pagan festivals generally included over consumption of food, alcohol, and so on, gift giving, decoration of houses, and generosity to the poor — for that day only[217].

Pagan traditions of tree worship led to the invention of the Christmas tree. Santa Klaus or Father Christmas is another "folksy" invention that today distracts from the intended meaning of Christmas and fuels the world's biggest shopping season. Parents of the less affluent, in Africa as elsewhere, now dread the coming of Christmas.

The Christmas card was invented by a Briton in 1842 and today, the card-making industry employs up to half a million Britons alone. These cards are eagerly bought by Africans, thus creating a large market for imported cards[218]. Of course, the very image of Christmas as a snowy, northern event is a sign of cultural imperialism and mental colonization.

---

215. Watch Tower Bible Tract Society of Pennsylvania, *The Truth that Leads to Eternal Life*, New York, 1968. Also M. Ranji, "Origins of some Christmas practices," Young Nation Magazine, *Sunday Nation*, December 21 1997, p. 6.

216. *Ibid.*

217. Watch Tower, *The Truth that Leads to Eternal Life* and Ranji, "Origins of some Christmas practices".

218. Asif Khan, "Cards: Billion dollar industry," Wednesday Magazine, *Daily Nation*, December 24 1997, p. 2.

Easter

Nowhere is Jesus recorded to have instructed anyone to celebrate his resurrection from the dead. Nor can the term Easter be found in the bible. The holiday was concocted to supplant a number of pre-Christian celebrations and may derive its name from the Anglo-Saxon spring goddess, Eostre[219]. Eggs, a symbol of new life and springtime, are decorated with the sun's rays in imitation of earlier worship of the sun. Chocolate was eventually added to this pagan ritual after the Catholic Europeans under Don Hernando Cortes invaded the Aztec Empire. The Aztecs used cocoa beans to produce a brew called chocolate, and it was used in connection with human sacrifice. Chocolate was specifically used in Easter because Easter involves a human sacrifice — Christ.

Valentine's Day

As a festival celebrating the coming of spring, fertility, and by extension, love and romantic coupling, this festival dating from about AD 496 has nothing to do with Christianity or spiritual or moral teachings of any kind. It originated from the ancient pagan Roman festival of *Lupercalia*, which was similar to older Chaldean rituals. The festival is pagan both in origin and content, and serves principally today to create a market for flowers, cards, restaurants and so on.

Worship Aids

Western Churches in Africa are particularly keen on the use of material objects and worship of images during worship, raising questions of idolatry as well as commercialism. Of course, the images nearly always depict European-looking figures for the holy family, saints, and angels and the devil is black. This adds up to a powerful propaganda message. Worship aids such as rosaries do not originate in early Christianity. As for images, the Old testament says, "You shall not make for yourself a graven image, or any likeness of anything that is in heaven above, or that is in the earth beneath or that is in the water under the earth; you shall not bow down to them or serve them." (Exodus 20:3-5)[220]. All these anti-Christian worship aids are manufactured in Europe. "Christian" books, rosaries, magazines, pamphlets, crucifixes, chains and other parapher-

---

219. Watch Tower, *The Truth that Leads to Eternal Life*.
220. Revised Standard Version, *The Holy Bible*, Collins Bible, Glasgow, 1971.

nalia are imported into Africa; and sites of pilgrimage are all found outside of Africa. This industry provides thousands of jobs to Westerners.

The Attack on African Culture and the Implanting of Western Culture in the Guise of Christianity

During colonialism European missionaries aimed at "civilizing" Africans through the systematic destruction of African culture and its replacement with European culture. Today, foreign-controlled Churches in Africa are in the final stages of demolishing African culture and even using new versions of the bible to justify this[221]. At least, their extreme "modernism" is finally raising questions among parishioners who draw the line at the appointment of homosexuals as pastors and priests[222].

Hence there is nothing Christian in the practice of monogamy or enforced celibacy. The church has also fought against clitoridectomy, which promotes or guarantees chastity, while abortion is promoted as simply another medical procedure. There is nothing un-Christian in polygamy. However, the African family has already lost a battle in its war for survival and the cultural imperialists have destroyed polygamy. Africans always believed the family to be a sacred union between a man and a woman or a man with several women. The European Churches are trying to establish and popularize the notion that a family may be a union between a man and another man, or a woman with a woman, but not one man and more than one woman.

Names are one of the oldest and most fundamental ways of proclaiming identity an affiliation. Yet, European names are routinely given, or adopted, by Africans. Often this is in the mistaken belief that there is such a thing as a "Christian" name; but fashion is a large part of the trend. There are even European-sounding names arising out of recent innovations, so that one may encounter an African named Internet Kituti, or others baptized in honor of European pagan gods such as Diana.

---

221. "Church promoted erotic bible flies in the face of traditionalists," Lifestyle Magazine, *Sunday Nation*, March 17 1996, p. 12. The bible in question is called "Bible for Children" published by Darton, Longman and Todd, respected Catholic publishers. It features scenes of nudity and rape.

222. George Cornell, "US liberal Churches ordaining active gays," *Daily Nation*, May 28 1990, p. 16.

RELIGIOUS FOLLIES

Foreign missionaries working in Kenya have been guilty of all manner of crimes including promoting religious conflict in the country. In September 1986, a container destined for the Associated Christian Churches of East Africa, a US organization, was discovered to contain to rifles, shotguns and military uniforms. This Church had also imported a powerful transmitter and two-way radio and a map. The missionaries claimed the weapons had been brought to fight "vermin and rodents"[223]. One missionary insulted the Muslims, provoking armed conflict between Kenyans of different faiths in 1998[224].

During colonialism, the European missionaries conditioned the oppressed Africans into accepting their place. This was aimed at creating a docile rural labor force. By contrast, in South America throughout the 1970s and 1980s, the local Catholic missionaries and priests and their few Protestant counterparts found themselves identifying with the poor people in their fight against the CIA and US-sponsored oppression. They were condemned as "communists" and were variously sent home, arrested and de-frocked.

Foreign, mainly American, religious organizations have considerable experience of work in Africa. After most African countries attained independence, their activities increased tremendously. They publish books, newsletters, magazines, and newspapers. They have been constructing schools, wells, and hospitals. Their intrusion into this temporal sphere was aimed at forestalling an anti-West social revolution. They also used to use public projects as a method of combating "communist subversion". Paying tribute to the activities of the American Church in Africa, the former ambassador W. Atwood recalled in his book that the missionaries working in Guinea proudly told him that as a result of their sermons, "the people in their area were finally saying nice things about America"[225]. Today in Kenya, all Western-controlled Churches fulfill this public relations role. During a meeting organized by the National Council of Churches at Uhuru Park in mid 1998, the mainstream foreign-controlled Churches "pleaded with the US and Britain to intervene directly" in Kenya and take over the country.

---

223. Kwendo Opanga, "It's a long history of schemes and plots," *Sunday Nation,* October 29 1995, p. 8.

224. *Daily Nation,* July 31 1998.

225. E. A. Tarabrin, *"The New Scramble for Africa,"* Progress Publishers, Moscow 1974.

In summary, the continued existence of religion in its current form is detrimental and harmful to efforts at national psychological rehabilitation. This is because popular contemporary cultural forms in Africa are obstacles to self reliance and the establishment of an internally responsive economic structure, the only type capable of self sustaining growth. To encourage African populations to look inward, systems that cause responsiveness to external forces must be discouraged. In that vein, detrimental religious forms should be constitutionally banned.

When one looks at the phenomenal recovery and growth of countries such as South Korea and Japan, the issue of national psychological disposition assumes great importance. The cultures of these two great manufacturing nations are known to promote a high degree of self sufficiency. This means that the impetus for their growth is internal rather than external. They believe in themselves and their abilities. In the USA, this sense of independence and national self confidence is even more evident. Americans are accused of arrogance and their ignorance of the outside world is legendary. They are very much inward looking and believe that what they have and what they know is the biggest and the best.

On the other hand, Africans believe that what they have is the worst, poorest, weakest, and most hopeless in the world. Therefore, development efforts must first rectify this lack of self confidence. Contemporary religious forms encourage the negative tend. When Africans are persuaded each week in religious services that all heavenly beings are anything but African and when they are made to worship Europeans as God, self hatred and loss of national self confidence is induced. Such "religion" should have no place in Africa.

CHAPTER 11. EDUCATION

Education is a key to industrial development. It is important to have a significant core of educated people but it is even more important to ensure that the education they receive is geared towards economic advancement and not just literacy. Yet, the West has demanded that African governments reduce the amount spent on education as a condition for receiving aid. They have also become, themselves, the provider of education in Africa. Thus it is the West that decides what Africans are taught. Students end up without any industrial skills or patriotic framework and become agents of neocolonialism. Lack of proper education therefore is one of the factors sustaining neocolonialism.

The West controls what African students learn in schools in various ways such as:

- determining the education system
- influencing the language used
- controlling the education content
- providing books used in classrooms and
- directly educating African students

THE EDUCATION SYSTEM

As soon as Kenya became independent, the system of education was changed to become anti-colonial and it was designed to impart to students industrial skills necessary to replace the leaving British. This was partly the reason why the economy grew very fast and Kenya was said by the World Bank to be one of the "NICs", the Newly Industrializing Countries.

The industrial powers then literally ordered African governments to change the education systems. In Kenya, this took the form of the 8-4-4 educational system[226] characterized by maximum rote learning and minimal industrial content. This system is not producing competent school graduates but it succeeds in keeping Africa "down".

In primary schools, children are required to study eleven different subjects, in a language that is alien to them. The secondary school students are also overloaded: over 17 subjects are taught in high school. The knowledge imparted is shallow and artificial, and the examinations are so difficult that many students breakdown. Many have to repeat a grade, and many more drop out before graduating. This system discourages students rather than inspiring them. Secondary school graduates emerge as experts at needle-work, cooking, agriculture using the hoe, and are generally armed with skills useful only in a colonial economy. In addition, this alien education system strips the students their sense of right and wrong.

All neocolonial education systems are designed to frustrate students and prevent them from developing talents which have no room in a colonial economy. Nearly all Kenyan students have a negative attitude to school and the attitude of a student determines his performance. The apathy or sense of defeat is so great that the average mark for examinable subjects has fallen dramatically over the past decade.

Universities, like secondary schools, are modeled on Western institutions. In addition, they discourage research. Apathy to learning and research is one of the causes of economic and technological stagnation. A country cannot develop properly or be a source of innovations if the majority of its literate populace has a distaste for books and learning. The people who should lead in advancement cannot do so when they are not motivated to acquire more knowledge. After World War II, Japan was able to develop rapidly because the people were hard working and acquired new skills and knowledge; that requires education and reading.

In Kenya there are also foreign education systems. There is the Cambridge University International General Certificate Secondary Education, and The

---

226. 8-4-4 refers to the time spent at each level by students, that is, 8 years in primary, 4 in secondary and 4 in university.

British General Certificate of Education, where students are taught nothing about Africa and everything about Europe. This represents classic education colonialism and is a threat to any country.

For an African to gain "acceptable" credentials, he must first do an examination set in the U.K. The course is learnt in Kenya but the exams imported from Europe. This is common and represents the most direct form of intellectual imperialism since foreign States control the education of some of our citizens in their own interest. In fact, there are some schools in Kenya which are inspected by the British Government.

LANGUAGE

The West has managed to make Africa use its languages in spite of all the difficulties that creates. Africans imagine that it is European languages are "better" than African languages and there is a prestige associated with them. When obliged to use Swahili or their mother tongues, the elites do so with an American or British accent.

The use of European languages exacerbates the mental colonization; language is a very efficient vehicle for the most virulent forms of cultural imperialism. When all modern spheres of life are monopolized by European languages, modernity becomes confused with the European languages and African tongues become "backward". This creates a racial and cultural inferiority complex in Africans. These complexes are reinforced by the alien economy, because the use of a European tongue in the education system results in the entire economy using that foreign tongue. Africans who are fluent in that language automatically qualify for prestigious jobs and are guaranteed upward social mobility. The European language becomes valuable in opening employment opportunities and African languages become worthless, since their knowledge, in the neocolonial economy, brings neither profit nor prestige.

Today, Africans are socially defined by their knowledge or ignorance of European rather than African tongues. This is part of the reason why the use of European languages is widespread throughout the continent. African countries have found it impossible to eliminate the use of foreign languages. What's more, the alien language helps the elite maintain its exclusive preserve. Furthermore, the extreme poverty of the region makes it impossible to introduce new programs to effect the shift from alien to African languages. And besides, Western countries promote the use of their languages.

Even language training becomes a business, in which Africans are persuaded to pay Westerners to extend their cultural influence. A Minister for Defense in the Royal Navy of Britain once said that, "In the battle for international influence, we shall at last be fully deploying our most powerful weapon — the English language. [Africa's] demand for...English will be insatiable and will provide Britain with a superb opportunity to sell books, newspapers, magazines, TV programs to these African countries"[227].

There are various reasons why the West strongly campaigns for the use of their tongues in Africa:

- to secure lasting influence and a sense of prestige in Africa
- to increase their power globally
- to strengthen and sustain neocolonialism
- to make money, and
- to spread cultural imperialism

A person is tied to the country whose language he speaks, for as long as he speaks their language. For example, it has become fashionable for many people to speak the Jamaican Creole. Those who do so become bound to Jamaica. They have an increased desire to get to know the country, its flag, its history and over time, their political allegiance shifts in favor of Jamaica. The neocolonial powers spread their languages in Africa to provide a positive connection or sense of allegiance between the colonizers and the colonized. This has been very successful and most Africans regard the West with friendship.

Today Kenya is tied to Britain while Senegal is tied to France. The only African country outside of European-headed international groupings is Ethiopia, although English is fast making inroads. The more a country uses a foreign language, the more it weakens. The use of a language native to a particular country is an important component of national pride, which is necessary in obtaining and maintaining sovereignty.

The use of foreign languages enhances the prestige and power of the "parent" country. The fact that Africa mainly uses English and French inflates the importance of the UK and France. It is through the Commonwealth and Francophone Summit that Britain and France keep a strong international profile. Germany is trying to have German introduced as a subject of study in Africa.

---

227. Tarabrin, *The New Scramble for Africa*.

Using European languages also sustains neocolonialism by perpetuating ignorance and illiteracy. Ignorance is their mainstay because ignorant people are easily convinced by fake economic theories. Although less than 30% of Kenya is literate in English, 90% of the books, newspapers, and magazines published in Kenya are issued in English. Thus, large segments of the population are denied access to knowledge. No wonder most people have little idea how the economy functions and malfunctions.

As a result of ignorance concerning the wider world, the people think their own lives are divorced from the wider reality. When they lack money for school or hospital fees, they accept their fate. They do not know that in Cuba, anti-colonialism has resulted in free healthcare and education.

Through the use of its languages, the West is able to control the political, economic, intellectual and cultural development of African countries. This is mainly achieved through the dissemination of pro-neocolonial stories through books, magazines, and imported movies, made possible by the shared language.

By using foreign languages, Africa is kept divided both between and within nations. The mere fact Africans from the four corners of the continent cannot communicate independently without translators makes it impossible that progressive African leadership could unite the continent. A more unified Africa would be a stronger Africa, and the West would lose influence. The West has an interest in encouraging and perpetuating the factors that divide Africans, and language is very effective for this purpose.

Within African countries, foreign languages have become mechanisms of social stratification. This adds to the divisions within these countries and aggravates the political instability and self hatred. Indigenous languages are despised. While those who speak alien languages fluently may enter the professional sector, those who speak African tongues fluently are denied access to any position with the potential for upward social mobility. African-language users are the poverty stricken. This fact is turned inside out so that African languages are associated with poverty and suffering while European languages are linked to privileged positions, wealth and comfort. European lifestyle and language are an index of social prestige. In secondary school, students are berated for speaking African languages and girls prefer boys who speak English exclusively. The preference becomes internalized.

The West accrues great monetary profit through the importation of books, magazines, movies, TV programs, and music made possible by the use of European languages. The book trade is so lucrative that the British formed the

English Language Book Scheme (ELBS) which sells millions of books to colleges and universities in Africa. Because these books are imported from Britain, British writers and publishers get the profits. Within Africa, publishing has long been dominated by Western firms. These firms also import books. This complete colonization of publishing in Africa is part of intellectual imperialism and information colonialism and is a large factor in the political underdevelopment of Africa. These foreign firms make it impossible for African publishers to grow; and they block political advancement by publishing and importing books which support neocolonialism. Books written by Africans are rarely promoted in the West but Western books are actively promoted in Africa.

Finally, the West campaigns for Africans to use Western languages because they are the best vehicles for cultural imperialism. Language reflects the culture of its native speakers. For example, in African societies, the reproductive organs were held sacred and notions such as "rape" did not exist. In English, there are whole vocabularies of words describing sexual debauchery and all manner of violence and death, like batter, hit, bludgeon, club, assault, smash, genocide, homicide, infanticide, regicide, pogrom, massacre, murder, assassinate, annihilate, holocaust, slaughter, and so on. When these languages are used by a different society, these concepts become known and their practice begins because a transfer of that language's culture also occurs. In addition, foreign languages open a wide avenue for other forms of cultural imperialism, especially through the mass media.

EDUCATION CONTENT

The West determines what African students learn in schools by controlling what is taught. In pre-unit and nursery school, children are taught European myths such as Cinderella and fairy godmothers. The imported pictorial books used in this propaganda have horrible effects. When these children are bombarded with pictures of blue-eyed, blond-haired fairies and other cartoon characters they react by hating their dark hair, black eyes and brown skin. Self hate in children is worse than in adults. The children of Africa are led to identify with and love the West and to hate themselves and Africa. The education in Africa is so pro-West that a children's chant that, in the US, featured the paradigmatically capitalist Macy's department store, substituted the bastion of communism, "Moscow," and was taught to nursery school children. The irony would be amusing, if only children were not so susceptible to even such bizarre propaganda.

> I won't go to Moscow
> anymore, more, more.
> There's a big bad policeman
> at the door, door, door.
> He'll take you by the collar
> And he'll make you pay a dollar
> So I won't go to Moscow
> anymore, more, more...

In primary school, pupils are encouraged to read Western novels and cartoon books. They have one common trait: they all teach disrespect to parents, elders and especially teachers. With time, the alienation of the pupils is accomplished and the sustained bombardment with images from the West creates a strong unreasonable desire to "escape" from Africa.

In secondary school, students are taught everything about the West. They are taught that Europeans invented the steam engine and weaving machines, and that their genius led to industrialization. In contrast, Africans are portrayed as misguided primitives who fought against the colonialists and resisted the technological advancements brought in by the generosity of the Europeans. The Euro-centric view extends to coverage of the Second World War, which had little direct impact on the world as seen from Africa, and topics like the Roman conquest of "the known world". Even in biology the norms are European, so that the Caucasian is the model human being and all other races are measured by that standard.

At the university level, the alienation is completed. The history of Greece, Rome, and medieval Europe forms the bulk of humanities studies. Universities in Kenya ignore non-colonial and pre-colonial African history, literature or philosophy. Any graduate can quote Virgil or give the birthday of Aristotle. But he cannot say who Mansa Musa was, much less when he became ruler. The state of extreme poverty in Africa is barely addressed. There is minimal explanation of events and nothing is put in its proper historical context. Take the example of the Congo Crisis of the 1960s. According to the KIE Form 3 History textbook, Mobutu is to be "commended because...the economy of [Zaire] improved. [In 1989] the country is stable and the economy has improved through....the support...by...the United States". The fact that the US (with UN help) assassinated Lumumba as well as several thousand Africans is omitted.

Books on science begin with a lengthy tribute to European scientists. For example, before studying gravity, the students are told that it was Isaac Newton who "discovered" gravity. The students are also asked to remember his country of origin, village and even date of birth. In history, the damage and misinformation is worse.

The education content attempts to explain the Caucasian world's developed state as a result of their efforts only. In Form 2 history, a common question is: What made the USA become an industrialized power? The answers include: (1) hardworking population, (2) entrepreneurs like Henry Ford. If development were the result of hard work, then the African slaves should be the richest group on earth. In Kenyan history, no mention is made of the capture and enslavement of individuals and whole families who were kidnapped and set to work in harsh conditions to develop America and feed the British economy, or the role that the slave trade played in the primary accumulation of capital, which was invested to bring about industrialization. European activities in Africa are discussed from an extremely biased perspective, so that Stanley, for instance, is described as a brave explorer who did not fear hostile tribes. That he gratuitously abused Africans is not mentioned. African native culture and social structure are ignored. Europe uses numerals invented by the Arabs, medicine invented in Egypt, rockets, gunpowder and paper invented in China — but none of this communicated to students. In addition, exercise book covers have portraits of European "great men of science" exclusively, with exhortations to the effect that the world would not be as we know it were it not for them. This leaves the students with the impression that no person of African descent has ever come up with any useful invention.

Kenyan schools also lack industrial education. In primary and secondary level, students are taught how to cook, wash clothes, construct walls and farm using the hoe, so that they can fill in the lowest level of the alien economy.

When the neocolonial powers educate the elite of African countries, they forge a strong bond with future African rulers. Most of those African rulers who collaborated with the West to destroy other African countries and support Apartheid had a history of being educated in the West. These include Jomo Kenyatta — who resided in Britain for 15 years, Mobutu — who had studied in Belgium, Kamuzu Banda — who had studied in Europe, "Leopold" Sedar Senghor — who studied, taught and lived in France, and Houphouet Boigny.

Today, the younger generation is the target for much of the campaign to shape public attitudes. Over half the Africans trained with the West's help are government officials and workers in ideological sectors like teaching and trade unions. Efforts are also concentrated on training army and police officers.

When African students are exposed to Western concepts, culture, literature, history, and the religious value system they are alienated from their own culture. They are left with confused morals and none of the skills that are necessary if industrialization is to occur.

Up to 15 percent of all students in primary schools in Kenya in 1993 were repeaters[228]; they are mostly from the rural areas, the areas where the chasm is greatest between reality at home and at school. Rural people are least exposed to cultural imperialism, and therefore they are unable to express themselves or develop their talents in the alien educational environment. Questions, examples, illustrations, content and the context of the education are all derived from the West or the Europeanized upper classes, an environment that is totally alien to them. Since 80% of the population lives in rural areas, this is extremely retarding to the social development and effective utilization of Kenya's human resources.

There are two fundamental differences between pre-colonial African education and neocolonial education. African education was relevant to the local environment and ultimately aimed to prepare the youth for their responsibilities adults; neocolonial education does not.

Books

The West determines what African students learn in school by controlling the books used from pre-unit to university. These books are either imported or authored by foreigners living in Africa. One way in which books are imported is through aid. In fact, the World Bank started a Volunteer Services Book Project, and on November 4, 1998, it donated over 20,000 books to 157 Kenyan schools[229].

The West also controls the writing and publishing of books within Africa. Many publishing firms are European owned. The European control of African property is fully supported by these publishing firms. In Kenya, most textbooks are written and published by the Kenya Institute of Education (KIE). The history of Africa as taught is the European history in Africa. KIE books describe the Dutch invasion of South Africa in pro-Dutch terms, praising the hardy Dutch

---

228. Mathiu, "Salary crisis: Is money the solution?"
229. *Daily Nation*, November 5 1998, p. 2.

settlers and saying not a word about the entire villages of Africans that they obliterated.

By authoring and providing textbooks, the West benefits commercially as well. Foreign books make a profit and also keep locally-written books from entering the market. "Aid" programs for books are designed to assist Western publishers to entrench themselves in Africa by giving buyers a distorted perception of the real cost of books, because the imported books are subsidized. This severely retards the local publishing industry.

The foreign books trivialize apartheid and promote historical amnesia. Even those books authored by Africans support colonialism. Chinua Achebe's *Things Fall Apart*[230] aims to show the futility of opposing colonialism, which is presented as natural and inescapable. In *Mine Boy* by Peter Abrahams, Xuma's suffering is not presented as the result of colonialism; rather, apartheid is credited with providing Africans with employment[231].

This kind of cultural imperialism is also common in secondary schools. Hence, the gap between curriculum and real life experience is very wide. To illustrate how confusing and wasteful such irrelevant education has become, imagine students reading an English-language version of Nikolai Gogol's *Government Inspector*[232] and encountering the term "lily white neck". After a protracted debate on what it could possibly mean, the students elected to consult their teacher. The teacher conceded that "white" meant a color but had no idea what "lily" was. They all went to ask the headmaster, who told them that a "lily" was a flower but did not understand what a flower had to do with a neck. And a new debate began on what the connection between flowers and necks is.

Neocolonial education in Africa is an avenue for leaving African culture behind.

EDUCATING AFRICAN STUDENTS DIRECTLY

The final way in which the West determines what African students learn in schools is by directly educating these students either in the West or in Africa.

---

230. Chinua Achebe, *Things Fall Apart*, Heinnemann Educational Books, 1962.

231. Peter Abrahams, *Mine Boy*, Heinnemann Educational Books, 1946.

232. Nikolai Gogol, *Government Inspector*, East African Educational Publishers, Translated by D. J. Campbell.

This is achieved by sending African students abroad through scholarships and other enticements.

Industrial countries sponsor the brightest students from Africa to study so that they become acculturated, and on returning home they act as agents of neo-colonialism. Their Westernized ways have a cumulative influence on the national life of their countries. Most are sponsored to study art subjects. Scholarships are never given to African students to go study in another African country. These programs do not help Africans develop their local talent; rather, they encourage the most gifted people — the very people who could help Africa develop — to emigrate. There is a constant stream of Africans into Western Universities, "a stream which must be preserved, whatever its marginal cost on the overstrained economies of British education", according to highly placed British government officials[233].

"Britain's major universities are still international centers of learning and if they do not remain such, the loss of this position will be as much disaster in the long run to Britain as a naval defeat would have been in the days when sea power was the dominant force in history"[234]. The British government has stepped up their efforts to bring in African students, as many Africans now seek to go to America instead. Other Western countries are also trying their hands. Enrollment in British institutions is falling as a result of the shrinking (and ageing) of the local populations; immigration is a partial answer to that, as well as other, challenges.

In the late 1970s and early 80s, African economies were growing rapidly and many employment opportunities were available. Few students were going abroad. When the economies were destroyed, African students were enticed to go abroad. The damage caused by the SAPs and the intensification of cultural imperialism made it easy. Currently, 80% of all students who enroll in Std 1 do not make it to university or other higher institutions of learning[235]. The majority of secondary school graduates are denied further education despite the fact that many actually pass in exams. When the West places newspaper notices such as the following encouraging the students to seek admission in foreign universities, the result is clear.

---

233. E. A. Tarabrin, (ed) *Neocolonialism and Africa in the 1970s*, Moscow, 1974.
234. *Ibid.*
235. Mathiu, "Salary crisis: Is money the solution?"

They have also opened their own schools in Africa and bring in teachers who take jobs that Africans could have filled. The main feature of aid to Kenya in the late 1960s and early 70s was extending the education system. The US has helped build youth clubs, schools and universities. After flag independence, the Americans constructed 17 schools, 6 colleges, 19 agricultural study centers, a medical school and an administrative institute[236].

In 1968, a faculty of engineering in the University of Nairobi was also opened[237]. These actions may seem benevolent but the underlying motive was political gain. Apart from the goodwill such projects generate, the Americans also take a controlling position on the syllabus. This eventually weakens the university. While the University of Dar-es-Salaam became a hub of African and development studies, the Nairobi University faded away and became insignificant. Kenya's education system has been taken over by foreigners. In fact, there is actually a United States International University and an American University Preparation Center in Kenya. Because of this re-colonization of the education system, scholars today enthusiastically subscribe to notions like encouraging foreign investor confidence and trade liberalization as the way to industrialization.

The schools controlled by foreigners are by their very names agents of neo-colonialism. Most high cost, upper class schools have European names such as Braeburn, Allen Grove, Brookhouse, and Strathmore, while low class schools have distinctly African names. This naming pattern perpetuates a racial inferiority complex in Africans.

Lastly, the West controls what African students learn by sending in teachers, sometimes in the guise of missionaries or volunteers. These teachers propagate cultural imperialism by the mere fact that they are foreigners. In 1969, USAID provided 166 primary and secondary school teachers and training college lecturers for work in Kenya, while in West Africa, the French government has sent teaching staff on a massive scale. In 1968, there were about 28,000[238] French teachers there.

In many Western-funded schools, the entire teaching staffs are European. The African governments purchase teaching materials and equipment from the

---

236. E. A. Tarabrin, (ed) *Neocolonialism and Africa in the 1970s.*
237. *Ibid.*
238. Tarabrin, (ed) *Neocolonialism and Africa in the 1970s.*

donor countries and lose the right to control cost, quality and content; meanwhile, the teachers take away jobs from educated locals.

In the early 1980s in Kenya, when the IMF imposed the SAPs, all university lecturers thought to oppose the SAPs were either sacked, driven into exile or detained[239]. No one openly informed ordinary Kenyans of the likely effects of the programs. Twenty years later, the majority of the scholars and economists have had a biased education and so they have no objective perspective from which to assess events in Kenya.

In colonial situations, the economy requires relatively few educated recruits. Where too many received an education, that colony usually faced political turmoil. The three best examples are Ghana, Kenya and Algeria. In these three instances, the colonized people managed to open up their own schools. In Kenya, the Kikuyu Karinga Educational Association and Kikuyu Independent Schools Association ran many schools in Central province. In Algeria, there was the reformist Ulema. The "excess" school leavers who were unable to find positions in the colonial economy became agitators for independence as early as 1945. In Algeria war broke out, as well as in Kenya. Ghana became the first African country to attain independence.

Something similar is happening today. The West pressured African governments to cut spending on education to avoid a repeat scenario. The international establishment fears that too many Africans will receive an advanced education and refuse to work in lower capacities. This would allow for the rise of Africa as a world power and threaten the West's dominant position. Today, illiteracy in most African countries is at more than 60%. The few skilled Africans work for Western companies and any "excess" are constantly enticed to migrate to the West.

CONSEQUENCES OF NEOCOLONIAL EDUCATION

Colonial education is one which is controlled externally, for the benefit of foreigners and not the nation or the educated. The West strengthens its hegemony over Africa through education, which is a powerful tool for brainwashing. The consequences of re-colonization of education are obvious.

Through cultural imperialism it alienates pupils and students.

---

239. Ochwada, "Why African scholars do not respond to the continent's woes."

Those who return from abroad are more dangerous and subversive than those who stayed home. The Kenyan education destroys logic and reason. Students come out believing that Kenya would have been more developed if it had been colonized for a longer period, and by the Americans. But, a country such as Mozambique, which had been colonized for several hundred years, is far poorer than Kenya. The harmful effects of colonialism are never mentioned. Poverty is presented to students as a fact of life.

Neocolonialism is most effective when it assimilates the elite of an African nation into the West[240]. By taking control of the education system, the West accelerates and strengthens this trend. Any potential for locally developing architects, engineers, or leaders in any field is vitiated.

Industrial or technical skills are generally not taught, and the development of critical judgment, creative adaptable thinking and capacity for sustained argument are discouraged[15]. Industrial and technical courses are excluded from the curriculum and the few institutions offering them are directly controlled by foreign countries (e.g., Jomo Kenyatta University of Agriculture and Technology) or are tied to the overall neocolonial economy and are meant to strengthen it. By controlling the education system and institutions, the West also controls the economy.

The alien education system has also been a contributing factor in the creation of a national culture that disdains books and the process of learning. This hampers innovation and economic development. This apathy to learning is mainly the result of the over-emphasis on exams. The entire system is geared to prepare students for examinations. Students are not taught with the aim of acquiring knowledge. This approach dulls and confuses students' memories, leading to historical amnesia[241].

Furthermore, the education creates an illusory bond with Europe, rather than establishing or recognizing natural links with neighboring peoples. Africans do not see themselves as "Africans". When a war is provoked in Angola, they do not realize that Africans are dying, not "Angolans." And they continue to respect Caucasians.

---

240. Harrison, *Inside the Third World*, p. 323.
241. P. G. Altbach and G. P. Kelly (eds), *Education and Colonialism*, Longman, New York, 1978. This excellent work has been used extensively in this chapter.

Possible Reforms

It would be politically and economically advantageous for Africa to regain control of the education sector. All foreign books, teachers, school education systems should be phased out and replaced by African products and teachers. The education content should be centered on Africa and the history needs to be rewritten. Linguistic purity should be enforced, especially in the media. Proverbs and songs reflecting and conserving African heritage can be integrated in lessons. The requirements for university admission could be changed to de-emphasize the learning of multiple European languages. Competence in at least two regional African languages should be rewarded.

Such ideas, however, will not be implemented in the foreseeable future. The West has all the cards in its hands, so pro-African ideas are unacceptable. Furthermore, most African governments do not recognize the extent to which this type of education contributes to economic stagnation, and where they do, the cost of dismantling the education system is too high. Even the vocabulary of African languages will need to be updated to include terms that can be used in science.

Chapter 12. Cultural Imperialism

Cultural imperialism mainly involves the transfer and establishment of Western culture into Africa. Its effect is to alienate Africans from themselves, so that they become confused in their allegiances and worldviews. The descendants of African slaves and other immigrants in the West are the most alienated Africans anywhere on the globe. Racism against them is well known but this has not stopped them from being acculturated. This has created ironical situations time and again. For example, they eagerly enlisted in the US army to kill the Vietnamese and "defend democracy", while back home they were discriminated against. Muhammad Ali, the champion boxer, was jailed for refusing to partake in the war because, as he said, "The Vietnamese never called me nigger."

The immediate direct benefit accrued by cultural imperialists is economic gain. Africans form a guaranteed market for products originating from the West. A magazine from the UK will have more sales in Kenya than one from, say, Tanzania.

The best way to destroy a society is to destroy the moral and ethical standards[242]. This is currently being achieved in Kenya. Before long, Africa shall become like the USA, where there appears to be increased violence because the saturation of pornography and graphic violence, disseminated even through video games, has been more complete.

Cultural exploitation and imperialism has saturated the information and entertainment industries, affecting everything from the way houses are con-

---

242. Prof. Eysenck, *Psychology is About People*, Allen Lane, 1972.

structed to the language employed by computers. When Africans become cul-turally alienated from themselves, they imagine that they are superior to other Africans who are less Westernized.

TELEVISION AS A CONDUIT OF CULTURAL IMPERIALISM

Since its introduction into Kenya in 1962, television has been taken over by various foreigners. Virtually nothing African is ever aired except for news, half of which is not African. In the pre-liberalization era, some African programs were shown but these days programs produced by Africans are un- and anti-African, both in content and context. They emulate the low-level Western staples except that the characters happen to be Africans. Imported programs portray loose living and rebellion against parental authority. Since young people tend to emulate what they see on TV, it is not surprising that 111 Africans between the ages of 15–35 are infected by HIV daily.

A study of TV programs aired in Kenya revealed some interesting things:

- Out of 1302 weekly television hours, as of mid 2004, only 5 hours, a mere 0.8%, are allocated to programs positively African. The remaining 99.2% continuously promote the loss of values and provide bad examples. In Kenya today, teenage pregnancies have increased by as much as 70%, as compared to two decades ago when the West did not control the media and many people did not own television sets. Reported rapes have increased by more than 1300 percent! Child rape has emerged as a new phenomenon.

- In KBC TV, out of 126 weekly hours, less than 20 are devoted to African content and of these, only 5 hours are positively African. On national holidays, a few extra hours are allocated to Africans. Thus, 116 hours per week are entirely devoted to Western music and mindless fantasies. The Swahili news has not been spared from dilution and distortion. Two KBC announcers present the Swahili news with an American accent.

- DSTV (M-NET), like all foreign-owned channels, has no time for Africa and Africans. It is not available to most Africans since it costs an initial sum which is about 20 months' wages for an ordinary worker, plus a monthly subscription fee.

The foreign television programs are just as habit-forming in Africa as else-where, even if the stories seem even more preposterous when viewed from afar. Long-running soap operas form a guaranteed future market; very little news or programs with constructive information are aired. Hence, very few Kenyans know anything about Kenya beyond the poverty they see around them. Rather, imported programs serve to instill an abnormal curiosity about the West, rather than in their own countries.

Imported shows also prevent Africans from developing their own actors and soaps. Imported programs do not employ creative writers, expand the local talent base, or employ local artists or performers.

Radio as a Conduit for Cultural Imperialism

The only difference between radio and TV is the fact that there are radio services produced and run by Africans, in African languages, and having total African content. The majority of average, that is, poor Africans prefer African to foreign radio stations, and thus they are insulated from some of the negative Western influences. Still, the West has moved into Africa and opened a whole array of radio stations aimed at the youth. BBC "World" Service is beamed in; among its programs is "Britain Today," which treats Africans sitting with transistor radios in mud huts to stories about the tribulations of the British royalty. Voice of America (VOA) seeks to legitimize the notion of colonization by America. The Germans, not to be left behind, offer Deutsche Welle, while France has Radio France Internationale (RFI). No African country beams any African programs even to any other African country, making a mockery of Union des Radiodiffusions et Televisions Nationales d'Afrique. The TV and radio stations in Africa are extensions of European and American stations in everything but name.

The lifestyles of Western musicians are very well known; so are the values that are promoted by music videos shown on TV. While of course it is not considered mentionable, it is also well known that many of these musicians are prostitutes, sodomites, perverts, drug addicts, and devil worshippers. Their assault on civilization in African is felt as surely as it is in their home countries.

The Cinema as a Conduit for Cultural Imperialism

In Kenya, European and American movies are readily accessible. Even those in remote areas are brought movies in open air venues known as *watoto kaeni chini*. The political consequences of a steady diet of foreign movies are subversive to any government. Most movies are produced with the tacit approval of the CIA, MI6 and other foreign intelligence agencies. American (or British, or French) enemies are routinely demonized. Africans watching the movie therefore become biased and are made to support the country that produced the movie, usually the Americans. They are influenced to hate the USA's enemies (most of whom are oppressed and exploited people who have the courage to resist colonialism).

In order to justify the exploitation and genocide that accompanied the colonization of North America, Hollywood created the myth of the "Wild West", in which the original inhabitants are demonized and depicted as bloodthirsty savages. For the African who has no other source of history, this produces a very peculiar distortion of perspective. By the same token, films produced during the 1950s US invasion and occupation of the Korean peninsula demonized the Koreans and Chinese who fought against the US. In an information vacuum, such films serve as far more than entertainment.

In a movie called "Independence Day", we are shown the Americans (the Caucasian ones) in conjunction with the Russians, Japanese and Europeans together defeating aliens from outer space, led by the gallant American president. Africans only come into the picture as half-naked savages emerging from the bush in grass skirts, armed with spears and clubs, celebrating the Western victory over the aliens.

Of late, Arabs and Muslims have been targeted as the Americans' enemies. In movies such as "Executive Decision," Muslims and Arabs are depicted as terrorists — thus denying the legitimacy of national defense. This movie depicts wild-eyed, panicky, fanatical Arabs, cool and calculating US heroes who spray bullets, and one Afro-American — who is critically injured as soon as the film starts.

In 1839, African slaves aboard a slave ship called *Le Amistad* revolted and attempted to sail back to Africa — to freedom. They were captured by the US Navy, which sold them back into slavery. The movie "Le Amistad" is based upon this historical fact. When its production was completed, it was blasted by film critics as propaganda[243]. Pro-African sentiments in the US usually invite strong attack.

It must not be forgotten that movies are primarily produced to make profit. In this respect, films are a tremendous success. The attendance of

---

243. "Spielberg's 'propaganda' film annoys critics", Lifestyle Magazine, *Sunday Nation*, January 4 1998.

Kenyans to watch the top ten films imported and screened in 1997 at the main foreign-owned cinema halls was 212,228 people. They spent a total of 42,445,600 Kshs ($707,427)[244]. This pattern continues today. The money wasted by Kenyans on imported movies and videos would be more than enough to eliminate malaria.

People, especially young people, imitate the lifestyles of actors and actresses, often with disastrous results. Gangsta-rap is decried even by Americans; but that rap music and its performers are extremely popular among youth in Kenya.

Reggae music was originally intended to promote and propagate Rastafarian philosophy. The pioneer bands and musicians had a deep attachment to Africa. For example, the group *Burning Spear* was formed in 1969 and named after the honorary title linked with the then Kenyan head of state, Jomo Kenyatta. *Black Uhuru*, formed in 1974, refers to a free Africa under African rule. Western governments became alarmed at this movement which was uniting Africans of Africa and the diaspora, both culturally and politically. They hijacked the trend, and the result is "Ragga muffin," a distortion of Reggae. This music peddles the underside of Western culture. In the original *Wailer* band, the back up female singers appeared on stage in flowing robes and headdress; they were stout in the true African way. When the raggamuffin singer Shabba Ranks staged a "family" show in Kenya, people were shocked at the thin and undressed "dancing girls".

Reggae music is as old as the history of Africans suffering in the Caribbean. But, as a result of the Americanization of this music to form raggamuffin, drugs are openly idolized. The singer called Bob Marley promoted the use of marijuana and among the African fans of raggamuffin, the use of marijuana is now standard.

Other types of music such as pop, rhythm & blues and others are not only un-African, they are anti-African. Michael Jackson, a descendant of Africans who were enslaved, seems to have decided that he would rather be Caucasian. He mutilated his hair, bleached his skin and deformed his nose and lips. Naturally, this example of self hate was picked up by his fans, and examples of this self-mutilation and self-destruction have proliferated. What happens when they imitate the rest of his lifestyle?

---

244. John Kariuki, "Field day for blockbuster films", Lifestyle Magazine, *Sunday Nation*, January 11 1998, pp. 10-11. This estimate has been arrived at by multiplying the attendance numbers and average cost of a ticket and other sales of videos. It is by no means definitive.

To increase their hold on African minds, Western governments have formed cultural centers linked to their embassies abroad. In Nairobi, the French center is always busy. It sponsors French language classes, plays, poems and films. Shocked by the American success in Kenya, the French changed the name from "French Cultural Center" to "French Cultural and Co-operation Center", and its director Guy Trezelix says the reason was to "widen its repertoire of activities to include cultural exchanges in music, drama and others. We intend to cultivate more genuine co-operation with Kenyan artistes and cultural institutions". He neglected to mention that Kenyans have no culture to speak of, in France's view; they can only absorb the French culture. It is a one-way "exchange".

The Germans have their own approach. They were deprived of their colonies after the First World War and are still eager to keep a hand in the game. The embassy of the Federal Republic of Germany looks after both economic exploitation and cultural imperialism. They bring in chamber music ensembles to promote the alien music of Mozart, Handel, and others. The Goethe Institute offers instruction in the German language, at a very steep fee; and it has given money to Nyeri schools to promote the German language. These activities are beyond the reach of ordinary Kenyans and are specifically aimed at the well-to-do — that is, at the sector that is expected to inherit the country's leadership. The high fees also prevent the formation of mobs of poor German-speaking Africans who might well seek to migrate to Germany. It is an investment designed to produce Africans who like Germans and who, once in power, will pursue policies favorable to Germany. Never mind the expansion of neo-Nazi groups in Germany who have been known to kill Africans.

Americans are less vigorous in pursuing that type of cultural exchange, since their culture has already taken root in the most affluent parts of Kenya. Poverty is the main obstacle that prevents the entire continent from being totally culturally alienated. Nevertheless, the US Information Service has imported some Euro-Americans in what they term the "Denver–Nairobi Artistic Exchange". It was never made clear what was being exchanged with this "Cleo Parker Robinson Dance Ensemble". The "Pamoja performance" was a wholly Euro-American cultural package in which Africans were not allowed to contribute anything African except, perhaps, their bodies[245]. For a full day's wages, an African worker could attend the show and get his bit of indoctrination.

---

245. *Sunday Nation*, January 14 1996.

The importation of video games has opened a new avenue for cultural imperialism. The games are often very Western both in content and context. One American described these made games as "spine ripping, flesh chilling, head clawing fun"[246]. Sadistic, violent games distort the children's sense of acceptable behavior and incite them to crime, and they, too, are addictive. One game aficionado explained that the effect of playing was so bad that he would imagine that his hand was a gun and point it at people[247].

Fashion and the promotion of a Western notion of beauty present another major avenue for cultural imperialism. Even in Western countries, it is well known that fashion has more to do with increasing seasonal spending than with making people look good. Fashion shows and beauty pageants are essentially anti-African. The models look undernourished — hardly an aesthetic ideal where food shortages are common — and are required to be practically nude[248]. The recent M-NET "Face of Africa" is not an African face at all; it is more the "Caucasian face of Africa". One model, who bore some resemblance to African norms of beauty, was disqualified because she was not thin. The contest was won by a girl who looked more Caucasian than African; Chief Judge Massimo Redaelli, a Caucasian, claimed that she met "international" requirements. The Sudanese model Alek Wek has become an outstanding success in the West, but this is not because Europeans have suddenly started loving Africans; rather, she exudes mystery to Europeans, who stare at her as one would stare at wild animals in a jungle.

Beauty is a complex issue, and its concept has been influenced by different cultures at different places and times. In the purest African traditions, dimples, the rolling gait and a gap in the teeth were considered beautiful. In some African communities women with shaven heads were admired, while long-haired men were handsome. Beauty in Africa was also seen in behavior such as kindness, generosity, compassion and patience. For Europeans, the physical traits were and still are more important.

Foreign companies have succeeded in creating a large market for a wide range of beauty products, products which mostly come from Europe and North America. This providing Westerners with jobs that are desperately needed in

246. "Should I play video games," *Awake!*, August 22 1996, p. 12.
247. "Should I play video games," *Awake!* p. 14.
248. Lifestyle Magazine, *Sunday Nation*, March 29 1998, p. 3.

Africa, and brings them profits and political advantage through the entrenchment of their culture in Africa.

A relatively new avenue for cultural imperialism has been developed. Smirnoff has been coming to Kenya to "advise" African designers on making clothes that depict the Western culture, based on themes provided by the cultural imperialists. In 1997, the theme was "decadence"[249] — presumably, to promote drinking as well as "fashion." Like college scholarships, this award encourages Africans to strive to emulate Westerners; "it gives them an enviable platform from which they can make a name for themselves if they are creative enough and can interpret the theme correctly,"[250] that is, with sufficient vulgarity.

THE FAMILY

At the heart of every society is the family, and even in different cultures, the structure of the family is essentially the same. The roles of the family members are also similar. But the main difference between Western and African families is the emphasis made on extended family relations. Where as Africans value strong extended family bonds, modern Westerners by and large focus on the immediate family members only. Demographic and economic factors did not create any advantage for polyandry, so both types of society shunned matriarchal formations.

In Africa, the extended family plays various roles such as providing dowry, assisting in times of crisis, maintaining discipline among all children, burying and honoring the dead, dividing and taking responsibility for a dead man's children and property. Polygamy was found, in some societies, to be helpful as a way of preventing male promiscuity and female helplessness. Wife inheritance was also practiced, so that a dead man's family would be protected from destitution (in which case, at best, the wife would be forced into prostituting to provide for the children). The African family was a self-sustaining, self-regulating unit. Africans married early, immediately after initiation. This headed off promiscuity and prevented unwanted pregnancies; bastards and street children were almost unheard of. Families had many children and were less likely to spoil,

---

249. Njoki Karuoya, and wa Gacheru, "Is this high fashion or wild creation", Lifestyle Magazine, *Sunday Nation*, March 29 1998, p. 2.
250. *Ibid.*

or even worship, their offspring as many people do now, in the West. (In the USA, a mother who disciplined her unruly nine-year-old son by slapping him was arrested and jailed on a charge of cruelty to children. Her husband had to pay the equivalent of Kshs 1,323,000 ($22,000) to secure her release[251].)

The family size in Africa is limited by economic constraints; otherwise, large families are considered better and polygamy would be encouraged. The attack on the African family has been accomplished through various means. Billboards, especially in rural areas, depict two different families — the European type, surreally happy, wealthy, with beautiful children, and the African type. The African family is always shown to be sorrowful, dirty, poor, — unplanned. Housing constructed in cities of Africa is designed along the European model to discourage African-type families by tightly limiting space and other facilities.

Relations within the Western family seem indulgent and counter-productive to Africans; many Western couples are quite open and sexual in front of their children, while modesty is still valued in the "dark continent." And then, the Western practice of marrying later in life is avoided in Africa; indeed, children born to older women are known to face medical disadvantages.

New family formats are being introduced, and it is doubtful they will strengthen the social fabric. Single-parent families used to be acceptable only if one parent died. Acceptance of promiscuity has given acceptance to the unwed mother phenomenon, and since Western ideas have become widely accepted in Africa, the rate of divorce is very high.

Mentally colonized Africans now base their marriages on the flimsy grounds of "love" and, at that, most often on the deliberate confusion of mature love with infatuation and carnal love. Traditional societies knew that practical, tangible reasons provided a stronger base.

The UN-sponsored 1992 Cairo Conference supported the promulgation of Western "values" throughout Africa. It was a maneuver by which Westerners seek to impose their culture and moral decay on Africans. Its conclusions covered many areas.

1. Family: The Westerners dictate that two homosexuals or lesbians can come together and form a legally accepted family. They can even adopt children[252].

---

251. *Daily Nation*, July 2004.
252. "The UN assaults life and family", *The Family*, August-December 1997.

2. Adolescent health and responsible sexual behavior: According to this document, "the child is adolescent from 10 years of age" and is to be allowed to indulge in "safe" sex without any hindrance with males, females and animals. In this document, sexuality is considered only in its physical aspects, with no moral or psychological consequences. "Safe sex" and promiscuity are encouraged and parents are to have no legal authority over their children. This means that it would be a crime for a parent to punish a deviant child[253].

3. Abortion: Abortion is supposed to be legalized by all African governments. Religious and cultural values and the views of the girls' parents are totally ignored[254].

In Kenya a seminar was sponsored in 1998 by Unicef but hosted by Kenya Women Judges Association. This seminar called for the legalization and institutionalization of Western cultural elements such as abortion. President Clinton also offered the equivalent of Kshs 23,100,000,000 ($385 million) to distribute condoms, IUDs and birth control pills in Africa[255]. Apart from the obvious aim of trying to cut down the number of Africans, this strategy couples economic gain with the encouragement of promiscuity as a way to widen the market for contraceptives and medicines for STDs.

Today, the Kenyan family is in a dilemma as a result of the intensification of cultural imperialism. As more and more African families go the European way, the fashionable activity for these families has emerged to be going to nightclubs and bars. In these family outings, children prance about with little supervision while the parents drink. After a while, the very young doze off despite the blaring music, while the slightly older ones go to the dance floor. These clubs appear harmless to the mentally colonized, but children who are exposed to drunkenness, vulgar language, lewd dancing and prostitutes at work are bound to be negatively affected. One 14-year-old girl in Kenya who lives near a disco admitted that she had already had two abortions[256]. Other children have become seasoned drunkards, drug addicts and sexually promiscuous — a leading cause of the rapid increase in AIDS cases.

---

253. "The UN assaults life and family", *The Family*.

254. *Ibid*.

255. AP, "Good news on teenage pregnancies," Lifestyle Magazine, *Sunday Nation*, February 16 1997, p. 7. Also look at J. Chweya, "We want children not dollars," *Sunday Nation*, March 16 1997, p. 18.

256. Peter Kimani, "Sending the youth down the drain", *Daily Nation*, January 12 1996.

HOTELS

Anti-Africanism is so widespread in Africa that anything of African origin or which is perceived to be is considered to be of low quality. Hotels in Africa are simply transplants of Western hotels in every way. A perusal of leading restaurants around Nairobi reveals that African foods are not offered. Many restaurants have Western names and the few which have African names reflect the colonial, racist view of Africans. There are Italian, German, Chinese and French restaurants but no Zambian or Zulu or Ugandan restaurants in Nairobi. Most of these hotels are peddlers of Western anti-African culture. On one Christmas day, Safari Park Hotel had a Christmas Eve Dinner at Le Bougainville. There was a Santa Claus to present gifts. There is virtually nothing African about such hotels except for their location.

The high prices also amount to cultural segregation whereby African culture is discriminated against and average Africans are kept out of the best places: all part of the process of mental colonization, especially of the ruling elite. Most of the drinks served in such establishments, by the way, have a terrible legacy. Jamaican rum, Captain Morgan and American whiskey (bourbon), among others, originated on slave farms. Bonne Esperance is advertised as being "the proud result of more than 300 years of wine tradition...of the southern tip of Africa"; that means 300 years of forced labor under apartheid.

CLASSIC WESTERN CULTURE

Western culture is youth oriented and has an abnormal value system in which old age is despised rather than respected, as it was in Africa. Ageism is therefore widely practiced. Enjoyment of, and promotion of, irrational pastimes including occult practices such as seances, satanism, and palm reading, flow directly into the endless fascination with, and creation of, pseudo-spiritual movements that range from a superficial take on yoga, Zen and other developments borrowed from non-Western cultures to the proliferation of cults, some of which are relatively innocuous, some of which are deadly. The loss of structure, the destruction of the very idea of standards and norms, and the weakness of the family have left many Westerners adrift to the point that unofficial worship of pets, personalities and objects becomes routine. There are also nudist camps and nude beaches, and occasional waves of "streakers" and "mooning".

Cheating and fraud have become fashionable, and the legal system is often used as a tool for injustice. An author was sued for the equivalent of Kshs 3600 million ($600 million) after writing a book about a convicted killer. Although this killer faced execution, he claimed that the book defamed his good name and would make it hard for him "to get a job". After the publisher had accrued Kshs 1.8 million ($30,000) in legal fees, the case was thrown out. In a different case, a surfer sued another surfer for taking "his" wave. After several days of intense deliberation, the case was dismissed because the jury *was unable to put a price on the pain and suffering endured by someone watching another person ride on the wave "intended for him"*[257].

We have already touched on the problem of pornography which is much debated, but pervasive, in the West. Pornography encourages promiscuity spreads AIDS, and crime. Effects of the influx of pornography are reported almost daily in Kenyan newspapers. Between 1999 and 2003, reported rape cases in Kenya, according to police statistics, increased by more than 5000%[258]. Pornography is addictive and, as with other stimulants, the user usually ends up craving more, and stronger, stuff. This can lead to dysfunctional social lives and in some cases to terrible crimes. Yet, pornography has become very common in Africa. This has partly been caused by the complicity of Africans; the government has allowed pornographic videos to be imported and distributed nationwide. It has also allowed local TV stations to air pornographic movies and music videos. Pornography also opens up new markets for contraceptives. Either way, the spread of pornographic material weakens Africa politically and economically.

The best way to destroy human society is to destroy the moral and ethical standards which alone maintain a society[259]. This is currently being achieved in Kenya. Before long, Africa shall become like the USA, where high levels of violence have been associated with the saturation of pornography and graphic violence in "entertainment" media.

Undoubtedly, Western culture is strongly anti-women. A study of cartoons produced for children showed that 90% of all "heroes" were male, and the female heroes were either passive sex symbols, over-reliant on males, or they modeled masculine characteristics in a bikini; secondary female characters are

---

257. *Daily Nation*, July 2004.
258. Kenya Police Statistics, 2004.
259. Prof. Eysenck, *Psychology is About People.*

ugly evil-doers or passive sex symbols. When boys (and girls) are exposed to this kind of chauvinism at an early age, prejudices and role confusion become indelible. Movies and television programs, and fashion, perpetuate the notion that women are valuable for as long as they are physically attractive and can be bought, sold or replaced when they age.

Researchers have discussed at length why men are violent towards women. Often, it has been concluded that a man uses violence as an instrument of control or a way to boost his ego. While this may sometimes be true, and regrettable, it is not entirely correct. In informal polling, men who were randomly asked what could make them hit their wives or partners repeatedly, they cited "disobedience", "insubordination" and "insolence" as the issues that engender the most rage within their marriages. This suggests that if women were less confrontational, there would be far less assault. Since the 1960s the confusion over what used to be accepted as natural family roles is a problem throughout the world, and it is largely the result of misguided education. While women must be accorded equal treatment and equal opportunity in many spheres, cooperation is always easier and more effective when every member in a partnership (whether construed as a hierarchy or a relation of equals) brings tact and charm rather than abrasiveness. This fact has been lost along the way and young people are no longer raised with that in mind.

THE SETTLER PROBLEM

Europeans first started to settle in Kenya in significant numbers in the 1890s. These days, most of the foreigners who have emigrated and settled in Kenya and elsewhere in African are descendants of the first invaders and expatriates. They have discovered that they can enjoy many privileges, courtesy of the admiring Africans. They own all the profitable tourist lodges, large farms and profitable business and generally live in secluded areas where any contact with Africans remains a master-servant relationship. A good example of the re-colonization of Kenya can be found in Naivasha. Here apartheid is the norm. "Whites" have their own exclusive hotels, schools, and hospitals in which Africans are not welcome (except as servants, of course). They even have a Lake Naivasha Riparian Owners Association. Africans are forced to live as squatters or on marginally productive land because these foreigners have taken possession of all the best land, which is dedicated to growing inedible crops, such as flowers. Africans are also denied access to the Lake Naivasha coastline[260].

As more Africans are co-opted, the foreigners have become more daring. The Karen and Lang'ata District Association was formed to agitate for the creation of an entire district to be controlled by the settlers only. Actually, this District Association is not new. In the 1940s, a fascist Ngong District Association existed. Its aim was the creation of a "white homeland" in which Africans were banned[261].

The Wilson Airport in Nairobi is a bastion of "White" supremacy in Kenya. Africans are only welcome as sweepers and other low cadre workers. Africans who work or have worked there report anti-African racism and racial discrimination. More than 20 companies employ no fewer than 400 pilots, but only 50 of these pilots are African[262]. Forty qualified Africans are forced to operate on a freelance basis so that the full-time jobs can be given to foreigners. One American employed by Skymaster, a Captain Mark Chase, emigrated to Kenya after being declared redundant in the US and was given full employment while freelancing African pilots were denied the job[263]. A sign at the de facto *mzungu*-only Aero Club has a list of men who died fighting to maintain colonialism in Africa. The sign says, "Their names live for everyone". The Chairmanship of this club has never been held by an African since it was begun in 1927[264].

All foreign-owned aircraft leasing firms have an open policy of not employing Africans. The "*wazungus* don't want anyone except themselves", lamented an African pilot. "All these foreigners must be reminded of what they are — foreigners." They also represent cultural imperialism in its most naked and pungent form. The Kenya Wildlife Service leadership is always dominated by a Caucasian, and its chief pilot has never been an African. All these Caucasian-controlled companies claim that Africans are professionally incompetent. Kenya Airways, before being taken over by the Germans through KLM, was 100% African from the ownership down to the stewards and pilots. And this airline had a 100% safety record under African control[265]. Nearly all aircraft acci-

---

260. Joe Ombuor, "No longer an island", *Daily Nation*, December 27 1996.

261. Mutuma Mathiu, "Milestone in city management", Lifestyle Magazine, *Sunday Nation*, March 1 1998, p. 4.

262. Mutegi Njau, "Wilson Airport: Colonial outpost in a free Kenya?"

263. *Ibid.*

264. *Ibid.*

dents that have occurred in Kenya have involved planes piloted by foreigners. The Kenya Pipeline Company bought a helicopter which was flown by an African, Captain Ithong'o, for three years without any accident. A *mzungu* was then given the job, and within two months he crashed, blowing himself up in the process[266].

Westerners are also known to pay bribes to pass exams and displace qualified African candidates. Early in 1998, the African teachers at Braeburn School, a Caucasian school, went public revealing extensive racism and racial discrimination. The foreign teachers were paid more than the African teachers doing the same work.

Most Caucasians working or living in Kenya appear to be quite indifferent to the country's problems and interests. They are ignorant of the country and its peoples. Their attitude is summed up in a *mzungu* settler farmer in the Rift Valley's declaration, "I don't care who's president!" The "once Whites-only" Nairobi suburb of Karen is named in honor of a British woman who imported syphilis into Kenya and was noted for her busy romantic life[267].

All the high class neighborhoods in Kenya and indeed the whole of Africa have European names. In Nairobi, the wealthy live in Karen, Lavington, Hurlingham, Westlands, Mountainview and so on. The slums and the filthy areas all have distinctly African names such as Dandora, Mathare, Kibera, or Kariokor.

Several European colonies have sprung up in Kenya. At Malindi, foreigners own more than 80% of the businesses. The ownership extends from the beachside hotels to tiny kiosks which sells curios, among other things[268]. This total control ensures that all profits derived from tourists are expatriated to Europe, leaving Africans nothing. The local people persistently complain about the noise level from discos which play only European and American music. The Watamu Turtle Conservation Group brought to public attention a foreign investor's plan to develop a large part of Watamu Marine Park, an important turtle nesting area.

Malindi police caught a so-called tourist a few years back who had raped and sodomized several primary school girls, infecting them with AIDS[269]. He did not have legal travel documents. Like the various drug traffickers who have been

---

265. "African pilots perform better", *Daily Nation*, April 29 1994, p. 7.
266. *Ibid.*
267. "The forgotten baron", Lifestyle Magazine, *Sunday Nation*, March 8 1998, p. 3.
268. Makau Niko, "The Italian invasion", Lifestyle Magazine, *Sunday Nation*, February 6 1994, pp. 8-9.

apprehended, he was, in effect, an invader. The number of criminal cases involving foreigners is alarming[270]. One pretended to be a doctor, and claimed to have over "45 years of experience in rural Africa"[271].

In 1968, five years after flag independence, a Mr. H. Preston openly referred to African women as "dogs". Thirty-five years later, Africans may not be openly referred to as "dogs" or "black monkeys" but racial discrimination against them is widespread. In Nairobi, African may be barred from renting in upscale apartment blocks or from shopping in the better stores.

The Americans have also established a colony in Kenya, at Naivasha. They follow American laws and are not bound by the Kenyan constitution. It is also a state within the Kenyan state[272]. When the US embassy was bombed on August 1998, Africans who rushed in to help the injured were blocked by American soldiers. Later on, Western anti-African racism was clearly displayed when the American refused to allow a tunnel to be dug through the embassy's compound in order to save the lives of some 40 Africans who were trapped under the rubble of the collapsed Ufundi House. All 40 died.

CONSEQUENCES OF CULTURAL IMPERIALISM

The consequences of cultural imperialism are wide and varied, but all are negative. Cultural imperialism guarantees Western political control of African governments, and therefore open markets and access to cheap sources of raw materials. The racial inferiority complex it induces in Africans ensures markets for Western products, including those that can as well be supplied locally. That means that African peasants lose the market and cannot work their way up from poverty. In Kenyan shops, hot items are always those labeled "imported", "new arrivals", "British" suits or "French" wines.

This pro-Western mindset makes it easy to take advantage of uncritical Africans. Neocolonialism is more powerful than colonialism was, because it has the built-in ability to blind its victims to the fact that it exists. In French (neo-

---

269. R. Nyagah, "Sex scandal: Foreign suspect questioned", *Sunday Nation*, February 22 1998, p. 4.

270. "Court orders German deported", *Daily Nation*, November 1997.

271. The Lincks To Good Health Clinic, Hurlingham, Rose Avenue, Nairobi.

272. Joe Ombuor, "A haven deep in rural Kenya for US students", *Sunday Nation*, June 7 1998, p. 14.

colonized) West Africa, a professor imported from France is paid more than ten times as much as the an African professor doing the same job. These expatriates are said to be "assisting Africa develop." In important ways, they actually hinder the development of the continent.

According to an article published in a local daily, an African woman was studying when electricity went off. She called the Kenya Power and Lighting Company, but the problem was ignored and the power remained off. She called again some time later, but this time with an American accent. Profuse apologies were given and in 15 minutes, the lights were back on. This is important as it shows how mental colonization has become institutionalized. The Utalii College in Nairobi commissioned a documentary film to show how a typical tourist lives back home in Europe or North America. This bit of reality programming was a necessary step toward piercing the African staff's illusions about the paradisical life and conduct of Caucasians.

Mental colonization involves self hatred, self destruction and mutilation. Africans have been convinced that they need to become Caucasian, both in physical looks and behavior. This damages self respect, dignity, and cultural and racial pride. Poverty has aggravated the situation by intensifying the negative self image.

African women pay large percentages of their income for skin lighteners, which work by destroying the skin pigmentation. The skin is then unable to withstand African sunlight; the skin later burns and develops black patches, causing disfigurement[273]. Skin cancer is obviously a risk, and the continued use of these chemicals may lead to immune suppression. Body organs such as the liver and kidneys are adversely affected[274]. Hypertension and diabetes are also aggravated by these "cosmetics", and these lighteners may contribute to a weakening of the bones and a wide range of other disorders. Eye makeup sold in Africa sometimes contains dangerous ingredients; some eye pencils are made out of lead sulphide, which can cause lead poisoning, while others contain polycyclic aromatic hydrocarbons (PAHs) which cause cancer. Lead sulphide poisoning is a major cause of nervous system disorders, convulsions and mental disorders. These compounds also interfere with the manufacture of blood cells. In other cases they may cause kidney failures[275].

---

273. Njoki Karuoya, "Lighter skin at what cost?" Lifestyle Magazine, *Sunday Nation*, August 10 1997, p. 7.

274. *Ibid.*

African women also pay for lipstick, which one might find redundant since their natural lips are already full, while the typical Caucasian has little to work with. Middle-class African women in Kenya may be spending up to Kshs 20,000 ($330) per person annually on imported "beauty" products. Assuming that a sixteenth of all Kenyan women spend similar amounts, this adds up to a Kshs 7 billion ($117 million) industry[276]. Most women say that they use these products "to make [them] more beautiful and to attract men," according to a survey by National Institute of Statistics and Economic Analyses[277]. The survey also revealed that women who are unable to buy the imported products make their own skin-lightening concoctions, using a mixture of baking soda and bleach. The immediate effect is infectious dermatosis and facial burns; long term effects include difficulty with lactation, skin cancer, obesity, ophthalmological trouble, nervous depression and sterility by inhibiting the normal functioning of ovaries.

The adoption of Western culture has very negative social consequences the world over, including the proliferation of sexually transmitted diseases, social violence, disrespect for other people and the law, the collapse of the family, and lack of self control.

Yet, the Western culture is propagated in ever more creative ways. Even international penpal programs foster it. In 1000 penpal requests posted in various major Kenyan newspapers over a period of several months, only two young Africans did not specifically request a European or American correspondent. None wanted an African; 99.8% wanted Westerners[278]. This idea of pen friends was an invention of the UN, which claimed that racial differences could only be overcome by having different people from various cultures intermixing and communicating. However, this can only work if the different people intermix as equals. Penpal services are promoted by the West as an avenue of cultural imperialism through personal assimilation, which was French policy during colonialism.

---

275. Dagi Kimani, "Beware of skin lightening cosmetics," Lifestyle Magazine, *Sunday Nation*, February 2 1997, p. 7 and "Skin trouble in the name of beauty," Lifestyle Magazine, *Sunday Nation*, December 22 1996, p. 7.

276. This figure is an estimate compiled from the average costs of all the oils, powders, lipstick and other cosmetics that the female urban elite uses on itself. Most "beauty" products cost between 650 and 4000 Kenya Shillings or $11 and $67.

277. This study was done in The Gambia.

278. Author's research.

Misinformation

In the media, cultural and information imperialism go hand in hand. Information or misinformation is a very potent weapon, which is used by the West to maintain global dominion.

Most of the news agencies that disseminate information in Africa are Western. There is no international news gathering organization controlled by Africans; all global news reaches Africa via the West and comes with that bias built in. The West also controls all the information flowing into Africa through the importation of books, magazines and newspapers from Europe and America. The presence of foreign television channels and radio stations, such as VOA, CNN, and M-NET, represents direct information imperialism. Information *within* African countries is also controlled by the West. The bulk of newspapers with large readership are not owned by Africans. In Kenya, the radio stations, cinemas and publishing firms are all controlled by foreigners.

All Government media organizations are indirectly controlled, because the state is also controlled by the West. This situation has led to expensive and ludicrous ironies, as most of the information in newspapers comes from the West — even when it comes to events happening in Kenya, itself. Information flowing between African countries is also controlled by the West. Little coverage is given to events in Africa, the wars that are being fought or who is behind them.

There are many powerful reasons why the West maintains its lock on information in Africa. By the end of the 1960s, the US government had concluded that economic aid was not achieving political goals effectively. The approach was changed to put more emphasis upon cultural and information imperialism. An extensive organization was set up for the ideological assault on the less developed regions of the world, and developed countries, too. The main building blocks of this organization are the US Information Agency (USIA) and the Peace Corps. Also included are various NGOs and foundations. The USIA has poured money into a wide variety of cultural exchanges with the Soviet Union and elsewhere, fostering elitist pro-American views and promoting divisive issues like feminism while publicizing and emphasizing the folk music and rustic culture of the target countries. One of USIA's main instruments is the VOA radio station. By 1980, this agency had more than 70 centers propagating pro-West propaganda. The largest ones are located in Kenya and Nigeria[279].

---

279. Tarabrin, *Neocolonialism in the 1970s*.

While granting Kenya independence, Britain ensured that all organizations that gather and distribute information were firmly in its (or its allies') control. The British also undertook to start new news organizations, to gain control of existing ones and increase its influence in those which it already had some control. In Kenya, the British managed to gain a share in the ruling party's newspaper, the *Kenya Times*. Nothing negative about the West and the British in particular ever appeared in newspapers. This remains the situation today.

Misinformation has been the cause of confusion and civil strife in several countries. In Bujumbura, Burundi, the US government produced large posters showing a military boot crushing tiny human figures. The headline was, "Down with Micombero, Dictator!" At the bottom of the posters was the symbol of a youth congress widely known to be backed by the USSR. This resulted in the Soviet ambassador being expelled. These posters were part of a CIA campaign that led to the 1972 genocide.

In Chile, the USA's media manipulation was an important factor in the overthrow of Allende and the massacre that followed. During a three year period between 1970–73, the US government gave more than $3.5 million to *El Mercurio* — a very influential newspaper — to publish a minimum of one story a day that was written by the CIA[280]. Political gain is also made through the use of catch-words that shift the news into favoring the West. Today, all reports from Algeria come with labels like "moderates", "extremists," "radicals", "fundamentalists", all assigned according to an American perspective. There is no "patriotism" or "homeland security" for them. Aggression by Western countries is not described as invasion or unprovoked hostilities; only "intervention" or "protecting a democracy". This is also why, when Africans become rulers, they form a "regime" while the Americans form "administrations".

Slogans such as "the US is the world's policeman" and "America is the world's melting pot" constitute powerful propaganda. America flouts international law and despises democracy as represented by global public opinion but sustained propaganda has elevated the West in the eyes of most Africans, who see it as the source of all that is admirable.

---

280. www.foia.state.gov/default.asp

CHAPTER 13. MILITARY AND POLITICAL THREATS

INTRODUCTION

Poorer countries are coerced by military and political threats from the wealthy states into following certain policies. Effectively, they are made to obey orders. This tactic is normally used as a last resort. The threats are directed at leaders or entire countries to bully them into accepting and implementing policies favorable to the industrialized nations but harmful and detrimental to the impoverished nations. These threats are used to ensure the furthering and reinforcement of neocolonialism. Threats are sometimes manifested in the elimination of leaders who opted for a non-neocolonial path as the route to genuine development. They come in various forms and guises, including "civil" wars, coups, assassinations, economic destabilization and outright military invasion, or a combination of the above. A rebellion may be fomented against a certain leader while assassinations on him are attempted simultaneously.

Coups: Within the first two decades of flag independence, the West sponsored 31 coups in Africa directly and indirectly. Only a few have been the result of internal politics, and political instability caused by economic collapse (which is the result of neocolonial exploitation). Coups are the means of interference that is least expensive and most difficult to trace. Successful coups are often engineered by operatives who have been in the respective African country for long periods and have developed an infrastructure of reliable contacts in the local military establishment.

The sponsoring of coups generally takes two forms. The instigator country may hire mercenaries or use its own trained operatives to execute a coup. A well-known mercenary is the Frenchman called Denard. In 1977, he led a coup that overthrew the government in Benin. He was also hired to overthrow the government in Comoros, and in 1981 he attempted to topple the government in Seychelles. All these coups were sponsored by France. Progressive leaders such as Ben Bella, Kwame Nkrumah were all victims of Western-sponsored coups. The Western country may also bribe soldiers and officers in the victim country's army to stage a coup, promising assistance and support. Major Western countries like Britain, France and the US practice this form of state-sponsored terrorism.

Only when the African leader targeted for a coup is immensely popular among his people and the armed forces do the Western states foment a civil war to oust him or reduce his effectiveness as a leader. Attempts to overthrow a popular leader are not guaranteed to succeed, and the resulting investigation may unearth information that damages the West's credibility among other African countries.

Civil Wars

The fomenting of civil wars is a mode of coercion commonly employed by Western countries. It is a weapon of choice because Western involvement is difficult to detect. The cost is also relatively low, since the sponsoring country does not suffer casualties. These wars always achieve a certain degree of success, regardless of who wins; the victim country is always ruined and is unable to develop in any meaningful way. One way to detect whether a civil war in Africa is genuine or externally sponsored is its duration. Only a suspiciously well-funded rebel group can fight for any length of time.

Prominent examples of civil wars in Africa that were fueled by foreign interests include:

- The war in Angola, sponsored by the USA.
- The bloody short war in Congo (1997) that overthrew elected president Lissouba, sponsored by France.
- The ongoing bloody confrontation in Algeria sponsored by France and USA.
- The genocidal Biafran war in Nigeria sponsored by the UK.

On top of the loss of life, maiming, and destruction of property, these wars leave psychological scars on children who see their parents raped or butchered. The sheer terror of war is mentally damaging.

Assassinations

Before or during a coup, leaders who seem to be unmanageable and candidates that the West considers a threat may be assassinated. Among those progressive Africans killed by Westerners are Amilcar Cabral, Walter Rodney, Patrice Lumumba, Felix Moumie, Ben Barka, Mondlane, Marien Ngouabi, Samora Machel, and Murtala Muhammed. Others, like Al-Qathafi, have been the target of Western assassins for many years.

Assassinations do not always achieve their goals. Even when the leader is killed, the government may fail to change its pro-African policy. That invites further Western terrorist actions, in the form of a coup or civil war, as happened in Mozambique. After President Samora Machel was killed, the government led by Joaquim Chissano persisted in following Samora's policies. This led to further USA/SA military attacks that included the bombing of suburbs.

Economic Destabilization

The Western states use their influence in the UN to persuade other African and "Third World" states to impose economic sanctions on a country which rejects neocolonialism. The best example of this situation in Africa is Libya. When its government declared that Libyan oil would be owned by Libyans and not Americans (effectively closing the door to foreign investment), the US government started a secret war on Libya and pressured all African countries to break diplomatic links and impose economic and travel sanctions on Libya, which they quickly did.

Economic destabilization also takes the form of financial harassment. When a country abandons neocolonialism, major lending organizations and banks refuse to extend loans to that country and begin to press for the repayment of outstanding debts. Any products the victim country exports are subjected to price reductions in the world markets, preventing the country from earning money legitimately. The country then experiences economic upheavals and collapse. Western propaganda, assassins, money, training and arms move in to foment a war to overthrow the progressive government and return that country into neocolonialism. This is what happened in Chile during Allende's presidency from 1970 until his assassination on September 11, 1973.

Military invasion: When all else fails, a progress-minded poor country is invaded militarily. A prime example was the US invasion of Korea in 1950, followed by the US invasion of Vietnam in 1965. From 1975, the US- and European-controlled South Africa invaded and occupied large swathes of Angola. The Anglo–French–Israeli attempt at invasion of Egypt in 1956 is another example, and the 1960 US invasion by proxy of Congo, Kinshasa. In other continents, European and American military invasions are common. In the Middle East, Lebanon and Iraq have been invaded repeatedly, while the South Americans have suffered tremendously from repeated invasions especially by the Americans.

The UN as an Arm of Imperialism and Neocolonialism

The UN has long been colonized by Western Europe and the US, which use it to further their exploitation and oppression of weaker countries. No pro-African person has ever held the post of Secretary General. Boutros Ghali was an Egyptian but not an African; Kofi Annan looks like an African but he has done nothing to fight for the end of neocolonialism in Africa. He fervently promotes the interests of the industrialized nations. He even has a blond, European wife.

The UN has been used to invade Iraq, Korea and other countries to "restore democracy," but it never invaded South Africa to end Apartheid. The UN has implemented an economic embargo and blockaded Libya, but it never opposed US, EU and Japan trade with South Africa.

Today, the US and EU are the greatest threats to world peace and development. Dictators such as Uganda's Idi Amin, "Emperor" Jean Bedel Bokassa of Central African Republic, apartheid South Africa, the Nigerian military rulers, Mobutu of Zaire, Ghana's Samuel Doe and many more were encouraged by the US and EU to terrorize their own people.

The West threatens world peace by fomenting wars, political upheavals and desperate poverty among what West describes as "Third Worlders" (a term that seems to imply that a three-quarters of mankind are third-rate citizens on this planet). The West also has large stocks of those arms and "weapons of mass destruction" that the UN forbid Iraq to own. Apart from nuclear weapons, America maintains an arsenal of all types of poisonous chemicals. We are denied to own any nuclear weapons because Africans are "not responsible". It is often forgotten that the West has the only countries to have used nuclear weapons.

The US is not shy to use biological and chemical agents and even poisonous gas, all of which are banned by various international treaties. In Vietnam, America used millions of tons of Agent Orange and defoliants to destroy plant life over great expanses of the country, causing widespread hunger and, later, cancer in the Vietnamese population. US forces bombed Vietnamese villages with poisonous gasses and with bombs that sucked all the oxygen from the air. A few years ago, France exploded nuclear bombs on an atoll far — away from France. The water polluted by this "test" has reached the coast of Africa and Asia.

EXAMPLES OF AMERICAN AND EUROPEAN INTERVENTION

The following is a brief and necessarily very incomplete survey of a few of the countries in Africa which have been subjected to interference and attack.

Egypt

In 1956, Nasser, a progressive president, decided to nationalize the Suez Canal, rejecting foreign investment and thus refusing to play Egypt's allotted role in the structure of international capitalism.

Since 1949, the Suez Canal Company's payment to Egypt was a meager 7% of the canal's gross profits and Egypt had five directors (compared to 25 French and British board members). Even this was an improvement over the past, but it was hardly acceptable to the Egyptian government. After all, it was constructed in Egypt by Egyptian labor. More than 100,000 Egyptians died while the canal was being constructed. There was a 20% shortage of pilots to steer ships through the canal, but they were not allowed to increase of the number of Egyptian pilots. Foreign investment meant that, of the Kshs 5,460 million ($91 million) revenue in 1955, only Kshs 382.2 million ($6.37 million) went to Egypt, while British and French investors received Kshs 5,077.8 million ($84.6 million).

When Nasser nationalized the canal, the British parliament compared him to Mussolini and Hitler. Western vessels passing through the canal refused to pay their transit dues to Egypt, and paid the European-controlled Suez Canal Company's accounts in Paris and London instead.

The British and French government encouraged all the foreign pilots — 165 out of the total 205 — to quit, bringing traffic in the canal to a standstill. To this purpose they were offered bribes of up to the equivalent of their 3 years annual salary. The pilots who refused to quit were threatened with losing their pensions. All the foreign contingent resigned *en masse*. The original 40 Egyptian pilots, working round the clock, kept the ships moving and even increased the traffic.

Meanwhile in Paris, London and Tel Aviv, moves were made to prepare to overthrow Nasser by direct military invasion and occupation the aim to "restore the Suez Canal to European control", among other things. Some 25,000 reservists were recalled to Britain's army of the military. Radio broadcasts were begun, inciting the Egyptian people to rise and overthrow Nasser. Israel invaded Egypt October 29, 1956, and Britain and France issued an ultimatum to Israel and Egypt requiring them to cease fire and that Egypt accept the "temporary" occupation of Port Said, Ismailia and the Suez Canal.

Egypt refused to accept the terms of the cease-fire and continued fighting the Israeli and Anglo-French units in the Sinai area. The next plan was to have British bombers destroy the Egyptian air force, communications, and military capability in preparation of a general European invasion. The plan was to occupy the Suez Canal from Port Said to Suez. A further attack was contemplated, aimed at the occupation of Cairo. And if Nasser had not been overthrown by this time, a radio and leaflet campaign was to be pursued to rouse the people against him. On November 1, two radio stations were destroyed by British warplanes and immediately a British radio transmitter tuned in on the vacant wavelength with exhortations to the Egyptians to rebel against Nasser, who had "gone mad and seized the Suez Canal ... [and] betrayed Egypt". The broadcast concluded that the Egyptians should accept the proposal of the Europeans, which would bring them "prosperity .... [or] bear the consequences of Nasser's mad behavior". The propaganda failed. Meanwhile, the joint efforts by Israel, France and Britain reinforced the belief in many Arab and African minds that there is an ongoing alliance between Zionism and European imperialism.

Nasser maintained that, "Just as Egypt is determined to have political independence, so also Egypt is determined to maintain independence from all foreign ideologies such as Marxism, racism, colonialism, imperialism, atheism, all of which are European in origin". The invasion failed to achieve any of its stated objections, and Nasser's stature grew. However, the loss of Egyptian life was staggering and there was extensive destruction of infrastructure. Now, the Egyptian government asked for emergency supplies of food, fuel and medicines. The US rejected the request, and refused to release any of the Government's dollar funds to enable them to purchase desperately needed supplies. But, the Suez Canal remained Egypt's property.

Abdel Nasser's achievements transformed a nation of backward peasants into a community of citizens with a stake in their own future. The construction of the High Dam and land reclamation programs have increased the cultivable land by more than a million acres. As a result of the land reform that Nasser introduced, 75% of land is now owned by Egyptians. Egypt today is well on the way to becoming an industrial society with factories producing various sophisticated products. The value of industrial output quadrupled during Nasser's presidency, illiteracy dropped from 80% to about 30%. Nasser created conditions for economic expansion by refusing to accept any political conditions for foreign economic or military assistance. In other words, he avoided the detrimental and destructive proposals of the IMF and World Bank. Only a strong leader, with a nationalist agenda, could change the country's direction — against the tide of outside pressures[281].

Nigeria

At independence, the British government handed power to a neo-colonized group, which proceeded to abandon the drive toward political and economic independence. It protected the interests of those who were exploiting the workers and peasants. These were the local rich, allied with the foreign companies as represented by the Shell and BP monopoly. The exploitation of the rural areas by the cities continued unabated, with widespread corruption and dependency. They capitalized on parochial and ethnic loyalties, directly causing increased ethnic hostilities.

The coup of January 1966 was welcomed by many Nigerians, with the greatest outburst of national enthusiasm ever seen in the country. Similar to what they had done in colonial Kenya during the Mau Mau war for land and liberation, the British depicted the coup as an Ibo plot designed to destroy Hausa-Fulani power. This misinformation campaign was spearheaded by the BBC and the British embassy.

Hostility towards the Ibo increased, since it was an Ibo — General Ironsi — who had overthrown the British-appointed government. Waves of killing ensured, directed at the Ibos in all areas of Nigeria except the eastern part from which they originated. Nigeria began to disintegrate as the Ibos fled to eastern

---

281. Jean Lacoutre, *Nasser: A Biography*, Knopf, New York, 1970.

Nigeria. British actions led to the death of 3 million Nigerian Africans during the Biafran war. Tribalism and ethnic tensions were trumped up and exaggerated, preventing the Nigerian people from uniting as Africans in conflict with Europeans; the conflict was broken down to rivalry between the Hausa, Ibos, Yorubas and so on. The Ibos sought to form their own state, isolated from foreign meddling — but the foreign companies in Nigeria moved to prevent the secession of Biafra, with its oil fields. The leader of the Biafran secession was Lieutenant Colonel Chukwuemeka Ojukwu.

British pressured Nigeria to attack Biafra, even after it had accepted the secession. The conflict became so Europeanized that its solution depended on decisions made in London, Paris and Washington. At first, the British and the Americans claimed to be neutral, believing that Nigeria would achieve a speedy military triumph. A victory for Nigeria was a victory for Britain. When Biafra withstood the initial Anglo-Nigerian invasion and threatened Lagos and British political and economic interests after capturing the Midwestern part of the country, Britain took further steps aimed to bring about the collapse of Biafra.

The British had better control of Lagos than of the progressive leaders of Biafra. All the foreign companies developing Nigerian oil stepped in, creating an embargo by shipping lines and commercial companies against Biafra. Britain declared itself publicly, as militarily, economically and morally in support of Nigeria. The war dragged on for more than two years, resulting in 2 million Africans dead and another million injured. The UK had assisted Nigeria on the understanding that British oil companies would have unlimited rights to Biafran oil. In fact, British and Dutch oil companies, mainly Shell and BP, aided the Nigerians in their invasion of oil rich sections of Biafra.

Shell and BP company were taking Biafran oil but paying the royalties to Nigeria to help it buy weapons and ammunition. The United Africa Company (UAC — a subsidiary of Unilever, which is also engaged in Kenya through the East Africa Industries), John Holt, and Elder Dempster, all assisted the Nigerian invasion of the riverine areas of Biafra by providing navigational charts, weather information and up-to-date maps of the areas, as well as transportation for the invading troops which were led by British soldiers. Even as the Biafrans started to die of mass starvation, the UK blocked all food aid. Nigeria was able to defeat starving Biafran soldiers and neocolonialism won the war. The entire country reverted to the pre-war situation, in which European ownership of enterprises in Nigeria was 92.9%.

When Nigeria was urged to help push the Angolan government toward collapse, Nigerian president Murtala Mohammed bitterly attacked the US president. Talking before the Organization of African Unity, he said that the US president had "taken upon himself to instruct African heads of states and government by a circular letter, to insist on the withdrawal of Soviet and Cuban advisors from Angola as a precondition for the withdrawal of South African and other military adventurers. This constitutes a most intolerable presumption and a flagrant insult on the intelligence of African rulers". A short time later, this bold Nigerian leader was dead.

When a small group of Nigerians from the Ogoni Community started to speak out against the pollution of their land, Ken Saro Wiwa and several other leaders of the protests were arrested. Several days later, despite international calls for their release, Saro Wiwa and the others were killed. One thousand members of the Ogoni Community were also killed.

The relentless exploitation of Nigerian oil by foreign oil companies has given very little back to the ordinary people. Because the Western oil companies export all the oil, even oil and petrol shortages are very common. Today, Nigerian oil is still owned by foreign companies. while most Africans in Nigeria live in desperate poverty[282].

Zaire

Belgium, the colonial power in Zaire, did nothing to prepare Africans to take over at the end of the colonial era. In fact, they deliberately encouraged ethnic divisions by inciting one community against the other. Zaire had no basis on which to found any national political parties.

After independence in 1960, the country's civil service remained dominated by the Belgians. In the armed forces the top officers were all Belgian. Every company was owned by *wazungus* and the top government posts were filled by Belgians. African soldiers mutinied in reaction to the continued presence of Caucasians in top echelons of the army, who persisted in their habit of referring to Africans as macaques (monkeys). The mutiny spread towards other parts of the country and the demand for total independence, that is, a switch from neocolonialism to another path to genuine development was made. At this juncture,

---

282. References include Joseph Okpaku (Ed), Nigeria: *Dilemma of Nationhood*, Greenwood Publishing Co., Westport, CT: 1972. "Shell actions feed unrest," *East African Standard*, June 14, 2004, p. 15.

Belgium invaded Zaire. Belgian troops occupied Luluaburg, Kamina, Jadotville and Elizabethville. On July 11, 1960, Belgian naval forces bombed the area of Matadi, killing many Africans. They then annexed the mineral rich Katanga region. The Belgium government then looked for a reliable man to install as the leader of the Katanga region, to look after Europeans interests in the minerals. The man chosen was "Moise" Tshombe. He declared the secession of Katanga.

This caused the Congo Crisis. The Zairean president at that time, Kasavubu, and his Prime Minister Lumumba requested UN intervention. Secessionist troops with the help of Belgian forces started fighting government troops. The UN refused to help, claiming a policy of non-interference in the "internal" affairs of member countries. (In 1950, the UN had attacked and invaded Korea to "defend democracy" when American interest were threatened, but it could not respond to the request of a sovereign government in Africa to help resist the Belgians.) When the UN finally did send in troops, they arrested Lumumba, making him a prisoner in the country that he was supposed to govern and paving way for his assassination.

After the Katanga secession (which was by now being aided by France's Union Minière and British and American mining interests), Belgium and the US extended massive military and technical assistance to ensure the permanent disintegration of the Congo. On July 12, 1960, Lumumba and Kasavubu, Prime Minister and President respectively, were refused authorization to land at Elisabethville by the Belgian troops that had invaded and occupied 28 localities. Most of the European population of the Congo was in the Katanga region, which Belgium planned to make into a state modeled on Ian Smith's Rhodesia or South Africa's apartheid system. But, the Katanga secession ended on January 14, 1961 when some 338 European mercenaries and the European civilian population were driven from the land.

Patrice Lumumba had openly declared that, as the Congolese Prime Minister, he would work to exclude foreign interests and direct the country to follow an alternative path to genuine development by repossessing the vast mineral resources from colonial interests; this no doubt sealed his fate. At a meeting of the National Security Council's Special Group, CIA Director Allen Dulles began to attack Lumumba, saying:

....that in Lumumba we are faced with a person who is Castro or worse[283].

Robert Johnson, a member of the NSC, testified to the Church Committee that in 1960 at an NSC meeting he heard President Eisenhower make a statement that sounded to him like an order to murder Lumumba.

> At some time during that discussion, President Eisenhower said something – I can no longer remember his words – that came across to me as an order for the assassination of Lumumba.... I remember my sense quite clearly because the President's statement came as a great shock to me[284].

Dulles later called the CIA's Kinshasa station chief Lawrence Devlin, demanding Lumumba's "removal" as an "urgent and prime objective," and saying that under existing conditions "this should be a high priority covert action". Using the facilities of the US Army chemical warfare laboratories at Fort Derrick, Maryland, CIA science advisor put together an "assassination kit" that included poison to produce a fatal disease indigenous to Lumumba's area. Dulles reported to the NSC that "Mobutu appears to be the effective power in Congo for the moment, but Lumumba is not yet disposed of and remains a grave danger."[285]

In Kinshasa, the American assassin failed to get close enough to Lumumba to poison him, and the chemicals expired and were disposed of. The CIA station chief in Kinshasa then explored several other lethal possibilities, including the use of a high powered non-American rifle with telescopic sights and silencer. But Lumumba's residence was guarded by concentric rings of Congolese and UN troops. The course of action agreed to in Washington was to get the UN troops to stop guarding Lumumba so as to facilitate his elimination[286].

At the General Assembly of the UN, the US persuaded several states to vote for Mobutu as the legitimate ruler of Congo, even though he had not been elected. Rajeshwar Dayal, the UN's chief diplomat in Congo, admitted that, "it was common knowledge in the corridors and lounges that the intensest of pressures had been applied to force countries to change their votes, if not their convictions ... it is a sad commentary on the weakness and venality of countries that

---

283. Church Committee, *Alleged Assassination Plots Involving Foreign Leaders*, US Government Printing Office, Washington, 1975.

284. *Ibid.* Also Pease, "Midnight in the Congo."

285.Kelly, *America's Tyrant.*

286. Mutuma Mathiu, "The story of two giants," *Sunday Nation*, March 23 1997, pp. 16-17. Also, Kelly, *America's tyrant.*

so many succumbed." Lumumba was not recognized as prime minister of Congo and the UN troops guarding him were pulled out. Lumumba was arrested and killed. With Lumumba's death, the country with the richest reserves of rare and precious minerals succumbed to neocolonialism.

In 1963, the Belgians returned to Congo to train the Congolese Army in preparation for a coup to bring Mobutu into power. Belgium and the US pressured President Kasavubu to appoint the pro-Belgian Tshombe to be prime minister; Tshombe was appointed, but the country rebelled. Various nationalist rebel groups were formed and tried to throw him out. The Council of National Liberation (CNL) was formed in Brazzaville in 1963 and led attacks into Kinshasa. Lumumba's former Education Minister, P. Mulele, formed an army that stormed Kinshasa in 1963 and 1964. By mid 1964, the national army controlled by Mobutu and Tshombe had disintegrated in the face of lightly armed "rebels" who had become a force of some 6,000 fighters. The fall of Kinshasa and neocolonialism seemed imminent.

At this point, the Americans, French and Belgians launched a massive invasion of Congo. They left several thousand Africans dead and Mobutu remained effective ruler. South African mercenaries, US pilots and the Belgian Air Force bombed African huts. The US supplied trucks, armored vehicles and heavy machine guns to Mobutu's army. "Volunteers" from South Africa, Rhodesia, Belgium, Germany, UK and France were all involved. After this invasion, Tshombe disappeared and left Mobutu to rule Congo as prime minister.

In November 1965, Mobutu staged a coup and overthrew president Kasavubu and the civilian government and declared himself president. US ambassador G. McMurtrie urged Mobutu to establish new contacts with other African countries as quickly as possible, to "explain the reasons for his coup and his government's policies." It is rumored that the Americans not only helped Mobutu pay his troops in 1960 and later organized his mercenary army, navy and air force, but gave him an early warning intelligence system to protect against threats to his regime. The Americans gave military, financial and technological support to the anti-African regime of Mobutu for decades[287]. Of course, it is important to note that the actual murder of Lumumba was never achieved by the Americans, but by the Belgians.

Belgium and the US were now in a contest over the mineral wealth. When Tshombe showed up again, the US got him to lead another secession of the

---

287. Kelly, *America's Tyrant*.

Katanga region. A series of attempted coups and followed. In 1977, former Katangese gendarmes launched a revolt to oust Mobutu. They were crushed by the US and European forces. Later, the West avoided supporting Mobutu in the war led by Kabila because they knew that Mobutu was dying of cancer. They decided to ensconce themselves with Kabila.

Zaire is the world's largest supplier of industrial diamonds and cobalt. In addition, there are major deposits of gold, zinc, tin, copper, uranium and other valuables. It is also a well-watered country and has the capacity to feed the entire continent. But, the encouragement of foreign investment and toleration of an externally-responsive economy means that all the wealth went elsewhere. The Congolese Africans remain poor, illiterate, and without piped water, electricity, schools, and hospitals. Unemployment is high, infant mortality is elevated, and mass hunger is common.

When Kabila came to power, the US looked for increased access to the mineral deposits for US companies. Kabila refused, and another war ensued. Kabila is dead but the war is still being fought[288].

South Africa

Many have wondered why apartheid South Africa survived for so long. Apartheid was institutionalized racism, and racism was institutionalized all over Europe and North America until 1960. Ever since the legalization of anti-African racism in South Africa in 1948, the West and Japan supported White South Africa. Many companies in South Africa are owned by Europeans and Americans, to that any gains apartheid made were direct benefits to the West. The UN, which blockaded Iraq for violating the rights of Kuwaitis, refused for 40 years to move against the white government in South Africa which had denied Africans their rights for 300 years.

Relations between apartheid South Africa and Israel were so good that by 1967, Pretoria had relaxed its foreign exchange rules in order to allow some 21.5 million rand to flow out to Israel. In 1968, the chief of staff of the Israeli Air Force, General Mordecai Hod, visited an apartheid staff college to teach military skills. Now, the apartheid Air Force could threaten Zambia with aerial bombardment. Trade between apartheid South Africa and Israel was extensive. In

---

288. Additional reference; Ludo de Witte, *The Assassination of Lumumba*, (Translated by Ann Wright and Renee Fenby) Verso Books, New York, 2001.

1969, one time Israeli prime minister David Ben Gurion and former intelligence Chief Haim Herzog, visited South Africa.

In 1970, trade in arms was started. The Israelis trained apartheid soldiers. The Sharpeville massacre is one incident where Israel and American riot control methods were fully. South Africa began to manufacture the HK-11 (Uzi) machine gun and were supplied with the latest warplanes. In the period 1972–1973, among the Israeli dignitaries constantly visiting apartheid South Africa was Chief Rabbi Shlomo Goren, who held meetings with P.W. Botha and various top apartheid officials. Apartheid personalities also visited Israel, including General Van den Bergh, the head of Bureau of State Security (BOSS) of apartheid. During the Yom Kippur War, over R 20 million was given to Israel, and several thousand Caucasian medical teams and soldiers were also supplied to Israel.

Israel, whose defense and intelligence departments work closely with the CIA, maintains a large scale diplomatic and aid effort throughout Africa. Israel is a country that has developed firmly within the confines of neocolonialism, posing for Africans the image of a technically impressive model of development which is pro-West. This image is not dimmed by any hint that Israel receives more aid than any "developing" country.

Israel allowed apartheid South Africa to use it as a base for exports of products to other countries, mocking the international embargo before it was lifted by the West. Apartheid South Africa provided Israel with millions of tons of coal and uranium, and constructed a railway for Israel in the Negev, in exchange for Israeli gunboats equipped and other military technology.

Several African rulers aided apartheid by collaborating with Israel, including Kamuzu Banda, Leopold Sedar Senghor, Jomo Kenyatta and Houphouet Boigny. In 1976, Kenya cooperated with an Israeli and apartheid South Africa attack on Uganda by allowing war planes to refuel in Kenya. George Githii, editor of *Daily Nation*, published details of the attack but was ordered to stop. Four years later in 1980, the Jewish owned Norfolk Hotel in Nairobi was bombed, killing twenty people.

The European Union aided apartheid South Africa by continuing to trade with it even after an international embargo was instituted. Japan and Britain even granted apartheid South Africa the Most Favored Nation status, while denying such status to African-governed nations. France supplied apartheid South Africa with five Daphne submarines, Mirage jet fighters and a whole range of military hardware, and nuclear technology. The IMF and World Bank and other Western lending agencies assisted apartheid financially. The US National

Security Council and NATO led joint military maneuvers between the apartheid group's and French fleets, while Britain kept an air force base in South Africa. London was the center of joint operations between the apartheid secret police, the BOSS, the CIA and British MI5. This support strengthened apartheid, and emboldened the South Africa leadership to launch military attacks on other African countries such as Botswana, Zimbabwe, Mozambique and Angola.

In 1974, Admiral Hugo Bierman, Chief of Staff of apartheid's armed forces, met with Admiral Thomas Moorer, Chairman of US Joint Chiefs of Staff to discuss strengthening their cooperation; a similar meeting took place two years later between Kissinger and Forster in Germany. UN Security Council resolutions aimed at expelling apartheid South Africa from the UN were consistently vetoed by the US, and America supplied two nuclear reactors to South Africa in 1976. The US and EU continued to oppose the imposition of more general UN economic sanctions against apartheid South Africa. US Assistant Secretary of State Donald Easum said in 1974 that it was US policy to exert pressure on South Africa to dismantle apartheid, but he was soon replaced by Nathaniel Davies, who had played a crucial role in the economic and political problems in Chile between 1971–73 that led to the assassination of Chilean president Salvadore Allende and the massacre and disappearance of at least 90,000 Chileans.

In the commonwealth, African countries achieved a victory by persuading Canada, Australia and New Zealand to oppose Britain and support the imposition of sanctions against apartheid South Africa. At summit conferences in Nassau (1985) Vancouver (1987), and Kuala Lumpur (1989), the apartheid issue dominated the proceedings and Mrs. Thatcher found herself in a minority of one. Britain's isolation within the Commonwealth helped force the Caucasians in South Africa to abandon apartheid; and in 1986, the US president Ronald Reagan was overruled by the US Congress which, for a variety of political reasons, insisted on imposing more extensive sanctions against apartheid[289].

Angola

In 1961, a guerilla war began and was fought separately by the Peoples Movement for the Liberation of Angola (MPLA), the Front for the National Lib-

---

289. R. W. Johnson, *How Long Will South Africa Survive?* Macmillan Limited, London, 1977. Also Gwendolen, M. Carter and P. Omeara (Eds), *International Politics in South Africa*, Indiana University Press, Bloomington, 1982.

eration of Angola (FNLA) and the National Union for the Total Independence of Angola (UNITA).

Holden Roberto's FNLA and Jonas Savimbi's UNITA were little more than tribal groupings. Agostinho Neto's MPLA was the best organized and had immense national support. The guerilla war had begun because the Portuguese refused to grant their colony independence. The Portuguese army fought with arms supplied by the US. By 1974, it seemed that Portugal had been defeated; this defeat discredited the government in Portugal and the new leaders announced November 11, 1975 as the independence day of Angola. Elections were also scheduled for early 1975. The main contenders were MPLA, UNITA and FNLA. However, the Americans were unwilling to allow Neto, an independent-minded candidate, win. They intervened to prevent the elections — as they had done in Vietnam in 1964, preventing Ho Chi Minh from being elected.

In January 1975, the MPLA, UNITA and FNLA signed the Alvor Accord in which they all agreed to peaceful competition through elections, which were to be supervised by the Portuguese. The Americans stepped up pressure on the FNLA, inciting it to attack the MPLA. On July 14, apartheid's troops invaded Angola from the south. They moved up several hundred kilometers and annexed Cunene Dam. And on July 20, 17,000 heavily armed, thoroughly trained FNLA troops invaded Angola from the northeast and attacked MPLA positions in Luanda, leaving 20,000 dead.

With these twin invasions, the elections were forestalled. On July 26, the Front for the Liberation of the Cabinda Enclave (FLEC) troops, armed and backed by France, announced in Paris the "independence of Cabinda." This enclave is rich in oil. French support for the anti-MPLA groups increased when Jacques Chirac became the Prime Minister. UNITA was allowed to open an office in Paris. France also offered apartheid South Africa four Agosta submarines as an inducement to invade Angola.

In Luanda, the MPLA was struggling against UNITA troops. MPLA launched a counter offensive and ousted FNLA and UNITA troops (plus Mobutu's forces) from Luanda. MPLA quickly gained control of 12 out of 16 provincial capitals.[290] War material was supplied by the US government to the rebels in Angola. The Americans formed a loose coalition of UNITA, FNLA and Mobutu's troops reinforced by mercenaries and apartheid troops. Massive

---

290. John Stockwell, *In Search of Enemies, A CIA Story*, Andre Deutsch, London, 1978.

attacks on the MPLA were launched simultaneously all over. The plan was to destroy the MPLA before November 11, 1975 — independence day[291].

The United States ignored Senegal's proposal of ending the war in Angola by UN or OAU intervention in July 1975 and also prevented UNITA/MPLA discussion of a peaceful solution and ignored MPLA calls for a cease-fire. On October 6, a large force of Mobutu's troops, FNLA forces and mercenaries hired by the US, attacked Luanda and moved so fast that the MPLA units frequently found themselves behind enemy lines; but they prevailed. On November 11, 1975, the Peoples Republic of Angola was declared by MPLA in Luanda, while in Huambo, UNITA declared the formation of the Social Democratic Republic of Angola. The FNLA, in Ambriz, proclaimed the Democratic Republic of Angola, and in the Cabindan enclave, the FLEC declared the existence of the "Cabinda Republic." The Portuguese then withdrew their colonial apparatus[292].

At the start of 1975, the number of Portuguese settlers in Angola was about 340,000. Most of them had arrived in the early 1960s and 1970s. Between the beginning of 1975 and 1976, about 300,000 of them left Angola, taking with them consumer durables, vehicles, boats, and machinery, and sabotaging what they left behind.

The MPLA formed the first legitimate government of Angola. The new government tried to negotiate the formation of a coalition with the UNITA and FNLA, aimed at restoring peace. But the rebels acquired more arms and the war was escalated, with military and intelligence involvement of the US, France, apartheid South Africa and others. The US government refused to recognize the MPLA Government of Angola and vetoed Angola's entry to the UN.

The Angolan government sent an international appeal for military assistance; Cuba and the Soviet Union responded and by the November 27, 1975, the first Cuban troops had arrived in Luanda. The Congolese (Brazzaville) president Marien Ngouabi allowed the Cubans to disembark in Congo and provided them with transshipment bases at Brazzaville and Pointe Noire inviting much ire from the US government. President Ngouabi did not survive long; he was killed on March 18, 1977.

By April 1976, with the help of Cuban troops, the Angolan army had effectively defeated the FNLA, FLEC, European mercenaries, Mobutu troops, Cau-

---

291. *Ibid.*
292. http://www.wsws.org/articles2002/apr2002/ango-13_prn.shtml

casian apartheid army and the UNITA, and peace had returned to most areas. Apartheid forces were withdrawn.

The Gulf Oil Company, owned by the Americans, had been pumping Angolan oil since 1968 at a rate of 150,000 barrels a day and paying the Portuguese government the equivalent of Kshs 30,000 million ($500 million) a year in royalties. When MPLA formed the first African government of Angola, all these payments ceased, denying the Government funds with which it could prosecute its defense. Gulf Oil Company withheld payment of Kshs 12,000 million ($200 million). Two Boeing 737s which the MPLA government had bought were not delivered — US government withdrew the licenses for the export of the planes to Luanda. Meanwhile, a Lear jet was provided for the UNITA's leader Jonas Savimbi[293].

All these actions failed to break the Angolan government. Apartheid South Africa finally withdrew its troops in January 1976, but the machinations continued. UNITA lost 600 men in one battle alone, but somehow Savimbi still had funds, and arms. It was revealed in late 1998 that the US was fueling the war in Angola by purchasing diamonds from the UNITA and thus providing millions of dollars that went to buy arms and ammunition.

After Carter became US President, direct interference in Angola diminished. FNLA and the UNITA started to dissipate and were joining the mainstream society. In 1981, under President Reagan, the war began all over again. Attacks were aimed at the economic and social infrastructure such as industrial plants, electricity generating stations, electricity transmission lines, schools, hospitals, and oil wells in the southern provinces and in the central high plateau. For more than twenty years, violence has prevailed in place of reconstruction and development work[294].

Angola, now at peace, stands a very good chance of becoming a viable nation, with sufficient natural resources to help it avoid the aid trap. Although Angola exports some Kshs 240 billion ($4 billion) worth of oil per year, it is one of the poorest countries in the world[295].

---

293. Article by Oleg Artyukov in *Pravda* translated by Maria Gousseva, *Pravda,* http://www.english.pravda.ru/main/2002/02/26/2663.html

294. http://www.fronlineonnet.com/fl1905/119051340.htm

Mozambique

Here, American influence came mainly through South Africa. This took the form of direct military aggression by apartheid's troops on Mozambique and also the fomenting and sustaining of a "civil" war by supporting Renamo (MNR — National Resistance Movement). Like Angola, at the time of independence Mozambique had a large Portuguese population. When the tide turned and Africans took over, the foreigners left the country almost overnight. They left behind little of value, and most important, they took their skills and expertise. The Frelimo (Front for the Liberation of Mozambique) government inherited a non-functioning economy and a population of several million illiterate peasants.

The new government acted quickly to restructure the economy. Foreign investment and liberalization were rejected. The foreign exchange reserves were no longer used to import luxuries for a tiny urban elite but were used to pay wages in industry and to fund health and education programs. To keep food prices down, massive agricultural projects were started which utilized local resources more efficiently and increased food production.

Those funds had been earned from the sale of cash crops such as cotton, cashew nuts, seafood and tropical fruits that were exported. Just as the government had achieved the restructuring of Mozambique's economy, the world prices of these crops fell and they became unprofitable. Then, the apartheid government expelled Mozambican miners from South African gold mines, where many of them had worked for decades. This cut off another major source of foreign exchange, increasing poverty and unemployment and depriving the government of revenue. Economic destabilization left Mozambique vulnerable.

The National Resistance Movement (MNR) was formed to bring down the Frelimo government by military means and to destroy the country's infrastructure. Renamo terrorists sabotaged transport links between Mozambique and its landlocked neighbors, forcing the whole subcontinent to depend on the infrastructure and industry of apartheid South Africa, most of which is owned

---

295. Additional references: M. R. Bhagavan, *Angola's Political Economy 1975–1985*, Scandinavian Institute of African Studies, Uppsala, 1986.

John Fleming, "Angola limps on despite peace accord," *Daily Nation*, November 21 1997. Reuters, "Cabinda provides rare mix for war, wealth and poverty," *Daily Nation*, 1994. Jeff Mackler, "Files opened on 27 years of US terror in Angola" *Socialist Action*, April 2002, whose story is based on the article "From old files: A new story of US role in Angolan War," *New York Times*, March 31, 2002.

by European and American companies. During the "civil" war in Mozambique, Renamo sought out teachers and health workers and killed them. Schools and health posts were destroyed. Grotesque forms of torture and mutilation have been heavily documented.

The Mozambican president, Samora Machel, died October 20, 1986, when his airplane was downed in suspicious circumstances near the Maputo airport. Joachim Chissano was promptly appointed president in a smooth transition of power. In January 1983, the government appealed for food aid. The UN World Food Program supplied food to Maputo but refused to work in the worst effected areas. The Renamo stepped up its attacks on the civilian population in food producing areas while the donor agencies withheld food aid. An estimated 100,000 people died of starvation.

The 1974 famine in Ethiopia resulted in the fall of Emperor Haile Sellasie. The government of Mozambique did not fall, but it was greatly weakened. The government had to accept defeat and begin restructuring the economy into an externally responsive, neocolonial format. The Nkomati Accord was signed by Mozambique and apartheid South Africa in 1983. World Bank and IMF programs were begun, and rapid devaluation and inflation followed. The government was obliged to end food subsidies; health and education budgets were also cut. In a country where teachers and doctors were hunted down and killed by the rebels, this reduction in spending has effectively raised the death toll, and as of 2004 only 14% graduate from secondary school[296]. Trade liberalization and foreign investment have also been allowed. Now the country is a net importer of food[297].

Libya

After Libya received its independence in 1951, King Idris retained leadership. Over the years, the country came increasingly under neocolonialism until the September 1969 revolution. Libyan oil was owned by Europeans and Americans and the average Libyan was mired in poverty. Cultural imperialism and deleterious economic policies were pursued. Corruption was common at high levels. The import policy permitted all commodities to be brought in and the

---

296. World Bank, Africa Development Indicators, 2004 and also UNFPA, *State of the World Population 2004*, UNFPA.

297. For further information; Joseph Hanlon, Mozambique: *The Revolution Under Fire*, Zed Books, London, 1990.

port facilities were often strained, with ships queuing for berths and the storage and handling facilities congested. Import substitution was opposed by the government because the profits to be gained from importing and factoring foreign products were high, and these imports were so much in demand that in terms of short term politics, it made no sense for the government to stop the importation.

The oil revenue was largely channeled to the foreign oil companies and a small clique of government officials, leaving little for the government and the nation as a whole. Instead of the government seeking to increase the percentage it should receive, or raising the price, production was increased.

Before the revolution, the USA and UK both had military bases in Libya. In 1968, the teaching of English was introduced in schools at all levels. This meant that Libya was slowly sinking into cultural imperialism.

In September 1969, a group of young officers led by Muammar Al-Qathafi overthrew the government of King Idris. The US and British bases were shut down.

Al-Qathafi noted that:

> The conditions of the pre-revolutionary Libyan society are known to everybody. It is a fact that the Libyan society was controlled by favoritism, corruption and dominated by foreign elements, as well as intellectual and cultural imperialism. Foreigners were everything. Foreign languages were the rule. This involved humiliation to our dignity. It also represented cultural and intellectual imperialism with the conditions of backwardness being the common trait in society. The Libyan person has not reached even the minimum standard of decent human life. People live in shacks and tents despite all their enormous riches, and the crude oil flowing into Europe was denied to the people, who lived in abject poverty, misery, disease, ignorance and backwardness at a time when the twentieth century man reached the moon, the Arab man in Libya is unable to get bare necessities of life.

> Source: J. Allan, *Libya: The Experience of Oil*, Westview Press, Boulder, 1981.

This revolution brought immediate assertions of Libya's cultural independence. A cultural revolution was declared, "to implant values on all aspects of life politically, socially and culturally". Arabic script was enforced everywhere; foreign languages were eliminated from schools and the country's history was rewritten. The Italian settlers were also thrown out. Laws were enacted specifically designed to dismantle cultural imperialism. Women began to be included in all aspects of public life.

Al-Qathafi gained the enmity of the West, in particular the US, when he stopped the importation of luxury products and wrested control of oil production from the Western companies. Oil revenues increased despite reductions in the level of output.

By May 1970, Al-Qathafi's government had directed the Western oil companies to cut back production because they had been pumping oil at a rate inconsistent with optimal development of the fields and with Libya's national interests. This resulted in price increases. Income derived from oil sales was now directed to development of the country. The following is a comparison of government spending on social services under neocolonialism and under freedom after September 1969.

Government Spending On Social Services

	Neocolonial state	Independent state
Education	14.6m	470.4m
Public health	7.4m	171.4m
Social Affairs	2.0m	43.2m
Housing	22.2m	794.2m

(in Libyan dinars)[298]
Source: J. Allan, Libya: The Experience of Oil, Westview Press, Boulder, 1981

At the same time Libya's financial reserves accumulated, and by 1980 they stood at Kshs 600 billion ($10 billion). Before the revolution, during neocolonialism, Libya used to receive aid and had a large external debt and little or no reserves. Al Qathafi's government's policy from the outset was to provide every family with one decent house, regardless of family income or location. Rents were controlled and reduced, and spending on housing increased. Two years after the revolution, all male children were attending school. Agriculture was also improved by increased spending on educating farmers and the provision of farm inputs such as machinery. The standard of living was tremendously improved.

In 1983, the Libyan leader was blocked from taking his turn as Chairman of the OAU. Over the next several years, the CIA sought to find a way to kill Al-Qathafi and in April 1986, nine F-111 stealth warplanes swooped down from Britain and crossed into Libyan airspace. They bombed Al-Qathafi's house within the Aziziya barracks. His house was obliterated and one of his daughters was killed; his wife plus eight children were hospitalized with serious injuries.

---

298. One US dollar = 1.3 Libyan dinars

Outside Aziziya, 100 people were killed and 226 injured. The US claimed that it was attacking military installations, but in the Aziziya Barracks, no other building was hit except Al-Qathafi's house. The day after, the US denied that any civilians had been killed or injured, but as evidence mounted the US claimed that Libyan deaths had been caused by Libyans themselves. After the bombing, Western European states expelled Libyan diplomats and imposed economic sanctions on Libya. African countries eager to show their loyalty followed suit.

Early in the 2000s, Al-Qathafi made a major policy shift in relation with Libya's erstwhile Western enemies. After renouncing all ties to terrorism, Libya has now been rehabilitated into "acceptable" international circles and is emerging as a leader within the African continent.

Kenya

Kenya has never been subjected to a civil war, coup or economic sanctions because it has never deviated from the path set for it by the West. However, the Kenya Government has been obliged to legalize multi-partyism and the East African Community was terminated (later re-created), thus voiding the economic benefits that it could have provided. The British benefited by receiving contracts to help Kenya, Uganda and Tanzania set up separate national airlines, railway corporations, and port services to replace the collapsed regional bodies.

Kenya is also occupied by foreign troops. The Kenyan armed forces are fully controlled by the British and Americans who train them physically and psychologically. Kenya is scarcely a sovereign state since its armed forces can be called upon by the West to attack what would normally be Kenya's allies (as in Algeria), or to overthrow a government (as happened in Ghana and numerous other African countries). With the EAC revived under greater foreign control, more than 1,500 soldiers from Kenya, Tanzania and Uganda have held joint operations with US involvement. The American ambassador to Kenya attended the military exercises.

Why are British and American troops in Kenya? Kenya has no African enemies, and in any case, no African country has the military capability to invade and occupy Kenya. These British and American troops serve to ensure that Kenyans never stray from the course of neocolonialism.

The new 2004 Bomas constitution that is being written does not address ownership of the country. For any meaningful development to occur, Kenya must limit foreign ownership of land and other means of producing wealth. The constitution must also adequately protect Kenya's sovereignty and culture, and resolve the gross inequalities that are current. Democracy is an empty term where there is no semblance of economic equality.

In a reflection of concerns that are more pertinent in the West, the constitution makers have focused on questions such as women's rights and the creation of a prime minister's post, while ignoring fundamental needs like reviving the economy, eliminating social problems like poverty, and dealing with AIDS. Reserving 25% of parliamentary seats for women is little solace when so many have to prostitute because of joblessness or the illness or death of the husband. Reserving a percentage of seats defeats democracy, in any case; women (and men) are free to vote for female candidates if they find them good choices.

When the US embassy was bombed on August 7, 1998, the toll on Africans was heavy. Ordinary people rushed to rescue the injured but the US marines insulted them with racist remarks and the US ambassador later claimed that the Africans were there as "thieves and looters." The dead were treated after the traditional American manner: Africans were dumped in a warehouse in the industrial area while the dead Caucasians were taken to the most expensive funeral home in Nairobi. Forty Africans died when they were trapped in a collapsed building adjacent to the embassy because the US would not permit a tunnel to be dug through the US embassy compound to extract them.

Others

Algeria attained independence in 1962, after 130 years of French domination. Immediately after independence, the new government of Houari Boumedienne nationalized French oil and gas interests. When Challi Benjedid replaced Boumedienne, neocolonialism was soon reinstituted by the usual means of unrestricted foreign investment and trade liberalization resulting in economic decline where unemployment increased to more than 50% in most cities. The foreign debt increased to Kshs 1500 billion ($25 billion), accounting for over 83% of annual export earnings. The living standards steadily declined and the government became dictatorial. By the late 1980s, riots were common. Through constitutional reforms, Algeria became a multiparty state in 1990[299].

The Islamic Salvation Front (FIS) was formed in 1990. That June, elections were held for 1539 municipal assemblies and 48 provincial assemblies. The main

---

299. Rami G. Khouri, "Algeria's terrifying agony not surprising," *Daily Nation,* January 14 1998, p. 6.

contender was the National Liberation Front (FLN), which was also the ruling party. The first round of elections saw FIS win an absolute majority of 54%. The next elections for the national parliament were held in December 1991. The FLN government boosted its chances by having FIS candidates arrested.

The Algerian parliament has a combined total of 430 seats, and elections are held in two rounds, for 231 seats and then for the remaining 200 seats. In the first round FIS won 81% or 188 out of the 231 seats. The second round was scheduled for January 16, 1992[300]. It seemed a clear victory for the Islamic Salvation Front. But, an Islamic government would have ended Western cultural and economic influences. The Algerian military was called out to destroy FIS. The elections were nullified and more than 5000 FIS activists and their leaders were detained; FIS was banned and a state of emergency was declared[301]. The government started to kill those who were thought to have voted for FIS.

An Islamic Algeria would have provided a natural ally to Libya and would have stood as an example to other nations seeking to rid themselves of foreign manipulation. In Algeria, over 18,000 Islamists have "disappeared" and more than 65,000 people were massacred[302] in areas thought to be sympathetic with FIS. The attacks were often within a few meters of police stations and would go on for more than ten hours without the "security" forces intervening. No one has ever been arrested for these crimes[303].

The Western press, which is the only source of information for Africans, came out strongly in support of the Algerian government. The newspaper *Liberte* (quoted by local dailies in Kenya) claimed that "Algeria has been shaken by almost daily violence since the 'authorities' in January 1992 cancelled a general election in which 'radical' Islamists had taken a commanding lead"[304] while a Reuters article talked of the army stepping in to "halt elections that would have brought the 'fundamentalist' FIS to power".

When Sudan under the democratically elected President Ali Mahdi opened diplomatic relations with Libya in the 1980s, the US government recalled

---

300. *Ibid.*

301. *Ibid.*

302. *Ibid.*

303. Haji Admani and B. Adan, "Algerian government guilty of killings," *Daily Nation*, January 28 1998, p. 7. Also "Europe gropes warily into Algeria's murky tragedy," *Daily Nation*, January 20 1998, p. 11.

304. "Eight killed in Algeria violence," *Daily Nation*, December 12 1997, p. 9.

its ambassador and withdrew 300 of its embassy staff from Khartoum. Coincidentally, the civil war in Sudan with the SPLA rebels in the south was escalated.

The rebellion in the south had been peacefully ended in 1972 through the Addis Ababa Accord, but in 1983 Sudan's Nimeiry, who was pro-American, imposed a strict form of Sharia law. Even worse, he divided the South into three parts, which contravened the 1972 Accord that declared the Upper Nile and Equatoria to be united and autonomous. This caused the formation of the Sudan's People Liberation Army (SPLA).

After the Nimeiry regime was replaced, the new government refused to implement IMF policies and scrapped those that had already been implemented. The Sudan Central Bank estimated in 1986 that since 1978, the year Sudan introduced an IMF "economic reform" program, capital flight from the country was equal to Kshs 900 billion ($15 billion). In response, the international community denied Sudan loans and the US government blocked a USAID scheme to provide quality guarantees for Sudanese cotton so as to promote its sale. Sudan is the world's second largest producer of cotton.

In 1989, General Omar el Bashir seized power in a bloodless coup, apparently with external help. However, seven years later, el Bashir showed himself to be less compliant than expected and the US started to peddle propaganda claiming that Sudan backed terrorist groups and was therefore a terrorist state.

The Americans began to support the SPLA and other rebel groups to encourage them to overthrow the government[305]. When the US Secretary of State, Madeleine Albright, went to Uganda in late 1997, she pledged military aid to SPLA and NDA and urged them to bury their differences "in order to provide a credible alternative to the Sudanese government"[306]. The result of this increased military aid has been clearly evident. One of the worst famines in history is still ongoing in southern Sudan.

This famine is not as a result of drought; it is the consequence of a combination of two factors. Arable land cannot be farmed because there is no one to farm it — the people are either half dead or are living in refugee camps elsewhere.

---

305. *Daily Nation*, July 30 1998.
306. AFP, "Albright meets Sudanese opposition," *Daily Nation*, 1998. Also Reuters, "Albright, Garang talks annoy Sudan," *Daily Nation*, December 12 1997, p. 8.

In Ghana, Sierra Leone, Somalia and others, coups and wars have been fomented with evidence that points to initiatives by the US, Britain and/or France. Foreign governments continue to actively shape African political and economic reality to favor their own companies. When the Congolese president Lissouba liberalized the oil sector to dismantle the French monopoly and increased the competition, he was able to negotiate better terms[307]. Congo's share in its own oil increased from 15% to 33%. Then the French president, Chirac, demanded that Lissouba exclude any non-French oil companies and accept a lesser share of 17%. Chirac also demanded that the pro-French Sassou Nguesso be appointed chief of the armed forces. Lissouba noted that the Congolese constitution did not allow former presidents to be appointed to lead the army. Chirac reported replied to the effect that Lissouba could "chuck the constitution into a dustbin!"[308]

A few weeks later, Congo was engulfed in a bloody "civil" war that killed over 10,000 Africans. Sassou Nguesso was returned to power. Media reports gave the impression that the people of Congo had suddenly started killing each other on the basis of tribalism. The role of France was not considered worth mentioning. The UN war crimes tribunal has ignored Africa's when plight when it comes to prosecuting Westerners, but African war criminals acting in concert with Westerners are quickly hunted down. Today, Congo gets only 15% of its own oil, and the French still disappear with the rest. Then the nation's leaders go to France and seek loans, which have to be repaid at exorbitant interest rates. The French lend them money from the oil revenues.

This is the story of modern Africa: the reality of poverty, underdevelopment and the donor community.

---

307. *New African*, 1997.
308. *Ibid.*

TABLE OF CONTENTS

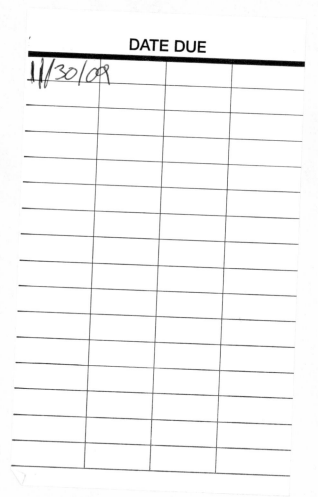

DATE DUE

11/30/09			

Printed in the United States
46962LVS00006B/156

9 780875 863191